Essays and Lectures on English Literature

ESSAYS AND LECTURES ON ENGLISH LITERATURE

By

CHARLES KINGSLEY

DISCOVERY PUBLISHING HOUSE
NEW DELHI–1100 02

Published by:
Namit Wasan
DISCOVERY PUBLISHING HOUSE PVT. LTD.
4383/4B, Ansari Road, Darya Ganj
New Delhi-110 002 (India)
Phone : +91-11-23279245; 23253475; 43596065
E-mail : discoverybooksindia@gmail.com
discoverypublishinghouse@gmail.com
namitwasan9@gmail.com
web www.discoverypublishinggroup.com

***Edition:* 2020**

ISBN: 978-81-7141-507-6

Essays and Lectures on English Literature

Printed at:
Infinity Imaging Systems
Delhi

CONTENTS.

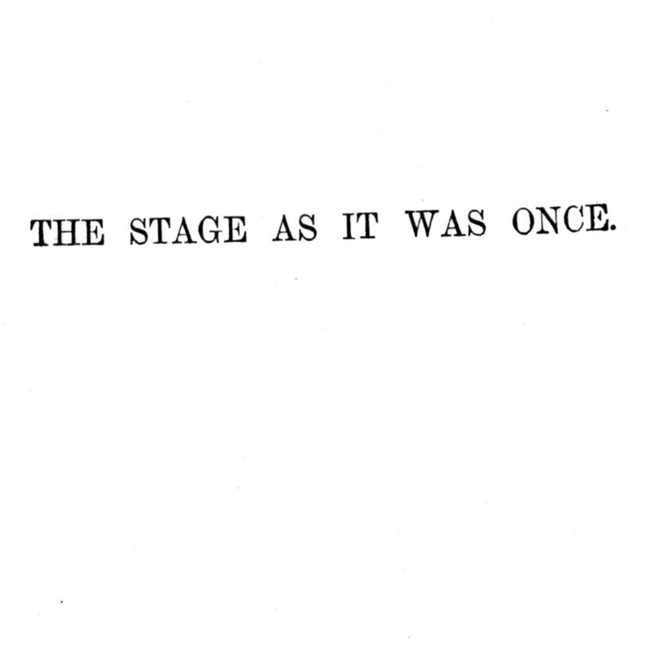

THE STAGE AS IT WAS ONCE.

THE STAGE AS IT WAS ONCE.*

Let us think for a while upon what the Stage was once, in a republic of the past—what it may be again, I sometimes dream, in some republic of the future. In order to do this, let me take you back in fancy some 2314 years—440 years before the Christian era, and try to sketch for you—alas! how clumsily—a great, though tiny people, in one of their greatest moments—in one of the greatest moments, it may be, of the human race. For surely it is a great and a rare moment for humanity, when all that is loftiest in it—when reverence for the Unseen powers, reverence for the heroic dead, reverence for the fatherland, and that reverence, too, for self, which is expressed in stateliness and self-restraint, in grace and courtesy; when all these, I say, can lend themselves, even for a day, to the richest enjoyment of life—to the enjoyment of beauty

* This Lecture was given at Harrow in 1873, and in America in 1874.

in form and sound, and of relaxation, not brutalising, but ennobling.

Rare, alas! have such seasons been in the history of poor humanity. But when they have come, they have lifted it up one stage higher thenceforth. Men, having been such once, may become such again; and the work which such times have left behind them becomes immortal.

A thing of beauty is a joy for ever.

Let me take you to the then still unfurnished theatre of Athens, hewn out of the limestone rock on the south-east slope of the Acropolis.

Above are the new marble buildings of the Parthenon, rich with the statues and bas-reliefs of Phidias and his scholars, gleaming white against the blue sky, with the huge bronze statue of Athenė Promachos, fifty feet in height, towering up among the temples and colonnades. In front, and far below, gleams the blue sea, and Salamis beyond.

And there are gathered the people of Athens—fifty thousand of them, possibly, when the theatre was complete and full. If it be fine, they all wear garlands on their heads. If the sun be too hot, they wear wide-brimmed straw hats. And if a storm comes on, they will take refuge in the porticoes beneath; not without wine and cakes, for what they have come to see will last for many an hour, and they intend to feast their eyes and ears from sunrise to sunset. On the highest seats are slaves and freedmen, below them the free citizens; and on the lowest seats of all are the dignitaries of the republic—the priests, the magistrates, and the other καλοὶ κἀγαθοί—the fair and good men—as the citizens of the highest rank were called, and with them foreign ambassadors and distinguished strangers. What an audience! the rapidest, subtlest, wittiest, down to the very cobblers and tinkers, the world has ever seen. And what noble figures on those front seats; Pericles, with Aspasia beside him, and all his friends—Anaxagoras the sage, Phidias the sculptor, and many another immortal artist; and somewhere among the free citizens, perhaps beside his father Sophroniscus the sculptor, a short, square, pug-nosed boy of ten years old, looking at it all with strange eyes—"who will be one day," so said the Pythoness at Delphi, "the wisest man in Greece" —sage, metaphysician, humorist, warrior, patriot, martyr—for his name is *Socrates.*

All are in their dresses of office; for this is not merely a day of amusement, but of religious ceremony; sacred to Dionysos—Bacchus, the inspiring god, who raises men above themselves, for good—or for evil.

The evil, or at least the mere animal aspect of that inspiration, was to be seen in forms grotesque and sensuous enough in those very festivals, when the gayer and coarser part of the population, in town and country, broke out into frantic masquerade—of which the silly carnival of Rome is perhaps the last paltry and unmeaning relic—"when," as the learned O. Müller says, "the desire of escaping from self into something new and strange, of living in an imaginary world, broke forth in a thousand ways; not merely in revelry and solemn though fantastic songs, but in a hundred disguises, imitating the subordinate beings—satyrs, pans, and nymphs, by whom the god was surrounded, and through whom life seemed to pass from him into vegetation, and branch off into a variety of beautiful or grotesque forms—beings who were ever present to the fancy of the Greeks, as a convenient step by which they could approach more nearly to the presence of the Divinity." But even out of that seemingly bare chaos, Athenian genius was learning how to construct, under Eupolis, Cratinus, and Aristophanes, that elder school of comedy, which remains not only unsurpassed, but unapproachable, save by Rabelais alone, as the ideal cloudland of masquerading wisdom, in which the whole universe goes mad—but with a subtle method in its madness.

Yes, so it has been, under some form or other, in every race and clime—ever since Eve ate of the magic fruit, that she might be as a god, knowing good and evil, and found, poor thing, as most have since, that it was far easier and more pleasant to know the evil than to know the good. But that theatre was built that men might know therein the good as well as the evil. To learn the evil, indeed, according to their light, and the sure vengeance of Até and the Furies which tracks up the evil-doer. But to learn also the good—lessons of piety, patriotism, heroism, justice, mercy, self-sacrifice, and all that comes out of the hearts of men and women not dragged *below*, but raised *above* themselves; and behind all—at least in the nobler and earlier tragedies of Æschylus and Sophocles, before Euripides had introduced the tragedy of mere human passion; that sensation tragedy, which is the only one the world knows now, and of which the world is growing rapidly tired—behind all, I say, lessons of the awful and unfathomable mystery of human existence —of unseen destiny; of that seemingly capricious distribution of weal and woe, to which we can find no solution on this side the grave, for which the old Greek could find no solution whatsoever.

Therefore there was a central object in the old Greek theatre, most important to it, but which did not exist in the old Roman, and does not exist in our theatres, because our tragedies, like the Roman, are mere plays concerning love, murder, and so forth, while the Greek were concerning the deepest relations of man to the Unseen.

The almost circular orchestra, or pit, between the benches and the stage, was empty of what we call spectators—because it was destined for the true and ideal spectators—the representatives of humanity; in its centre was a round platform, the θυμελή—originally the altar of Bacchus—from which the leader of these representatives, the leader of the Chorus, could converse with the actors on the stage and take his part in the drama; and round this thymelé the Chorus ranged with measured dance and song, chanting, to the sound of a simple flute, odes such as the world had never heard before or since, save perhaps in the temple-worship at Jerusalem. A chorus now, as you know, means merely any number of persons singing in full harmony on any subject. The Chorus was then in tragedy, and indeed in the higher comedy, what Schlegel well calls "the ideal spectator"—a personified reflection on the action going on, the incorporation into the representation itself of the sentiments of the poet, as the spokesman of the whole human race. He goes on to say (and I think truly), "that the Chorus always retained among the Greeks a peculiar national signification, publicity being, according to their republican notions, essential to the completeness of every important transaction." Thus the Chorus represented idealised public opinion; not, of course, the shifting hasty public opinion of the moment—to that it was a conservative check, and it calmed it to soberness and charity—for it was the matured public opinion of centuries; the experience, and usually the sad experience, of many generations; the very spirit of the Greek race.

The Chorus might be composed of what the poet would. Of ancient citizens, waiting for their sons to come back from the war, as in the "Agamemnon" of Æschylus; of sea-nymphs, as in his "Prometheus Bound;" even of the very Furies who hunt the matricide, as in his "Eumenides;" of senators, as in the "Antigone" of Sophocles; or of village farmers, as in his "Œdipus at Colonos"—and now I have named five of the greatest poems, as I hold, written by mortal man till Dante rose. Or it may be the Chorus was composed—as in the comedies of Aristophanes, the greatest humorist the world has ever seen—of birds, or of frogs, or even of clouds. It may rise to the level of Don Quixote, or sink to that of Sancho Panza; for it is always the incarnation of such wisdom, heavenly or earthly, as the poet wishes the people to bring to bear on the subject-matter.

But let the poets themselves, rather than me, speak awhile. Allow me to give you a few specimens of these choruses—the first as an example of that practical and yet surely not un-divine wisdom, by which they supplied the place of our modern preacher, or essayist, or didactic poet.

Listen to this of the old men's chorus in the "Agamemnon," in the spirited translation of my friend Professor Blackie:

> 'Twas said of old, and 'tis said to-day,
> That wealth to prosperous stature grown
> Begets a birth of its own:
> That a surfeit of evil by good is prepared,
> And sons must bear what allotment of woe
> Their sires were spared.
> But this I refuse to believe: I know
> That impious deeds conspire
> To beget an offspring of impious deeds
> Too like their ugly sire.
> But whoso is just, though his wealth like a river
> Flow down, shall be scathless: his house shall rejoice
> In an offspring of beauty for ever.
>
> The heart of the haughty delights to beget
> A haughty heart. From time to time
> In children's children recurrent appears
> The ancestral crime.
> When the dark hour comes that the gods have decreed
> And the Fury burns with wrathful fires,
> A demon unholy, with ire unabated,
> Lies like black night on the halls of the fated;
> And the recreant Son plunges guiltily on
> To perfect the guilt of his Sires.

But Justice shines in a lowly cell;
In the homes of poverty, smoke-begrimed,
With the sober-minded she loves to dwell.
    But she turns aside
From the rich man's house with averted eye,
The golden-fretted halls of pride
Where hands with lucre are foul, and the praise
Of counterfeit goodness smoothly sways;
And wisely she guides in the strong man's despite
    All things to an issue of RIGHT.

Let me now give you another passage from the "Eumenides"—or "Furies"—of Æschylus.

Orestes, Prince of Argos, you must remember, has avenged on his mother Clytemnestra the murder of his father, King Agamemnon, on his return from Troy. Pursued by the Furies, he takes refuge in the temple of Apollo at Delphi, and then, still Fury-haunted, goes to Athens, where Pallas Athené, the warrior-maiden, the tutelary goddess of Athens, bids him refer his cause to the Areopagus, the highest court of Athens, Apollo acting as his advocate, and she sitting as umpire in the midst. The white and black balls are thrown into the urn, and are equal; and Orestes is only delivered by the decision of Athené—as the representative of the nearer race of gods, the Olympians, the friends of man, in whose likeness man is made. The Furies are the representatives of the older and darker creed—which yet has a depth of truth in it—of the irreversible dooms which underlie all nature; and which represent the Law, and not the Gospel, the consequence of the mere act, independent of the spirit which has prompted it.

They break out in fury against the overbearing

arrogance of these younger gods. Athené bears their rage with equanimity, addresses them in the language of kindness, even of veneration, till these so indomitable beings are unable to withstand the charm of her mild eloquence. They are to have a sanctuary in the Athenian land, and to be called no more Furies (Erinnys), but Eumenides—the *well-conditioned*—the kindly goddesses. And all ends with a solemn procession round the orchestra, with hymns of blessing, while the terrible Chorus of the Furies, clothed in black, with blood-stained girdles, and serpents in their hair, in masks having perhaps somewhat of the terrific beauty of Medusa-masks, are convoyed to their new sanctuary by a procession of children, women, and old men in purple robes with torches in their hands, after Athené and the Furies have sung, in response to each other, a chorus from which I must beg leave to give you an extract or two:

Eldest Fury (Leader of the Chorus).

Far from thy dwelling, and far from thy border,
By the grace of my godhead benignant I order
The blight which may blacken the bloom of the trees.
Far from thy border, and far from thy dwelling,
Be the hot blast which shrivels the bud in its swelling,
The seed-rotting taint, and the creeping disease.
Thy flocks be still doubled, thy seasons be steady,
And when Hermes is near thee, thy hand be still ready
The Heaven-dropt bounty to seize.

Athené.

Hear her words, my city's warders—
Fraught with blessings, she prevaileth
With Olympians and Infernals,
Dread Erinnys much revered.

Mortal faith she guideth plainly
To what goal she pleaseth, sending
Songs to some, to others days
With tearful sorrows dulled.

Furies.

Far from thy border
The lawless disorder
That sateless of evil shall reign ;
Far from thy dwelling,
The dear blood welling,
That taints thine own hearth with the slain.
When slaughter from slaughter
Shall flow like the water,
And rancour from rancour shall grow
But joy with joy blending,
Live, each to all lending ;
And hating one-hearted the foe.
When bliss hath departed ;
From love single-hearted,
A fountain of healing shall flow.

Athené.

Wisely now the tongue of kindness
Thou hast found, the way of love.
And these terror-speaking faces
Now look wealth to me and mine.
Her so willing, ye more willing,
Now receive. This land and city,
On ancient right securely throned,
Shall shine for evermore.

Furies.

Hail, and all hail, mighty people, be greeted,
On the sons of Athena shines sunshine the clearest.
Blest people, near Jove the Olympian seated.
And dear to the maiden his daughter the dearest.
Timely wise 'neath the wings of the daughter ye gather,
And mildly looks down on her children the Father.

Those of you here who love your country as well as the old Athenians loved theirs, will feel at once the grand political significance of such a scene, in which patriotism and religion become one—and feel, too, the exquisite dramatic effect of the innocent, the weak, the unwarlike, welcoming among them, without fear, because without guilt, those ancient snaky-haired sisters, emblems of all that is most terrible and most inscrutable, in the destiny of nations, of families, and of men:

To their hallowed habitations
'Neath Ogygian earth's foundations
In that darksome hall
Sacrifice and supplication
Shall not fail. In adoration
Silent worship all.

Listen again, to the gentler patriotism of a gentler poet, Sophocles himself. The village of Colonos, a mile from Athens, was his birthplace; and in his "Œdipus Coloneus," he makes his Chorus of village officials sing thus of their consecrated olive grove:

In good hap, stranger, to these rural seats
Thou comest, to this region's blest retreats,
Where white Colonos lifts his head,
And glories in the bounding steed.
Where sadly sweet the frequent nightingale
Impassioned pours his evening song,
And charms with varied notes each verdant vale,
The ivy's dark-green boughs among,
Or sheltered 'neath the clustering vine
Which, high above him forms a bower,
Safe from the sun or stormy shower,
Where frolic Bacchus often roves,
And visits with his fostering nymphs the groves.

Bathed in the dew of heaven each morn,
Fresh is the fair Narcissus born,
Of those great gods the crown of old;
The crocus glitters, robed in gold.
Here restless fountains ever murmuring glide,
And as their crispèd streamlets play,
To feed, Cephisus, thine unfailing tide,
Fresh verdure marks their winding way.
Here oft to raise the tuneful song
The virgin band of Muses deigns,
And car-borne Aphrodite guides her golden reins.

Then they go on, this band of village elders, to praise the gods for their special gifts to that small Athenian land. They praise Pallas Athené, who gave their forefathers the olive; then Poseidon—Neptune, as the Romans call him—who gave their forefathers the horse; and something more—the ship—the horse of the sea, as they, like the old Norse Vikings after them, delighted to call it:

Our highest vaunt is this—Thy grace,
Poseidon, we behold,
The ruling curb, embossed with gold,
Controls the courser's managed pace,
Though loud, oh king, thy billows roar,
Our strong hands grasp the labouring oar,
And while the Nereids round it play,
Light cuts our bounding bark its way.

What a combination of fine humanities! Dance and song, patriotism and religion, so often parted among us, have flowed together into one in these stately villagers; each a small farmer; each a trained soldier, and probably a trained seaman also; each a self-governed citizen; and each a cultured gentleman, if ever there were gentlemen on earth.

But what drama, doing, or action—for such is the meaning of the word—is going on upon the stage, to be commented on by the sympathising Chorus?

One drama, at least, was acted in Athens in that year—440 B.C.—which you, I doubt not, know well—"Antigone," that of Sophocles, which Mendelssohn has resuscitated in our own generation, by setting it to music, divine indeed, though very different from the music to which it was set, probably by Sophocles himself, at its first, and for aught we know, its only representation; for pieces had not then, as now, a run of a hundred nights and more. The Athenian genius was so fertile, and the Athenian audience so eager for novelty, that new pieces were demanded, and were forthcoming, for each of the great festivals, and if a piece was represented a second time it was usually after an interval of some years. They did not, moreover, like the moderns, run every night to some theatre or other, as a part of the day's amusement. Tragedy, and even comedy, were serious subjects, calling out, not a passing sigh, or passing laugh, but all the higher faculties and emotions. And as serious subjects were to be expressed in verse and music, which gave stateliness, doubtless, even to the richest burlesques of Aristophanes, and lifted them out of mere street-buffoonery into an ideal fairyland of the grotesque, how much more stateliness must verse and music have added to their tragedy! And how much have we lost, toward a true appreciation of their dramatic art, by losing almost utterly not only the laws of their melody and harmony, but even the true metric time of their odes!—music and metre, which must have surely been as noble as their poetry, their sculpture, their architecture, possessed by the same exquisite sense of form and of proportion. One thing we can understand—how this musical form of the drama, which still remains to us in lower shapes, in the oratorio, in the opera, must have helped to raise their tragedies into that ideal sphere in which they all, like the "Antigone," live and move. So ideal and yet so human; nay rather, truly ideal, because truly human. The gods, the heroes, the kings, the princesses of Greek tragedy were dear to the hearts of Greek republicans, not merely as the founders of their states, not merely as the tutelary deities, many of them, of their country: but as men and women like themselves, only more vast; with mightier wills, mightier virtues, mightier sorrows, and often mightier crimes; their inward free-will battling, as Schlegel has well seen, against outward circumstance and overruling fate, as every man should battle, unless he sink to be a brute. "In tragedy," says Schlegel—uttering thus a deep and momentous truth—"the gods themselves either come forward as the servants of destiny and mediate executors of its decrees, or approve themselves godlike only by asserting their liberty of action and entering upon the same struggles with fate which man himself has to encounter." And I believe this, that this Greek tragedy, with its godlike men and manlike gods, and heroes who had become gods by the very vastness of their humanity, was a preparation, and it may be a necessary preparation, for the true Christian faith in a Son of Man, who is at once utterly human and utterly divine. That man is made in the likeness of God—is the root idea, only half-conscious, only half-expressed, but instinctive, without which neither the Greek Tragedies nor the Homeric Poems, six hundred years before them, could have been composed. Doubtless the idea that man was like a god degenerated too often into the idea that the gods were like men, and as wicked. But that travestie of a great truth is not confined to those old Greeks. Some so-called Christian theories—as I hold—have sinned in that direction as deeply as the Athenians of old.

Meanwhile, I say, that this long acquiescence in the conception of godlike struggle, godlike daring, godlike suffering, godlike martyrdom; the very conception which was so foreign to the mythologies of any other race—save that of the Jews, and perhaps of our own Teutonic forefathers—did prepare, must have prepared men to receive as most rational and probable, as the satisfaction of their highest instincts, the idea of a Being in whom all those partial rays culminated in clear, pure light; of a Being at once utterly human and utterly divine; who by struggle, suffering, self-sacrifice, without a parallel, achieved a victory over circumstance and all the dark powers which beleaguer man without a parallel likewise.

Take, as an example, the figure which you know best—the figure of Antigone herself—devoting herself to be entombed alive, for the sake of love and duty. Love of a brother, which she can only prove, alas! by burying his corpse. Duty to the dead, an instinct depending on no written law, but springing out of the very depth of those blind and yet sacred monitions which prove that the true man is not an animal, but a spirit; fulfilling her holy purpose, unchecked by fear, unswayed by her sisters' entreaties. Hardening her heart magnificently till her fate is sealed; and then after proving her godlike courage, proving the tenderness of her womanhood by that melodious wail over her own untimely death and the loss of marriage joys, which some of you must know from the music of Mendelssohn, and which the late Dean Milman has put into English thus:

Come, fellow-citizens, and see
The desolate Antigone.
On the last path her steps shall tread,
Set forth, the journey of the dead,
Watching, with vainly lingering gaze,
Her last, last sun's expiring rays.

Never to see it, never more,
For down to Acheron's dread shore,
A living victim am I led
To Hades' universal bed.
To my dark lot no bridal joys
Belong, nor e'er the jocund noise
Of hymeneal chant shall sound for me,
But death, cold death, my only spouse shall be.

Oh tomb! Oh bridal chamber! Oh deep-delved
And strongly-guarded mansion! I descend
To meet in your dread chambers all my kindred,
Who in dark multitudes have crowded down
Where Proserpine received the dead. But I,
The last—and oh how few more miserable!—
Go down, or ere my sands of life are run.

And let me ask you whether the contemplation of such a self-sacrifice should draw you, should have drawn those who heard the tale nearer to, or farther from, a certain cross which stood on Calvary some 1800 years ago? May not the tale of Antigone heard from mother or from nurse have nerved ere now some martyr-maiden to dare and suffer in an even holier cause?

But to return. This set purpose of the Athenian dramatists of the best school to set before men a magnified humanity, explains much in their dramas which seems to us at first not only strange but faulty. The masks which gave one grand but unvarying type of countenance to each well-known historic personage, and thus excluded the play of feature, animated gesture, and almost all which we now consider as "acting" proper; the thick-soled cothurni which gave the actor a more than human stature; the poverty (according to our notions) of the scenery, which usually represented merely the front of a palace or other public place, and was often though not always unchanged during the whole performance; the total absence, in fact, of anything like that scenic illusion which most managers of theatres seem now to consider as their highest achievement; the small number of the actors, two, or at most three only, being present on the stage at once,—the simplicity of the action, in which intrigue (in the playhouse sense) and any complication of plot are utterly absent; all this must have concentrated not the eye of the spectator on the scene, but his ear upon the voice, and his emotions on the personages who stood out before him without a background, sharp-cut and clear as a group of statuary, which is the same, place it where you will, complete in itself—a world of beauty, independent of all other things and beings save on the ground on which it needs must stand. It was the personage rather than his surroundings, which was to be impressed by every word on the spectator's heart and intellect; and the very essence of Greek tragedy is expressed in the still famous words of Medea:

Che resta? Io.

Contrast this with the European drama—especially with the highest form of it—our own Elizabethan. It resembles, as has been often said in better words than mine, not statuary but painting. These dramas affect colour, light, and shadow, background whether of town or country, description of scenery where scenic machinery is inadequate, all, in fact, which can blend the action and the actors with the surrounding circumstances, without letting them altogether melt into the circumstances; which can show them a part of the great whole, by harmony or discord with the whole universe, down to the flowers beneath their feet. This, too, had to be done: how it became possible for even the genius of a Shakespeare to get it done, I may with your leave hint to you hereafter. Why it was not given to the Greeks to do it, I know not.

Let us at least thank them for what they did. One work was given them, and that one they fulfilled as it had never been fulfilled before; as it will never need to be fulfilled again; for the Greeks' work was done not for themselves alone but for all races in all times; and Greek Art is the heirloom of the whole human race; and that work was to assert in drama, lyric, sculpture, music, gymnastic, the dignity of man—the dignity of man which they perceived for the most part with their intense æsthetic sense, through the beautiful in man. Man with them was divine, inasmuch as he could perceive beauty and be beautiful himself. Beauty might be physical, æsthetic, intellectual, moral. But in proportion as a thing was perfect it revealed its own perfection by its beauty. Goodness itself was a form—though the highest form—of beauty. Καλός meant both the physically beautiful and the morally good; *αἰσχρός* both the ugly and the bad.

Out of this root-idea sprang the whole of that Greek sculpture, which is still, and perhaps ever will be, one of the unrivalled wonders of the world.

Their first statues, remember, were statues of the gods. This is an historic fact. Before B.C. 580 there were probably no statues in Greece save those of deities. But of what form? We all know that the usual tendency of man has been to represent his gods as more or less monstrous. Their monstrosity may have been meant, as it was certainly with the Mexican idols, and probably those of the Semitic races of Syria and Palestine, to symbolise the ferocious passions which they attributed to those objects of their dread, appeasable alone by human sacrifice. Or the monstrosity, as with the hawk-headed or cat-headed Egyptian idols, the winged bulls of Nineveh and Babylon, the many-handed deities of Hindostan—merely symbolised powers which could not, so the priest and the sculptor held, belong to mere humanity. Now, of such monstrous forms of idols, the records in Greece are very few and very ancient—relics of an older worship, and most probably of an older race. From the earliest historic period, the Greek was discerning more and more that the divine could be best represented by the human; the tendency of his statuary was more and more to honour that divine, by embodying it in the highest human beauty.

In lonely mountain shrines there still might linger, feared and honoured, dolls like those black virgins, of unknown antiquity, which still work wonders on the European continent. In the mysterious cavern of Phigalia, for instance, on the Eleatic shore of Peloponnese, there may have been in remote times—so the legend ran—an old black wooden image, a woman with a horse's head and mane, and serpents growing round her head, who held a dolphin in one hand and a dove in the other. And this image may have been connected with old nature-myths about the marriage of Demeter and Poseidon—that is, of encroachments of the sea upon the land; and the other myths of Demeter, the earth-mother, may have clustered round the place, till the Phigalians were glad—for it was profitable as well as honourable—to believe that in their cavern Demeter sat mourning for the loss of Proserpine, whom Pluto had carried down to Hades, and all the earth was barren till Zeus sent the Fates, or Iris, to call her forth, and restore fertility to the world. And it may be true—the legend as Pausanias tells it 600 years after—that the old wooden idol having been burnt, and the worship of Demeter neglected till a famine ensued, the Phigalians, warned by the Oracle of Delphi, hired Onatas, a contemporary of Polygnotus and Phidias, to make them a bronze replica of the old idol, from some old copy and from a dream of his own. The story may be true. When Pausanias went thither, in the second century after Christ, the cave and the fountain, and the sacred grove of oaks, and the altar outside, which was to be polluted with the blood of no victim—the only offerings being fruits and honey, and undressed wool—were still there. The statue was gone. Some said it had been destroyed by the fall of the cliff; some were not sure that it had ever been there at all. And meanwhile Praxiteles had already brought to perfection (Paus. 1, 2, sec. 4) the ideal of Demeter, mother-like, as Heré—whom we still call Juno now—but softer-featured, and her eyes more closed.

And so for mother earth, as for the rest, the best representation of the divine was the human. Now, conceive such an idea taking hold, however slowly, of a people of rare physical beauty, of acutest eye for proportion and grace, with opportunities of studying the human figure such as exist nowhere now, save among tropic savages, and gifted, moreover, in that as in all other matters, with that innate diligence, of which Mr. Carlyle has said, "that genius is only an infinite capacity of taking pains," and we can understand somewhat of the causes which produced those statues, human and divine, which awe and shame the artificiality and degeneracy of our modern so-called civilisation—we can understand somewhat of the reverence for the human form, of the careful study of every line, the storing up for use each scattered fragment of beauty of which the artist caught sight, even in his daily walks, and consecrating it in his memory to the service of him or her whom he was trying to embody in marble or in bronze. And when the fashion came in of making statues of victors in the games, and other distinguished persons, a new element was introduced, which had large social as well as artistic results. The sculptor carried his usual reverence into his careful delineation of the victor's form, while he obtained in him a model, usually of the very highest type, for perfecting his idea of some divinity. The possibility of gaining the right to a statue gave a fresh impulse to all competitors in the public games, and through them to the gymnastic training throughout all the states of Greece, which made the Greeks the most physically able and graceful, as well as the most beautiful people known to the history of the human race,—a people who, reverencing beauty, reverenced likewise grace or acted beauty, so utterly and honestly, that nothing was too humble for a free man to do, if it were not done awkwardly and ill. As an instance, Sophocles himself—over and above his poetic genius, one of the most cultivated gentlemen, as well as one of the most exquisite musicians, dancers, and gymnasts, and one of the most just, pious, and gentle of all Greece—could not, by reason of the weakness of his voice, act in his own plays, as poets were wont to do, and had to perform only the office of stage-manager. Twice he took part in the action, once as the blind old Thamyris playing on the harp, and once in his own lost tragedy, the "Nausicaa." There in the scene in which the Princess, as she does in Homer's "Odyssey," comes down to the sea-shore with her maidens to wash the household clothes, and then to play at ball—Sophocles himself, a man then of middle age, did the one thing he could do better than any there—and, dressed in women's clothes, among the lads who represented the maidens, played at ball before the Athenian people.

Just sixty years after the representation of the "Antigone," 10,000 Greeks, far on the plains of Babylon, cut through the whole Persian army, as the railway train cuts through a herd of buffalo, and then losing all their generals by treacherous warfare, fought their way north from Babylon to Trebizond on the Black Sea, under the guidance of a young Athenian, a pupil of Socrates, who had never served in the army before. The retreat of Xenophon and his 10,000 will remain for ever as one of the grandest triumphs of civilisation over brute force: but what made it possible? That these men, and their ancestors before them, had been for at least 100 years in *training*, physical, intellectual, and moral, which made their bodies and their minds able to dare and suffer like those old heroes of whom their tragedy had taught them, and whose spirits they still believed would help the valiant Greek. And yet that feat, which looks to us so splendid, attracted, as far as I am aware, no special admiration at the time. So was the cultivated Greek expected to behave whenever he came in contact with the uncultivated barbarian.

But from what had sprung in that little state, this exuberance of splendid life, physical, æsthetic, intellectual, which made, and will make the name of Athens and of the whole cluster of Greek republics for ever admirable to civilised man? Had it sprung from long years of peaceful prosperity? From infinite making of money and comfort, according to the laws of so-called political economy, and the dictates of enlightened selfishness? Not so. But rather out of terror and agony, and all but utter ruin—and out of a magnificent want of economy, and the divine daring and folly of self-sacrifice.

In Salamis across the strait a trophy stood, and round that trophy, forty years before, Sophocles, the author of "Antigone," then sixteen years of age, the loveliest and most cultivated lad in Athens, undraped like a faun, with lyre in hand, was leading the Chorus of Athenian youths, and singing to Athené, the tutelary goddess, a hymn of triumph for a glorious victory—the very symbol of Greece and Athens, springing up into a joyous second youth after invasion and desolation, as the grass springs up after the prairie fire has passed. But the fire had been terrible. It had burnt Athens at least, down to the very roots. True, while Sophocles was dancing, Xerxes, the great king of the East, foiled at Salamis, as his father Darius had been foiled at Marathon ten years before, was fleeing back to Persia, leaving his innumerable hosts of slaves and mercenaries to be destroyed piecemeal, by land at Platea, by sea at Mycalé. The bold hope was over, in which the Persian, ever since the days of Cyrus, had indulged—that he, the despot of the East, should be the despot of the West likewise. It seemed to them as possible, though not as easy, to subdue the Aryan Greek, as it had been to subdue the Semite and the Turanian, the Babylonian and the Syrian; to rifle his temples, to destroy his idols, carry off his women and children as colonists into distant lands, as they had been doing with all the nations of the East. And they had succeeded with isolated colonies, isolated islands of Greeks, and the shores of Asia Minor. But when they dared, at last, to attack the Greek in his own sacred land of Hellas, they found they had bearded a lion in his den. Nay rather—as those old Greeks would have said—they had dared to attack Pallas Athené, the eldest daughter of Zeus—emblem of that serene and pure divine wisdom, of whom Solomon sang of old: "The Lord possessed me in the beginning of His way, before His works of old. When He prepared the heavens, I was there, when He appointed the foundation of the earth, then was I by him, as one brought up with Him, and I was daily His delight, rejoicing always before Him: rejoicing in the habitable part of His earth; *and my delight was with the sons of men*"—to attack Athené and her brother Apollo, Lord of light, and beauty, and culture, and grace, and inspiration—to attack them, not in the name of Ormuzd, nor of any other deity, but in the name of mere brute force and lust of conquest. The old Persian spirit was gone out of them. They were the symbols now of nothing save despotism and self-will, wealth and self-indulgence. They, once the children of Ormuzd or light, had become the children of Ahriman or darkness; and therefore it was, as I believe, that Xerxes' 1000 ships, and the two million (or, as some have it, five million) human beings availed naught against the little fleets and little battalions of men who believed with a living belief in Athené and Apollo, and therefore—ponder it well, for it is true—with a living belief, under whatsoever confusions and divisions of personality, in a God who loved, taught, inspired men, a just God who befriended the righteous cause, the cause of freedom and patriotism, a Deity, the echo of whose mind and will to man was the song of Athené on Olympus, when she

Chanted of order and right, and of foresight, and order of peoples;
Chanted of labour and craft, wealth in the port and the garner;
Chanted of valour and fame, and the man who can fall with the foremost,
Fighting for children and wife, and the field which his father bequeathed him.
Sweetly and cunningly sang she, and planned new lessons for mortals.
Happy who hearing obey her, the wise unsullied Athené.

Ah, that they had always obeyed her, those old Greeks. But meanwhile, as I said, the agony had been extreme. If Athens had sinned, she had been purged as by fire; and the fire—surely of God—had been terrible. Northern Greece had either been laid waste with fire and sword, or had gone over to the Persian, traitors in their despair. Attica, almost the only loyal state, had been overrun; the old men, women, and children had fled to the neighbouring islands, or to the Peloponnese. Athens itself had been destroyed; and while young Sophocles was dancing round the trophy at Salamis, the Acropolis was still a heap of blackened ruins.

But over and above their valour, over and above

their loyalty, over and above their exquisite æsthetic faculty, these Athenians had a resilience of self-reliant energy, like that of the French—like that of the American people after the fire of Chicago; and Athens rose from her ashes to be awhile, not only, as she had nobly earned by suffering and endurance, the leading state in Greece, but a mighty fortress, a rich commercial port, a living centre of art, poetry, philosophy, such as this earth has never seen before or since.

On the plateau of that little crag of the Acropolis some eight hundred feet in length, by four hundred in breadth—about the size and shape of the Castle Rock at Edinburgh—was gathered, within forty years of the battle of Salamis, more and more noble beauty than ever stood together on any other spot of like size.

The sudden relief from crushing pressure, and the joyous consciousness of well-earned honours, made the whole spirit-nature of the people blossom out, as it were, into manifold forms of activity, beauty, research, and raised, in raising Greece, the whole human race thenceforth.

What might they not have done—looking at what they actually did—for the whole race of man?

But no—they fell, even more rapidly than they rose, till their grace and their cultivation, for them they could not lose, made them the willing ministers to the luxury, the frivolity, the sentimentality, the vice of the whole old world—the Scapia or Figaro of the old world—infinitely able, but with all his ability consecrated to the service of his own base self. The

Greekling—as Juvenal has it—in want of a dinner, would climb somehow to heaven itself, at the bidding of his Roman master.

Ah what a fall! And what was the inherent weakness which caused that fall?

I say at once—want of honesty. The Greek was not to be depended on; if it suited him, he would lie, betray, overreach, change sides, and think it no sin. He was the sharpest of men. Sharp practice, in our modern sense of the word, was the very element in which he floated. Any scholar knows it. In the grand times of Marathon and Salamis, down to the disastrous times of the Peloponnesian war and the thirty tyrants, no public man's hands were clean, with the exception, perhaps, of Aristides, who was banished because men were tired of hearing him called the Just. The exciting cause of the Peloponnesian war, and the consequent downfall of Athens, was not merely the tyranny she exercised over the states allied to her, it was the sharp practice of the Athenians, in misappropriating the tribute paid by the allies to the decoration of Athens. And in laying the foundations of the Parthenon was sown, by a just judgment, the seed of ruin for the state which gloried in it. And if the rulers were such, what were the people? If the free were such, what were the slaves?

Hence, weakness at home and abroad, mistrust of generals and admirals, paralysing all bold and clear action, peculations and corruptions at home, internecine wars between factions inside states, and between states or groups of states, revolutions followed by despotism, and final exhaustion and slavery—slavery to a people who were coming across the western sea, hard-headed, hard-hearted, caring nothing for art, or science, whose pleasures were coarse and cruel, but with a certain rough honesty, reverence for country, for law, and for the ties of a family—men of a somewhat old English type, who had over and above, like the English, the inspiring belief that they could conquer the whole world, and who very nearly succeeded in that—as we have, to our great blessing, not succeeded—I mean, of course, the Romans.

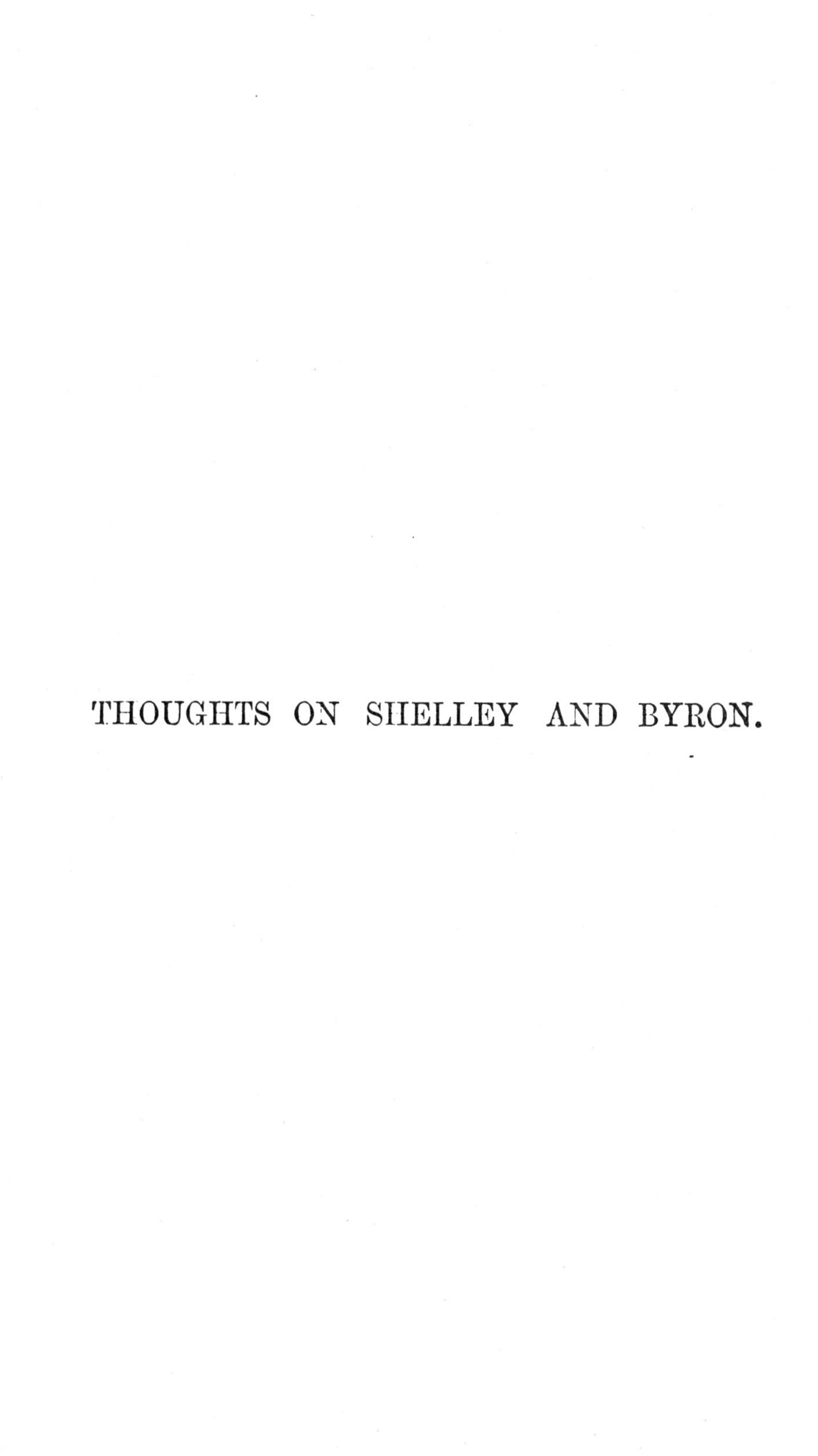

THOUGHTS ON SHELLEY AND BYRON.

THOUGHTS ON SHELLEY AND BYRON.*

THE poets, who forty years ago proclaimed their intention of working a revolution in English literature, and who have succeeded in their purpose, recommended especially a more simple and truthful view of nature. The established canons of poetry were to be discarded as artificial; as to the matter, the poet was to represent mere nature as he saw her; as to form, he was to be his own law. Freedom and nature were to be his watchwords.

No theory could be more in harmony with the spirit of the age, and the impulse which had been given to it by the burning words of Jean Jacques Rousseau. The school which arose expressed fairly the unrest and unruliness of the time, its weariness of artificial restraint and unmeaning laws, its craving after a nobler and a more earnest life, its sense of a glory and mystery in the physical universe, hidden from the poets of the two preceding centuries, and now revealed by science. So far all was hopeful. But

* Fraser's Magazine, November, 1853.

it soon became apparent, that each poet's practical success in carrying out the theory was, paradoxically enough, in inverse proportion to his belief in it; that those who like Wordsworth, Southey, and Keats, talked most about naturalness and freedom, and most openly reprobated the school of Pope, were, after all, least natural and least free; that the balance of those excellences inclined much more to those who, like Campbell, Rogers, Crabbe, and Moore, troubled their heads with no theories, but followed the best old models which they knew; and that the rightful sovereign of the new Parnassus, Lord Byron, protested against the new movement, while he followed it; upheld to the last the models which it was the fashion to decry, confessed to the last, in poetry as in morals, "Video meliora proboque, deteriora sequor," and uttered again and again prophecies of the downfall of English poetry and English taste, which seem to be on the eve of realisation.

Now no one will, we presume, be silly enough to say that humanity has gained nothing by all the very beautiful poetry which has been poured out on it during the last thirty years in England. Nevertheless, when we see poetry dying down among us year by year, although the age is becoming year by year more marvellous and inspiring, we have a right to look for some false principle in a school which has had so little enduring vitality, which seems now to be able to perpetuate nothing of itself but its vices.

The answer so easy twenty years ago, that the new poetry was spoiled by an influx of German bad taste, very ignorant people. It is now known, of course, that whatsoever quarrel Lessing, Schiller, and Goethe may have had with Pope, it was not on account of his being too severe an artist, but too loose a one; not for being too classical, but not classical enough; that English poets borrowed from them nothing but their most boyish and immature types of thought, and that these were reproduced, and laughed at here, while the men themselves were writing works of a purity, and loftiness, and completeness, unknown to the world—except in the writings of Milton—for nearly two centuries. This feature, however, of the new German poetry, was exactly the one which no English poet deigned to imitate, save Byron alone; on whom, accordingly, Goethe always looked with admiration and affection. But the rest went their way unheeding; and if they have defects, those defects are their own; for when they did copy the German taste, they, for the most part, deliberately chose the evil, and refused the good; and have their reward in a fame which we believe will prove itself a very short-lived one.

We cannot deny, however, that, in spite of all faults, these men had a strength. They have exercised an influence. And they have done so by virtue of seeing a fact which more complete, and in some cases more manly poets, did not see. Strangely enough, Shelley, the man who was the greatest sinner of them all against the canons of good taste, was the man who saw that new fact, if not most clearly, still most intensely, and who proclaimed it most boldly. His influence, therefore, is outliving that of his compeers, and growing and spreading, for good and for evil; and will grow and spread for years to come, as long as the present great unrest goes on smouldering in men's hearts, till the hollow settlement of 1815 is burst asunder anew, and men feel that they are no longer in the beginning of the end, but in the end itself, and that this long thirty years' prologue to the reconstruction of rotten Europe is played out at last, and the drama itself begun.

Such is the way of Providence; the race is not to the swift, nor the battle to the strong, nor the prophecy to the wise. The Spirit bloweth where He listeth, and sends on His errands—those who deny Him, rebel against Him—profligates, madmen, and hysterical Rousseaus, hysterical Shelleys, uttering words like the east wind. He uses strange tools in His cosmogony: but He does not use them in vain. By bad men if not by good, by fools if not by wise, God's work is done, and done right well.

There was, then, a strength and a truth in all these men; and it was this—that more or less clearly, they all felt that they were standing between two worlds; amid the ruins of an older age; upon the threshold of a new one. To Byron's mind, the decay and rottenness of the old was, perhaps, the most palpable; to Shelley's, the possible glory of the new. Wordsworth declared—a little too noisily, we think, as if he had been the first to discover the truth—the dignity and divineness of the most simple human facts and relationships. Coleridge declares that the new can only assume living form by growing organically out of the old institutions. Keats gives a sad and yet a wholesome answer to them both, as, young and passionate, he goes down with Faust "to the Mothers"—

> To the rich warm youth of the nations,
> Childlike in virtue and faith, though childlike in passion and pleasure,
> Childlike still, still near to the gods, while the sunset of Eden
> Lingered in rose-red rays on the peaks of Ionian mountains.

And there, amid the old classic forms, he cries: "These things, too, are eternal—

> A thing of beauty is a joy for ever.

These, or things even fairer than they, must have their place in the new world, if it is to be really a home for the human race." So he sings, as best he can, the half-educated and consumptive stable-keeper's son, from his prison-house of London brick, and in one mighty yearn after that beauty from which he is debarred, breaks his young heart, and dies, leaving a name not "writ in water," as he dreamed, but on all fair things, all lovers' hearts, for evermore.

Here, then, to return, is the reason why the hearts of the present generation have been influenced so mightily by these men, rather than by those of whom Byron wrote, with perfect sincerity:

> Scott, Rogers, Campbell, Moore, and Crabbe will try
> 'Gainst you the question with posterity.

These lines, written in 1818, were meant to apply only to Coleridge, Wordsworth, and Southey. Whether they be altogether just or unjust is not now the question. It must seem somewhat strange to our young poets that Shelley's name is not among those who are to try the question of immortality against the Lake School; and yet many of his most beautiful poems had been already written. Were, then, "The Revolt of Islam" and "Alastor" not destined, it seems, in Byron's opinion, to live as long as the "Lady of the Lake" and the "Mariners of England?" Perhaps not. At least the omission of Shelley's name is noteworthy. But still more noteworthy are these words of his to Mr. Murray, dated January 23, 1819:

"Read Pope—most of you don't—but do . . . . and the inevitable consequence would be, that you would burn all that I have ever written, and all your other wretched Claudians of the day (except Scott and Crabbe) into the bargain."

And here arises a new question—Is Shelley, then, among the Claudians? It is a hard saying. The present generation will receive it with shouts of laughter. Some future one, which studies and imitates Shakespeare instead of anatomising him, and which gradually awakens to the now forgotten fact, that a certain man named Edmund Spenser once wrote a poem, the like of which the earth never saw before, and perhaps may never see again, may be inclined to acquiesce in the verdict, and believe that Byron had a discrimination in this matter, as in a hundred more, far more acute than any of his compeers, and had not eaten in vain, poor fellow, of the tree of the knowledge of good and evil. In the meanwhile, we may perceive in the poetry of the two men deep and radical differences, indicating a spiritual difference between them even more deep, which may explain the little notice which Byron takes of Shelley's poetry, and the fact that the two men had no deep sympathy for each other, and could not in any wise "pull together" during the sojourn in Italy. Doubtless, there were plain outward faults of temper and character on both sides; neither was in a state of mind which could trust itself, or be trusted by those who loved them best. Friendship can only consist with the calm and self-restraint and self-respect of moral and intellectual health; and both were diseased, fevered, ready to take offence, ready, unwittingly, to give it. But the diseases of the two were different, as their natures were; and Shelley's fever was not Byron's.

Now it is worth remarking, that it is Shelley's form of fever, rather than Byron's, which has been of late years the prevailing epidemic. Since Shelley's poems have become known in England, and a timid public, after approaching in fear and trembling the fountain which was understood to be poisoned, has begun first to sip, and then, finding the magic water at all events sweet enough, to quench its thirst with unlimited draughts, Byron's fiercer wine has lost favour. Well—at least the taste of the age is more refined, if that be matter of congratulation. And there is an excuse for preferring champagne to waterside porter, heady with grains of paradise and quassia, salt and cocculus indicus. Nevertheless, worse ingredients than œnanthic acid may lurk in the delicate draught, and the Devil's Elixir may be made fragrant, and sweet, and transparent enough, as French moralists well know, for the most fastidious palate. The private sipping of eau-de-cologne, say the London physicians, has increased mightily of late; and so has the reading of Shelley. It is not surprising. Byron's Corsairs and Laras have been, on the whole, impossible during the thirty years' peace! and piracy and profligacy are at all times, and especially nowadays, expensive amusements, and often require a good private fortune—rare among poets. They have, therefore, been wisely abandoned as ideals, except among a few young persons, who used to wear turn-down collars, and are now attempting moustaches and Mazzini hats. But even among them, and among their betters—rather their more-respectables—nine-tenths of the bad influence which is laid at Byron's door really is owing to Shelley. Among the many good-going gentlemen and ladies, Byron is generally spoken of with horror—he is "so wicked," forsooth; while poor Shelley, "poor dear Shelley," is "very wrong, of course," but "so refined," "so beautiful," "so tender"—a fallen angel, while Byron is a satyr and a devil. We boldly deny the verdict. Neither of the two are devils; as for angels, when we have seen one, we shall be better able to give an opinion; at present, Shelley is in our eyes far less like one of those old Hebrew and Miltonic angels, fallen or unfallen, than Byron is. And as for the satyr; the less that is said for Shelley, on that point, the better. If Byron sinned more desperately and flagrantly than he, it was done under the temptations of rank, wealth, disappointed love, and under the impulses of an animal nature, to which Shelley's passions were

As moonlight unto sunlight, and as water unto wine.

At all events, Byron never set to work to consecrate his own sin into a religion and proclaim the worship of uncleanness as the last and highest ethical development of "pure" humanity. No—Byron may be brutal; but he never cants. If at moments he finds himself in hell, he never turns round to the world and melodiously informs them that it is heaven, if they could but see it in its true light.

The truth is, that what has put Byron out of favour with the public of late has been not his faults but his excellences. His artistic good taste, his classical polish, his sound shrewd sense, his hatred of cant, his insight into humbug above all, his shallow, pitiable habit of being always intelligible—these are the sins which condemn him in the eyes of a mesmerising, table-turning, spirit-rapping, spiritualising, Romanising generation, who read Shelley in secret, and delight in his bad taste, mysticism, extravagance, and vague and pompous sentimentalism. The age is an effeminate one, and it can well afford to pardon the lewdness of the gentle and sensitive vegetarian, while it has no mercy for that of the sturdy peer proud of his bull neck and his boxing, who kept bears and bull-dogs, drilled Greek ruffians at Missolonghi, and "had no objection to a pot of beer;" and who might, if he had reformed, have made a gallant English gentleman; while Shelley, if once his intense self-opinion had deserted him, would have probably ended in Rome as an Oratorian or a Passionist.

We would that it were only for this count that Byron has had to make way for Shelley. There is, as we said before, a deeper moral difference between the men, which makes the weaker, rather than the stronger, find favour in young men's eyes. For Byron has the most intense and awful sense of moral law—of law external to himself. Shelley has little or none; less, perhaps, than any known writer who has ever meddled with moral questions. Byron's cry is, I am miserable because law exists; and I have broken it, broken it so habitually, that now I cannot help breaking it. I have tried to eradicate the sense of it by speculation, by action; but I cannot—

> The tree of knowledge is not the tree of life.

There is a moral law independent of us, and yet the very marrow of our life, which punishes and rewards us by no arbitrary external penalties, but by our own consciousness of being what we are:

> The mind which is immortal, makes itself
> Requital for its good or evil thoughts;
> Is its own origin of ill, and end—
> And its own place and time—its innate sense
> When stript of this mortality derives
> No colour from the fleeting things about,
> But is absorbed in sufferance or in joy,
> Born from the knowledge of its own desert.

This idea, confused, intermitted, obscured by all forms of evil—for it was not discovered, but only in the process of discovery—is the one which comes out with greater and greater strength, through all Corsairs, Laras, and Parasinas, till it reaches its completion in "Cain" and in "Manfred," of both of which we do boldly say, that if any sceptical poetry at all be right, which we often question, they are right and not wrong; that in

"Cain," as in "Manfred," the awful problem which, perhaps, had better not have been put at all, is nevertheless fairly put, and the solution, as far as it is seen, fairly confessed; namely, that there is an absolute and eternal law in the heart of man which sophistries of his own or of other beings may make him forget, deny, blaspheme; but which exists eternally, and will assert itself. If this be not the meaning of "Manfred," especially of that great scene in the chamois hunter's cottage, what is?—If this be not the meaning of "Cain," and his awful awakening after the murder, not to any mere dread of external punishment, but to an overwhelming, instinctive, inarticulate sense of having done wrong, what is?

Yes; that law exists, let it never be forgotten, is the real meaning of Byron, down to that last terrible "Don Juan," in which he sits himself down, in artificial calm, to trace the gradual rotting and degradation of a man without law, the slave of his own pleasures; a picture happily never finished, because he who painted it was taken away before he had learnt, perhaps when he was beginning to turn back from—the lower depth within the lowest deep.

Now to this whole form of consciousness, poor Shelley's mind is altogether antipodal. His whole life through was a denial of external law, and a substitution in its place of internal sentiment. Byron's cry is: There is a law, and therefore I am miserable. Why cannot I keep the law? Shelley's is: There is a law, and therefore I am miserable. Why should not the law be abolished?—Away with it, for it interferes with my sentiments—Away with marriage, "custom and faith, the foulest birth of time."—We do not wish to follow him down into the fearful sins which he defended with the small powers of reasoning—and they were peculiarly small—which he possessed. Let any one who wishes to satisfy himself of the real difference between Byron's mind and Shelley's, compare the writings in which each of them treats the same subject—namely, that frightful question about the relation of the sexes, which forms, evidently, Manfred's crime; and see if the result is not simply this, that Shelley glorifies what Byron damns. "Lawless love" is Shelley's expressed ideal of the relation of the sexes; and his justice, his benevolence, his pity, are all equally lawless. "Follow your instincts," is his one moral rule, confounding the very lowest animal instincts with those lofty ideas of right, which it was the will of Heaven that he should retain, ay, and love, to the very last, and so reducing them all to the level of sentiments. "Follow your instincts"—But what if our instincts lead us to eat animal food? "Then you must follow the instincts of me, Percy Bysshe Shelley. I think it horrible, cruel; it offends my taste." What if our instincts lead us to tyrannise over our fellow-men? "Then you must repress those instincts. I, Shelley, think that, too, horrible and cruel." Whether it be vegetarianism or liberty, the rule is practically the same—sentiment: which, in his case, as in the case of all sentimentalists, turns out to mean at last, not the sentiments of mankind in general, but the private sentiments of the writer. This is Shelley; a sentimentalist pure and simple; incapable of anything like inductive reasoning; unable to take cognisance of any facts but those which please his taste, or to draw any conclusion from them but such as also pleases his taste; as, for example, in that eighth stanza of the "Ode to Liberty," which, had it been written by any other man but Shelley, possessing the same knowledge as he, one would have called a wicked and deliberate lie—but in his case, is to be simply passed over with a sigh, like a young lady's proofs of table-turning and rapping spirits. She wished to see it so—and therefore so she saw it.

For Shelley's nature is utterly womanish. Not merely his weak points, but his strong ones, are those of a woman. Tender and pitiful as a woman; and yet, when angry, shrieking, railing, hysterical as a woman. The physical distaste for meat and fermented liquors, coupled with the hankering after physical horrors, are especially feminine. The nature of a woman looks out of that wild, beautiful, girlish face—the nature: but not the spirit; not

> The reason firm, the temperate will,
> Endurance, foresight, strength and skill.

The lawlessness of the man, with the sensibility of the woman. . . . Alas for him! He, too, might have discovered what Byron did; for were not his errors avenged upon him within, more terribly even than without? His cries are like the wails of a child, inarticulate, peevish, irrational; and yet his pain fills his whole being, blackens the very face of nature to him: but he will not confess himself in the wrong. Once only, if we recollect rightly, the truth flashes across him for a moment, amid the clouds of selfish sorrow:

> Alas, I have nor hope nor health,
>   Nor peace within, nor calm around;
> Nor that content surpassing wealth
>   The sage in meditation found,
> And walked with inward glory crowned.

"Nor"—alas for the spiritual bathos, which follows that short gleam of healthy feeling, and coming to himself—

> —fame nor power, nor love, nor leisure,
> Others I see whom these surround,
> Smiling they live and call life pleasure,
> To me that cup has been dealt in another measure!

Poor Shelley! As if the peace within, and the calm around, and the content surpassing wealth, were things which were to be put in the same category with fame, and power, and love, and leisure. As if they were things which could be "dealt" to any man; instead of depending (as Byron, who, amid all his fearful sins, was a man, knew well enough) upon a man's self, a man's own will, and that will exerted to do a will exterior to itself, to know and to obey a law. But no, the cloud of sentiment must close over again, and

> Yet now despair itself is mild
>   Even as the winds and waters are;
> I could lie down like a tired child,
>   And weep away this life of care,
> Which I have borne, and still must bear,

Till death like sleep might seize on me,
And I might feel in the warm air,
My cheek grow cold, and hear the sea
Breathe o'er my dying brain its last monotony!

Too beautiful to laugh at, however empty and sentimental. True: but why beautiful? Because there is a certain sincerity in it, which breeds coherence and melody, which, in short, makes it poetry. But what if such a tone of mind be consciously encouraged, even insincerely affected as the ideal state for a poet's mind, as his followers have done?

The mischief which such a man would do is conceivable enough. He stands out, both by his excellences and his defects, as the spokesman and ideal of all the unrest and unhealth of sensitive young men for many a year after. His unfulfilled prophecies only help to increase that unrest. Who shall blame either him for uttering those prophecies, or them for longing for their fulfilment? Must we not thank the man who gives us fresh hope that this earth will not be always as it is now? His notion of what it will be may be, as Shelley's was, vague, even in some things wrong and undesirable. Still, we must accept his hope and faith in the spirit, not in the letter. So have thousands of young men felt, who would have shrunk with disgust from some of poor Shelley's details of the "good time coming." And shame on him who should wish to rob them of such a hope, even if it interfered with his favourite "scheme of unfulfilled prophecy." So men have felt Shelley's spell a wondrous one—perhaps, they think, a life-giving regenerative one. And yet what dream at once more shallow and more impossible?

Get rid of kings and priests; marriage may stay, pending discussions on the rights of women. Let the poet speak—what he is to say being, of course, a matter of utterly secondary import, provided only that he be a poet; and then the millennium will appear of itself, and the devil be exorcised with a kiss from all hearts—except, of course, those of "pale priests" and "tyrants with their sneer of cold command" (who, it seems, have not been got rid of after all), and the Cossacks and Croats whom they may choose to call to their rescue. And on the appearance of the said Cossacks and Croats, the poet's vision stops short, and all is blank beyond. A recipe for the production of millenniums which has this one advantage, that it is small enough to be comprehended by the very smallest minds, and reproduced thereby, with a difference, in such spasmodic melodies as seem to those small minds to be imitations of Shelley's nightingale notes.

For nightingale notes they truly are. In spite of all his faults—and there are few poetic faults in which he does not indulge, to their very highest power—in spite of his "interfluous" and "innumerous," and the rest of his bad English—in spite of bombast, horrors, maundering, sheer stuff and nonsense of all kinds, there is a plaintive natural melody about this man, such as no other English poet has ever uttered, except Shakespeare in some few immortal songs. Who that has read Shelley does not recollect scraps worthy to stand by Ariel's song—chaste, simple, unutterably musical? Yes, when he will be himself—Shelley the scholar and the gentleman and the singer—and leave philosophy and politics, which he does not understand,

and shriekings and cursings, which are unfit for any civilised and self-respecting man, he is perfect. Like the American mocking-bird, he is harsh only when aping other men's tunes—his true power lies in his own "native wood-notes wild."

But it is not this faculty of his which has been imitated by his scholars; for it is not this faculty which made him their ideal, however it may have attracted them. All which sensible men deplore in him is that which poetasters have exalted in him. His morbidity and his doubt have become in their eyes his differential energy, because too often, it was all in him with which they had wit to sympathise. They found it easy to curse and complain, instead of helping to mend. So had he. They found it pleasant to confound institutions with the abuses which defaced them. So had he. They found it pleasant to give way to their spleen. So had he. They found it pleasant to believe that the poet was to regenerate the world, without having settled with what he was to regenerate it. So had he. They found it more pleasant to obey sentiment than inductive laws. So had he. They found it more pleasant to hurl about enormous words and startling figures than to examine reverently the awful depths of beauty which lie in the simplest words and the severest figures. So had he.

And thus arose a spasmodic, vague extravagant, effeminate, school of poetry, which has been too often hastily and unfairly fathered upon Byron. Doubtless Byron has helped to its formation; but only in as far as his poems possess, or rather seem to possess, elements in common with Shelley's. For that conscious struggle against law, by which law is discovered, may easily enough be confounded with the utter repudiation of it. Both forms of mind will discuss the same questions; both will discuss them freely, with a certain plainness and daring, which may range through all grades, from the bluntness of Socrates down to reckless immodesty and profaneness. The world will hardly distinguish between the two; it did not in Socrates' case, mistaking his reverent irreverence for Atheism, and martyred him accordingly, as it has since martyred Luther's memory. Probably, too, if a living struggle is going on in the writer's mind, he will not have distinguished the two elements in himself; he will be profane when he fancies himself only arguing for truth; he will be only arguing for truth, where he seems to the respectable undoubting to be profane. And in the meanwhile, whether the respectable understand him or not, the young and the inquiring, much more the distempered, who would be glad to throw off moral law, will sympathise with him often more than he sympathises with himself. Words thrown off in the heat of passion; shameful self-revealings which he has written with his very heart's blood: ay, even fallacies which he has put into the mouths of dramatic characters for the very purpose of refuting them, or at least of calling on all who read to help him to refute them, and to deliver him from the ugly dream—all these will, by the lazy, the frivolous, the feverish, the discontented, be taken for integral parts and noble traits of the man to whom they are attracted, by finding that he, too, has the same doubts and struggles as themselves, that he has a voice and art to be their spokesman. And hence arises confusion on confusion, misconception on misconception. The man is honoured for his dishonour. Chronic disease is taken for a new type of health; and Byron is admired and imitated for that which Byron is trying to tear out of his own heart, and trample under foot as his curse and bane, something which is not Byron's self, but Byron's house-fiend, and tyrant, and shame. And in the meanwhile that which calls itself respectability and orthodoxy, and is—unless Augustine lied—neither of them, stands by; and instead of echoing the voice of Him who said: "Come to me ye that are weary and heavy laden, and I will give you rest," mumbles proudly to itself, with the Pharisees of old: "This people, which knoweth not the law, is accursed."

We do not seek to excuse Byron any more than we do Shelley. They both sinned. They both paid bitter penalty for their sin. How far they were guilty, or which of them was the more guilty, we know not. We can judge no man. It is as poets and teachers, not as men and responsible spirits; not in their inward beings, known only to Him who made them, not even to themselves, but in their outward utterance, that we have a right to compare them. Both have done harm. Neither have, we firmly believe, harmed any human being who had not already the harm within himself. It is not by introducing evil, but by calling into consciousness and more active life evil which was already lurking in the heart, that any writer makes men worse. Thousands doubtless have read Byron and Shelley, and worse books, and have risen from them as pure as when they sat down. In evil as well as in good, the eye only sees that which it brings with it the power of seeing—say rather, the wish to see. But it is because, in spite of all our self-glorifying pæans, our taste has become worse and not better, that Shelley, the man who conceitedly despises and denies law, is taking the place of Byron, the man who only struggles against it, and who shows his honesty and his greatness most by confessing that his struggles are ineffectual; that, Titan as he may look to the world, his strength is misdirected, a mere furious weakness, which proclaims him a slave in fetters, while prurient young gentlemen are fancying him heaping hills on hills, and scaling Olympus itself. They are tired of that notion, however, now. They have begun to suspect that Byron did not scale Olympus after all. How much more pleasant a leader, then, must Shelley be, who unquestionably did scale his little Olympus—having made it himself first to fit his own stature. The man who has built the hay-rick will doubtless climb it again, if need be, as often as desired, and whistle on the top, after the fashion of the rick-building guild, triumphantly enough. For after all Shelley's range of vision is very narrow, his subjects few, his reflections still fewer, when compared, not only with such a poet as Spenser, but with his own contemporaries; above all with Byron. He has a deep heart, but not a wide one; an intense eye, but not a catholic one. And, therefore, he never wrote a real drama; for in spite of all that has been said to the contrary, Beatrice Cenci is really none other than Percy Bysshe Shelley himself in petticoats.

But we will let them both be. Perhaps they know better now.

One very ugly superstition, nevertheless, we must mention, of which these two men have been, in England at least, the great hierophants; namely, the right of "genius" to be "eccentric." Doubtless there are excuses for such a notion; but it is one against which every wise man must set his face like a flint; and at the risk of being called a "Philister" and a "flunky," take part boldly with respectability and this wicked world, and declare them to be for once utterly in the right. Still there are excuses for it. A poet, especially one who wishes to be not merely a describer of pretty things, but a "Vates" and seer of new truth, must often say things which other people do not like to say, and do things which others do not like to do. And, moreover, he will be generally gifted, for the very purpose of enabling him to say and do these strange things, with a sensibility more delicate than common, often painful enough to himself. How easy for such a man to think that he has a right not to be as other men are; to despise little conventionalities, courtesies, even decencies; to offend boldly and carelessly, conscious that he has something right and valuable within himself which not only atones for such defects, but allows him to indulge in them, as badges of his own superiority!

This has been the notion of artistic genius which has spread among us of late years, just in proportion as the real amount of artistic genius has diminished; till we see men, on the mere ground of being literary men, too refined to keep accounts, or pay their butchers' bills; affecting the pettiest absurdities in dress, in manner, in food; giving themselves credit for being unable to bear a noise, keep their temper, educate their own children, associate with their fellow-men; and a thousand other paltry weaknesses, morosenesses, self-indulgences, fastidiousnesses, vulgarities—for all this is essentially vulgar, and demands, not honour and sympathy, but a chapter in Mr. Thackeray's "Book of Snobs." Non sic itur ad astra. Self-indulgence and exclusiveness can only be a proof of weakness. It may accompany talent, but it proves that talent to be partial and defective. The brain may be large, but the manhood, the "virtus," is small, where such things are allowed, much more where they are gloried in. A poet such a man may be, but a world poet never. He is sectarian, a poetical Quaker, a Puritan, who, forgetting that the truth which he possesses is equally the right and inheritance of every man he meets, takes up a peculiar dress or phraseology, as symbols of his fancied difference from his human brothers. All great poets, till Shelley and Byron, as far as we can discern, have been men especially free from eccentricities; careful not merely of the chivalries and the respectabilities, but also of the courtesies and the petty conventionalities, of the age in which they lived; altogether well-bred men of the world. The answer, that they learnt the ways of courts, does not avail; for if they had had no innate good-breeding, reticence, respect for forms and customs, they would never have come near courts at all. It is not a question of rank and fashion, but of good feeling, common sense, unselfishness. Goethe, Milton, Spenser, Shakespeare, Rabelais, Ariosto, were none of them high-born men; several of them low-born; who only rose to the society of high-born men because they were themselves innately high-bred, polished, complete, without exaggerations, affectations, deformities, weaknesses of mind and taste, whatever may have been their weaknesses on certain points of morals. The man of all men most bepraised by the present generation of poets, is perhaps Wolfgang von Goethe. Why is it, then, that of all men he is the one whom they strive to be most unlike?

And if this be good counsel for the man who merely wishes—and no blame to him—to sing about beautiful things in a beautiful way, it applies with tenfold force to the poet who desires honestly to proclaim great truths. If he has to offend the prejudices of the world in important things, that is all the more reason for his bowing to those prejudices in little things, and being content to be like his neighbours in outward matters, in order that he may make them like himself in inward ones. Shall such a man dare to hinder his own message, to drive away the very hearers to whom he believes himself to be sent, for the sake of his own nerves, laziness, antipathies, much more of his own vanity and pride? If he does so, he is unfaithful to that very genius on which he prides himself. He denies its divinity, by treating it as his own possession, to be displayed or hidden as he chooses, for his own enjoyment, his own self-glorification. Well for such a man if a day comes to him in which he will look back with shame and self-reproach, not merely on every scandal which he may have caused by breaking the moral and social laws of humanity, by neglecting to restrain his appetites, pay his bills, and keep his engagements;

but also on every conceited word and look, every gaucherie and rudeness, every self-indulgent moroseness and fastidiousness, as sins against the sacred charge which has been committed to him; and determine with that Jew of old, who, to judge from his letter to Philemon, was one of the most perfect gentlemen of God's making who ever walked this earth, to become "all things to all men, if by any means he may save some."

ALEXANDER SMITH AND ALEXANDER POPE.

ALEXANDER SMITH AND ALEXANDER POPE.

On reading this little book,* and considering all the exaggerated praise and exaggerated blame which have been lavished on it, we could not help falling into many thoughts about the history of English poetry for the last forty years, and about its future destiny. Great poets, even true poets, are becoming more and more rare among us. There are those even who say that we have none; an assertion which, as long as Mr. Tennyson lives, we shall take the liberty of denying. But were he, which Heaven forbid, taken from us, whom have we to succeed him? And he, too, is rather a poet of the sunset than of the dawn—of the autumn than of the spring. His gorgeousness is that of the solemn and fading year; not of its youth, full of hope, freshness, gay and unconscious life. Like some stately hollyhock or dahlia of this month's gardens, he endures while all other flowers are dying; but all

* "Poems," by Alexander Smith. London: Bogue. 1853. Fraser's Magazine, October, 1853.

around is winter—a mild one, perhaps, wherein a few annuals or pretty field weeds still linger on; but, like all mild winters, especially prolific in fungi, which, too, are not without their gaudiness, even their beauty, although bred only from the decay of higher organisms, the plagiarists of the vegetable world. Such is poetry in England; while in America the case is not much better. What more enormous scope for new poetic thought than that which the New World gives? Yet the American poets, even the best of them, look lingeringly and longingly back to Europe and her legends; to her models, and not to the best of them—to her criticism, and not to the best of that—and bestow but a very small portion of such genius as they have on America and her new forms of life. If they be nearer to the spring than we, they are still deep enough in the winter. A few early flowers may be budding among them, but the autumn crop is still in somewhat shabby and rain-bedrabbled bloom. And for us, where are our spring flowers? What sign of a new poetic school? Still more, what sign of the healthy resuscitation of any old one?

"What matter, after all?" one says to oneself in despair, re-echoing Mr. Carlyle. "Man was not sent into the world to write poetry. What we want is truth. Of the former we have enough in all conscience just now. Let the latter need be provided for by honest and righteous history, and as for poets, let the dead bury their dead." And yet, after all, man will write poetry, in spite of Mr. Carlyle: nay, beings who are not men, but mere forked radishes, will write it. Man is a poetry-writing animal. Perhaps he was meant to be one. At all events, he can no more be kept from it than from eating. It is better, with Mr. Carlyle's leave, to believe that the existence of poetry indicates some universal human hunger, whether after "the beautiful," or after "fame," or after the means of paying butchers' bills; and accepting it as a necessary evil which must be committed, to see that it be committed as well, or at least as little ill, as possible. In excuse of which we may quote Mr. Carlyle against himself, reminding him of a saying of Goethe once bepraised by him in print: "We must take care of the beautiful, for the useful will take care of itself."

And never, certainly, since Pope wrote his Dunciad, did the beautiful require more taking care of, or evince less capacity for taking care of itself; and never, we must add, was less capacity for taking care of it evinced by its accredited guardians of the press than at this present time, if the reception given to Mr. Smith's poems is to be taken as a fair expression of "the public taste."

Now, let it be fairly understood, Mr. Alexander Smith is not the object of our reproaches: but Mr. Alexander Smith's models and flatterers. Against him we have nothing whatsoever to say; for him, very much indeed.

Very young, as is said, self-educated, drudging for his daily bread in some dreary Glasgow prison-house of brick and mortar, he has seen the sky, the sun and moon—and, moreover, the sea, report says, for one day in his whole life; and this is nearly the whole of his experience in natural objects. And he has felt, too painfully for his peace of mind, the contrast between his environment and that of others—his means of culture and that of others—and, still more painfully, the contrast between his environment and culture, and that sense of beauty and power of melody which he does not deny that he has found in himself, and which no one can deny who reads his poems fairly; who reads even merely the opening page and key-note of the whole:

For as a torrid sunset burns with gold
Up to the zenith, fierce within my soul
A passion burns from basement unto cope.
Poesy, poesy, I'd give to thee
As passionately my rich laden years,
My bubble pleasures, and my awful joys,
As Hero gave her trembling sighs to find
Delicious death on wet Leander's lip.
Bare, bald, and tawdry, as a fingered moth
Is my poor life; but with one smile thou canst
Clothe me with kingdoms. Wilt thou smile on me?
Wilt bid me die for thee? Oh fair and cold!
As well may some wild maiden waste her love
Upon the calm front of a marble Jove.

Now this scrap is by no means a fair average specimen of Mr. Smith's verse. But is not the self-educated man who could teach himself, amid Glasgow smoke and noise, to write such a distich as that exquisite one which we have given in italics, to be judged lovingly and hopefully?

What if he has often copied? What if, in this very scrap, chosen almost at random, there should be a touch from Tennyson's "Two Voices?" And what if imitations, nay, caricatures, be found in almost every page?

Is not the explanation simple enough, and rather creditable than discreditable to Mr. Smith? He takes as his models Shelley, Keats, and their followers. Who is to blame for that? The Glasgow youth, or the public taste, which has been exalting these authors more and more for the last twenty years as the great poets of the nineteenth century? If they are the proper ideals of the day, who will blame him for following them as closely as possible—for saturating his memory so thoroughly with their words and thoughts that he reproduces them unconsciously to himself? Who will blame him for even consciously copying their images, if they have said better than he the thing which he wants to say, in the only poetical dialect which he knows? He does no more than all schools have done, copy their own masters; as the Greek epicists and Virgil copied Homer; as all succeeding Latin epicists copied Virgil; as Italians copied Ariosto and Tasso; as every one who can copies Shakespeare; as the French school copied, or thought they copied, "The Classics," and as a matter of duty used to justify any bold image in their notes, not by its originality, but by its being already in Claudian, or Lucan, or Virgil, or Ovid; as every poetaster, and a great many who were more than poetasters, twenty years ago, used to copy Scott and Byron, and as all poetasters now are copying the very same models as Mr. Smith, and failing while he succeeds.

We by no means agree in the modern outcry for "originality." Is it absolutely demanded that no poet shall say anything whatsoever that any other poet has said? If so, Mr. Smith may well submit to a blame which he will bear in common with Shakespeare, Chaucer, Pope, and many another great name; and especially with Raphael himself, who made no scruple of adopting not merely points of style, but single motives and incidents, from contemporaries and predecessors. Who can look at any of his earlier pictures, the Crucifixion for instance, at present in Lord Ward's gallery at the Egyptian Hall, without seeing that he has not merely felt the influence of Perugino, but copied him; tried deliberately to be as like his master as he could? Was this plagiarism? If so, all education, it would seem, must be a mere training in plagiarism. For how is the student to learn, except by copying his master's models? Is the young painter or sculptor a plagiarist because he spends the first, often the best, years of his life in copying Greek statues; or the schoolboy, for toiling at the reproduction of Latin metres and images, in what are honestly and fittingly called "copies" of verses? And what if the young artist shall choose, as Mr. Smith has done, to put a few drawings into the exhibition, or to carve and sell a few statuettes? What if the schoolboy, grown into a gownsman, shall contribute his share to a set of "Arundines Cami" or "Prolusiones Etonienses?" Will any one who really knows what art or education means complain of them for having imitated their models, however servilely? Will he not rather hail such an imitation as a fair proof, first of the student's reverence for authority—a more important element of "genius" than most young folks fancy—and next, of his possessing any artistic power whatsoever? For, surely, if the greater contains the less, the power of creating must contain that of imitating. A young author's power of accurate imitation is, after all, the primary and indispensable test of his having even the capability of becoming a poet. He who cannot write in a style which he does know, will certainly not be able to invent a new style for himself. The first and simplest form in which any metrical ear, or fancy, or imagination, can show itself, must needs be in imitating existing models. Innate good taste—that is, true poetic genius—will of course choose the best models in the long run. But not necessarily at first. What shall be the student's earliest ideal must needs be determined for him by circumstance, by the books to which he has access, by the public opinion which he hears expressed. Enough if he chooses, as Raphael did, the best models which he knows, and tries to exhaust them, and learn all he can from them, ready to quit them hereafter when he comes across better ones, yet without throwing away what he has learnt. "Be faithful in a few things, and thou shalt become ruler over many things," is one of those eternal moral laws which, like many others, holds as true of art as it does of virtue.

And on the whole, judging Mr. Alexander Smith by this rule, he has been faithful over a few things, and therefore we have fair hope of him for the future. For Mr. Smith does succeed, not in copying one poet, but in copying all, and very often in improving on his models. Of the many conceits which he has borrowed from Mr. Bailey, there is hardly one which he has not made more true, more pointed and more sweet; nay, in one or two places, he has dared to mend John Keats himself. But his whole merit is by no means confined to the faculty of imitation. Though the "Life Drama" itself is the merest cento of reflections and images, without coherence or organisation, dramatic or logical, yet single scenes, like that with the peasant and that with the fallen outcast, have firm self-consistency and clearness of conception; and these, as a natural consequence, are comparatively free from those tawdry spangles which deface the greater part of the poem. And, moreover, in the episode of "The Indian and the Lady," there is throughout a "keeping in the tone," as painters say, sultry and languid, yet rich and full of life, like a gorgeous Venetian picture, which augurs even better for Mr. Smith's future success than the two scenes just mentioned; for consistency of thought may come with time and training; but clearness of inward vision, the faculty of imagination, can be no more learnt than it can be dispensed with. In this, and this only it is true that poeta nascitur non fit; just as no musical learning or practice can make a composer, unless he first possess an innate ear for harmony and melody. And it must be said that it is just in the passages where Mr. Smith is not copying, where he forgets for awhile Shelley, Keats, and the rest, and is content to be simply himself, that he is best; terse, vivid, sound, manly, simple. May he turn round some day, and deliberately pulling out all borrowed feathers, look at himself honestly and boldly in the glass, and we will warrant him, on the strength of the least gaudy, and as yet unpraised passages in his poems, that he will find himself after all more eagle than daw, and quite well plumed enough by nature to fly at a higher, because for him a more natural, pitch than he has yet done.

True, he has written a great deal of nonsense; nonsense in matter as well as in manner. But therein, too, he has only followed the reigning school. As for manner, he does sometimes, in imitating his models, out-Herod Herod. But why not? If Herod be a worthy king, let him be by all means out-Heroded, if any man can do it. One cannot have too much of a good thing. If it be right to bedizen verses with metaphors and similes which have no reference, either in tone or in subject, to the matter in hand, let there be as many of them as possible. If a saddle is a proper place for jewels, then let the seat be paved with diamonds and emeralds, and Runjeet Singh's harness-maker be considered as a lofty artist, for whose barbaric splendour Mr. Peat and his Melton customers are to forswear pigskin and severe simplicity—not to say utility and comfort. If poetic diction be different in species from plain English, then let us have it as poetical as possible, and as unlike English; as ungrammatical, abrupt, involved, transposed, as the clumsiness, carelessness, or caprice of man can make it. If it be correct to express human thought by writing whole pages of vague and bald abstract metaphysic, and then trying to explain them by concrete concetti, which bear an entirely accidental and mystical likeness to the notion which they are to illustrate, then let the metaphysic be as abstract as possible, the concetti as fanciful and far-fetched as possible. If Marino and Cowley be greater poets than Ariosto and Milton, let young poets imitate the former with might and main, and avoid spoiling their style by any perusal of the too-intelligible common sense of the latter. If Byron's moral (which used to be thought execrable) be really his great excellence, and his style (which used to be thought almost perfect) unworthy of this age of progress, then let us have his moral without his style, his matter without his form; or—that we may be sure of never falling for a moment into his besetting sins of terseness, grace, and completeness—without any form at all. If poetry, in order to be worthy of the nineteenth century, ought to be as unlike as possible to Homer or Sophocles, Virgil or Horace, Shakespeare or Spenser, Dante or Tasso, let those too-idolised names be rased henceforth from the calendar; let the "Ars Poetica" be consigned to flames, and Martinus Scriblerus's "Art of Sinking" placed forthwith on the list of the Committee of Council for Education, that not a working man in England may be ignorant that, whatsoever superstitions about art may have haunted the benighted heathens who built the Parthenon, *nous avons changé tout cela.* In one word, if it be best and most fitting to write poetry in the style in which almost every one has been trying to write it since Pope and plain sense went out, and Shelley and the seventh heaven came in, let it be so written; and let him who most perfectly so "sets the age to music," be presented by the assembled guild of critics, not with the obsolete and too classic laurel, but with an electro-plated brass medal, bearing the due inscription, "Ars est nescire artem." And when, in twelve months' time, he finds himself forgotten, perhaps decried, for the sake of the next aspirant, let him reconsider himself, try whether, after all, the common sense of the many will not prove a juster and a firmer standing-ground than the sentimentality and bad taste of the few, and read Alexander Pope.

In Pope's writings, whatsoever he may not find, he will find the very excellences after which our young poets strive in vain, produced by their seeming opposites, which are now despised and discarded; naturalness produced by studious art; sublimity by strict self-restraint; depth by clear simplicity; pathos by easy grace; and a morality infinitely more merciful, as well as more righteous, than the one now in vogue among the poetasters, by honest faith in God. If he be shocked by certain peculiarities of diction, and by the fondness for perpetual antitheses, let him remember, that what seems strange to our day was natural and habitual in Pope's; and that, in the eyes of our grandchildren, Keats's and Shelley's peculiarities will seem as monstrous as Pope's or Johnson's do in ours. But if, misled by the popular contempt for Pope, he should be inclined to answer this advice with a shrug and a smile, we entreat him and all young poets, to consider, line by line, word by word, sound by sound, only those once well-known lines, which many a brave and wise man of fifty years ago would have been unable to read without honourable tears:

> In the worst inn's worst room, with mat half-hung,
> The floor of plaster, and the walls of dung,
> On once a flock-bed, but repaired with straw,
> With tape-tied curtains never meant to draw,
> The George and Garter, dangling from that bed,
> Where tawdry yellow strove with dirty red,
> Great Villiers lies. Alas! how changed from him,
> That life of pleasure, and that soul of whim!

Gallant and gay, in Cliveden's proud alcove,
The bower of wanton Shrewsbury and love;
Or just as gay, at Council, in a ring
Of mimic statesmen, and their merry king,
No wit to flatter, left of all his store!
No fool to laugh at, which he valued more.
There, victor of his health, of fortune, friends,
And fame, this lord of useless thousands ends.

Yes; Pope knew, as well as Wordsworth and our "Naturalisti," that no physical fact was so mean or coarse as to be below the dignity of poetry—when in its right place. He could draw a pathos and sublimity out of the dirty inn chamber, such as Wordsworth never elicited from tubs and daffodils—because he could use them according to the rules of art, which are the rules of sound reason and of true taste.

The answer to all this is ready nowadays. We are told that Pope could easily be great in what he attempted, because he never attempted any but small matters; easily self-restraining, because his paces were naturally so slow; above all, easily clear, because he is always shallow; easily full of faith in what he did believe, because he believed so very little. On the two former counts we may have something to say hereafter. On the two latter, we will say at once, that if it be argued, as it often is, that the reason of our modern poetical obscurity and vagueness lies in the greater depth of the questions which are now agitating thoughtful minds, we do utterly deny it. Human nature, human temptations, human problems, are radically the same in every age, by whatsoever outward difference of words they may seem distinguished.

Where is deeper philosophic thought, true or false, expressed in verse, than in Dante, or in Spenser's two cantos of "Mutabilities"? Yet if they are difficult to understand, their darkness is that of the deep blue sea. Vague they never are, obscure they never are, because they see clearly what they want to say, and how to say it. There is always a sound and coherent meaning in them, to be found if it be searched for.

The real cause of this modern vagueness is rather to be found in shallow and unsound culture, and in that inability, or carelessness about seeing any object clearly, which besets our poets just now; as the cause of antique clearness lies in the nobler and healthier manhood, in the severer and more methodic habits of thought, the sounder philosophic and critical training, which enabled Spenser and Milton to draw up a state paper, or to discourse deep metaphysics, with the same manful possession of their subject which gives grace and completeness to the "Penseroso" or the "Epithalamion." And if our poets have their doubts, they should remember, that those to whom doubt and inquiry are real and stern, are not inclined to sing about them till they can sing poems of triumph over them. There has no temptation taken our modern poets save that which is common to man—the temptation of wishing to make the laws of the universe and of art fit them, as they do not feel inclined to make themselves fit the laws, or care to find them out.

What! Do you wish, asks some one, a little contemptuously, to measure the great growing nineteenth century by the thumb-rule of Alexander Pope? No. But to measure the men who write in the nineteenth century by a man who wrote in the eighteenth; to compare their advantages with his, their circumstances with his: and then, if possible, to make them ashamed of their unmanliness. Have you young poets of this day, your struggles, your chagrins? Do you think the hump-backed dwarf, every moment conscious at once of his deformity and his genius—conscious, probably, of far worse physical shame than any deformity can bring, "sewed up in buckram every morning, and requiring a nurse like a child"—caricatured, lampooned, slandered, utterly without fault of his own—insulted and rejected by the fine lady whom he had dared to court in reality, after being allowed and allured to flirt with her in rhyme—do you suppose that this man had nothing to madden him—to convert him into a sneering snarling misanthrope? Yet was there one noble soul who met him who did not love him, or whom he did not love? Have you your doubts? Do you find it difficult to make your own speculations, even your own honest convictions, square with the popular superstitions? What were your doubts, your inward contradictions, to those of a man who, bred a Papist, and yet burning with the most intense scorn and hatred of lies and shams, bigotries and priestcrafts, could write that "Essay on Man"? Read that, young gentlemen of the Job's-wife school, who fancy it a fine thing to tell your readers to curse God and die, or, at least, to show the world in print how you could curse God by divine right of genius, if you chose, and be ashamed of your cowardly wailings.

Alexander Pope went through doubt, contradiction, confusion, to which yours are simple and light; and conquered. He was a man of like passions with yourselves; infected with the peculiar vices of his day; narrow, for his age was narrow; shallow, for his age was shallow; a bon-vivant, for his age was a gluttonous and drunken one; bitter, furious, and personal, for men round him were such; foul-mouthed often, and indecent, as the rest were. Nay, his very power, when he abuses it for his own ends of selfish spite and injured vanity, makes him, as all great men can be (in words at least, for in life he was far better than the men around him), worse than his age. He can outrival Dennis in ferocity, and Congreve in filth. So much the worse for him in that account which he has long ago rendered up. But in all times and places, as far as we can judge, the man was heart-whole, more and not less righteous than his fellows. With his whole soul he hates what is evil, as far as he can recognise it. With his whole soul he loves what is good, as far as he can recognise that. With his soul believes that there is a righteous and good God, whose order no human folly or crime can destroy; and he will say so; and does say it, clearly, simply, valiantly, reverently, in his "Essay on Man." His theodicy is narrow; shallow, as was the philosophy of his age. But as far as it goes, it is sound—faithful to God, and to what he sees and knows. Man is made in God's image. Man's justice is God's justice; man's mercy is God's mercy; man's science, man's critic taste, are insights into the laws of God himself. He does not pretend to solve the great problem. But he believes that it is solved from all eternity; that God knows, God loves, and God rules; that the righteous and faithful man may know enough of the solution to know his duty, to see his way, to justify God; and as much as he knows he tells. There were in that diseased sensitive cripple no vain repinings, no moon-struck howls, no impious cries against God: "Why hast thou made me thus?" To him God is a righteous God, a God of order. Science, philosophy, politics, criticism, poetry, are parts of His order—they are parts of the appointed onward path for mankind; there are eternal laws for them. There is a beautiful and fit order, in poetry, which is part of God's order, which men have learnt ages ago, for they, too, had their teaching from above; to offend against which is absolutely wrong, an offence to be put down mildly in those who offend ignorantly; but those who offend from dulness, from the incapacity to see the beautiful, or from carelessness about it, when praise or gain tempts them the other way, have some moral defect in them; they are what Solomon calls fools: they are the enemies of man; and he will "hate them right sore, even as though they were his own enemies"—which indeed they were. He knows by painful experience that they deserve no quarter; that there is no use giving them any; to spare them is to make them insolent; to fondle the reptile is to be bitten by it. True poetry, as the messenger of heavenly beauty, is decaying; true refinement, true loftiness of thought, even true morality, are at stake. And so he writes his "Dunciad." And would that he were here, to write it over again, and write it better!

For write it again he surely would. And write it better he would also. With the greater cleanliness of our time, with all the additional experience of history, with the greater classical, æsthetic, and theological knowledge of our day, the sins of our poets are as much less excusable than those of Eusden, Blackmore, Cibber, and the rest, as Pope's "Dunciad" on them would be more righteously severe. What, for instance, would the author of the "Essay on Man" say to anyone who now wrote p. 137 (for it really is not to be quoted) of the "Life Drama" as the thoughts of his hero, without any after atonement for the wanton insult it conveys toward him whom he dares in the same breath to call "Father," simply because he wants to be something very fine and famous and self-glorifying, and Providence keeps him waiting awhile? Has Pope not said it already?

> Persist, by all divine in man unawed,
> But learn, ye dunces, not to scorn your God!

And yet no; the gentle goddess would now lay no such restriction on her children, for in Pope's day no man had discovered the new poetic plan for making the divine in man an excuse for scorning God, and finding in the dignity of "heaven-born genius" free licence to upbraid, on the very slightest grounds, the Being from whom the said genius pretends to derive his dignity. In one of his immortal saws he has cautioned us against "making God in man's image." But it never entered into his simple head that man would complain of God for being made in a lower image than even his own. Atheism he could conceive of; the deeper absurdity of Authotheism was left for our more enlightened times and more spiritual muses.

It will be answered that all this blasphemy is not to be attributed to the author, but to the man whose spiritual development he intends to sketch. To which we reply that no man has a right to bring his hero through such a state without showing how he came out of the slough as carefully as how he came into it, especially when the said hero is set forth as a marvellously clever person; and the last scene, though full of beautiful womanly touches, and of a higher morality than the rest of the book, contains no amende honorable, not even an explanation of the abominable stuff which the hero has been talking a few pages back. He leaps from the abyss to the seventh heaven; but, unfortunately for the spectators, he leaps behind the scenes, and they are none the wiser. And next; people have no more right, even for dramatic purposes, to put such language into print for any purpose whatsoever, than they have to print the grossest indecencies, or the most disgusting details of torture and cruelty. No one can accuse this magazine of any fondness for sanctimonious cant or lip-reverence; but if there be a "Father in Heaven," as Mr. Smith confesses that there is, or even merely a personal Deity at all, some sort of common decency in speaking of Him should surely be preserved. No one would print pages of silly calumny and vulgar insult against his earthly father, or even against a person for whom he had no special dislike, and then excuse it by, "Of course, I don't think so: but if anyone did think so, this would be a very smart way of saying what he thought." Old Aristotle would call such an act "banauson"—in plain English, blackguard; and we do not see how it can be called anything else, unless in the case of some utter brute in human form, to whom "there is no cœnum, and therefore no obscœnum; no fanum, and therefore no profanum." The common sense of mankind in all ages has condemned this sort of shamelessness, even more than it has insults to parental and social ties, and to all which raises man above the brute. Let Mr. Smith take note of this, and let him, if he loves himself, mend speedily; for of all styles wherein to become stereotyped the one which he has chosen is the worst, because in it the greatest amount of insincerity is possible. There is a Tartarus in front of him as well as an Olympus; a hideous possibility very near him of insincere impiety merely for the purpose of startling; of lawless fancy merely for the purpose of glittering; and a still more hideous possibility of a revulsion to insincere cant, combined with the same lawless fancy, for the purpose of keeping well with the public, in which to all appearances one of our most popular novelists, not to mention the poet whose writings are most analogous to Mr. Smith's, now lies wallowing.

Whether he shall hereafter obey his evil angel, and follow him, or his good angel, and become a great poet, depends upon himself; and above all upon his having courage to be himself, and to forget himself, two virtues which, paradoxical as it may seem, are correlatives. For the "subjective" poet—in plain words, the egotist—is always comparing himself with every man he meets, and therefore momentarily tempted to steal bits of their finery wherewith to patch his own rents; while the man who is content to be simply what God has made him, goes on from strength to strength developing almost unconsciously under a divine education, by which his real personality and the salient points by which he is distinguished from his fellows, become apparent with more and more distinctness of form, and brilliance of light and shadow, as those well know who have watched human character attain its clearest and grandest as well as its loveliest outlines, not among hankerers after fame and power, but on lonely sickbeds, and during long unknown martyrdoms of humble self-sacrifice and loving drudgery.

But whether or not Mr. Smith shall purify himself —and he can do so, if he will, right nobly—the world must be purified of his style of poetry, if men are ever, as he hopes, to "set his age to music;" much more if they are once more to stir the hearts of the many by Tyrtæan strains, such as may be needed before our hairs are gray. The "poetry of doubt," however pretty, would stand us in little stead if we were threatened with a second Armada. It will conduce little to the valour, "virtus," manhood of any Englishman to be informed by any poet, even in the most melodious verse, illustrated by the most startling and pancosmic metaphors. "See what a highly-organised and peculiar stomach-ache I have had! Does it not prove indisputably that I am not as other men are?" What gospel there can be in such a message to any honest man who has either to till the earth, plan a railroad, colonise Australia, or fight his country's enemies, is hard to discover. Hard indeed to discover how this most practical, and therefore most poetical, of ages, is to be "set to music," when all those who talk about so doing persist obstinately in poring, with introverted eyes, over the state of their own digestion—or creed.

What man wants, what art wants, perhaps what the Maker of them both wants, is a poet who shall begin by confessing that he is as other men are, and sing about things which concern all men, in language which all men can understand. This is the only road to that gift of prophecy which most young poets are nowadays in such a hurry to arrogate to themselves. We can only tell what man will be by fair induction, by knowing what he is, what he has been.

And it is most noteworthy that in this age, in which there is more knowledge than there ever was of what man has been, and more knowledge, through innumerable novelists, and those most subtle and finished ones, of what man is, that poetry should so carefully avoid drawing from this fresh stock of information in her so-confident horoscopes of what man will be.

There is just now as wide a divorce between poetry and the common-sense of all time, as there is between poetry and modern knowledge. Our poets are not merely vague and confused, they are altogether fragmentary—disjecta membra poetarum; they need some uniting idea. And what idea?

Our answer will probably be greeted with a laugh. Nevertheless we answer simply, What our poets want is faith.

There is little or no faith nowadays. And without faith there can be no real art, for art is the outward expression of firm coherent belief. And a poetry of doubt, even a sceptical poetry, in its true sense, can never possess clear and sound form, even organic form at all. How can you put into form that thought which is by its very nature formless? How can you group words round a central idea when you do not possess a central idea? Shakespeare in his one sceptic tragedy has to desert the pure tragic form, and Hamlet remains the beau-ideal of "the poetry of doubt." But what would a tragedy be in which the actors were all Hamlets, or rather scraps of Hamlets? A drama of Hamlet is only possible because the one sceptic is surrounded by characters who have some positive faith, who do their work for good or evil undoubtingly while he is speculating about his. And both Ophelia, and Laertes, Fortinbras, the king, yea the very gravedigger, know well enough what they want, whether Hamlet does or not. The whole play is, in fact, Shakespeare's subtle reductio ad absurdum of that very diseased type of mind which has been for the last forty years identified with "genius"—with one difference, namely, that Shakespeare, with his usual clearness of conception, exhibits the said intellectual type pure and simple, while modern poets degrade and confuse it, and all the questions dependent on it, by mixing it up unnecessarily with all manner of moral weaknesses, and very often moral crimes.

But the poet is to have a faith nowadays of course —a "faith in nature." This article of Wordsworth's poetical creed is to be assumed as the only necessary one, and we are to ignore altogether the somewhat important fact that he had faith in a great deal besides nature, and to make that faith in nature his sole differentia and source of inspiration. Now we beg leave to express not merely our want of faith in this same "faith in nature," but even our ignorance of what it means. Nature is certain phenomena, appearances. Faith in them is simply to believe that a red thing is red, and a square thing square; a sine qua non doubtless in poetry, as in carpentry, but which will produce no poetry, but only Dutch painting and gardeners' catalogues—in a word, that lowest form of art, the merely descriptive; and into this very style the modern naturalist poets, from the times of Southey and Wordsworth, have been continually falling, and falling therefore into baldness and vulgarity. For mere description cannot represent even the outlines of a whole scene at once, as the daguerreotype does; they must describe it piecemeal. Much less can it represent that whole scene at once in all its glories of colour, glow, fragrance, life, motion. In short, it cannot give life and spirit. All merely descriptive poetry can do is to give a dead catalogue—to kill the butterfly, and then write a monograph on it. And, therefore, there comes a natural revulsion from the baldness and puerility into which Wordsworth too often fell by indulging his false theories on these matters.

But a revulsion to what? To the laws of course which underlie the phenomena. But again—to which laws? Not merely to the physical ones, else Turner's "Chemistry" and Watson's "Practice of Medicine" are great poems.

True, we have heard Professor Forbes's book on Glaciers called an epic poem, and not without reason: but what gives that noble book its epic character is neither the glaciers nor the laws of them, but the discovery of those laws: the methodic, truthful, valiant, patient battle between man and nature, his final victory, his wresting from her the secret which had been locked for ages in the ice-caves of the Alps, guarded by cold and fatigue, danger and superstitious dread. For Nature will be permanently interesting to the poet, and appear to him in a truly poetic aspect, only in as far as she is connected by him with spiritual and personal beings, and becomes in his eyes either a person herself or the dwelling and organ of persons. The shortest scrap of word-painting, as Thomson's "Seasons" will sufficiently prove, is wearisome and dead, unless there be a living figure in the landscape, or unless, failing a living figure, the scene is deliberately described with reference to the poet or the reader, not as something in itself, but as something seen by him, and grouped and subordinated exactly as it would strike his eye and mind. But even this is insufficient. The heart of man demands more, and so arises a craving after the old nature-mythology of Greece, the old fairy legends of the Middle Age. The great poets of the Renaissance both in England and in Italy had a similar craving. But the aspect under which these ancient dreams are regarded by them is most significantly different. With Spenser and Ariosto, fairies and elves, gods and demons, are regarded in their fancied connection with man. Even in the age of Pope, when the gods and the Rosicrucian Sylphs have become alike "poetical machinery," this is their work. But among the moderns it is as connected with Nature, and giving a soul and a personality to her, that they are most valued. The most pure utterance of this feeling is perhaps Schiller's

"Gods of Greece," where the loss of the Olympians is distinctly deplored, because it has unpeopled, not heaven, but earth. But the same tone runs through Goethe's classical "Walpurgis Night," where the old human "twelve gods," the antitypes and the friends of men, in whom our forefathers delighted, have vanished utterly, and given place to semi-physical Nereides, Tritons, Telchines, Psylli, and Seismos himself.

Keats, in his wonderful "Endymion," contrived to unite the two aspects of Greek mythology as they never had been united before, except by Spenser in his "Garden of Adonis." But the pantheistic notion, as he himself says in "Lamia," was the one which lay nearest his heart; and in his "Hyperion" he begins to deal wholly with the Nature gods, and after magnificent success, leaves the poem unfinished, most probably because he had become, as his readers must, weary of its utter want of human interest. For that, after all, is what is wanted in a poetical view of Nature; and that is what the poet, in proportion to his want of dramatic faculty, must draw from himself. He must—he does in these days—colour Nature with the records of his own mind, and bestow a factitious life and interest on her by making her reflect his own joy or sorrow. If he be out of humour, she must frown; if he sigh, she must roar; if he be—what he very seldom is—tolerably comfortable, the birds have liberty to sing, and the sun to shine. But by the time that he has arrived at this stage of his development, or degradation, the poet is hardly to be called a strong man. He who is so much the slave of his own moods that he must needs see no object save through them, is not very likely to be able to resist the awe which nature's grandeur and inscrutability brings with it, and to say firmly, and yet reverently:

> Si fractus illabatur orbis,
> Impavidum ferient ruinæ.

He feels, in spite of his conceit, that nature is not going his way, or looking his looks, but going what he calls her own way, what we call God's way. At all events, he feels that he is lying, when he represents the great universe as turned to his small set of Pan's pipes, and all the more because he feels that, conceal it as he will, those same Pan's pipes are out of tune with each other. And so arises the habit of impersonating nature, not after the manner of Spenser (whose purity of metaphor and philosophic method, when he deals with nature, is generally even more marvellous than the richness of his fancy), as an organic whole, but in her single and accidental phenomena; and of ascribing not merely animal passions or animal enjoyment, but human discursive intellect and moral sense, to inanimate objects, and talking as if a stick or a stone were more of a man than the poet is—as indeed they very often may be.

These, like everything else, are perfectly right in their own place—where they express passion, either pleasurable or painful, passion, that is, not so intense as to sink into exhaustion, or to be compelled to self-control by the fear of madness. In these two cases, as great dramatists know well enough, the very violence of the emotion produces perfect simplicity, as the hurricane blows the sea smooth. But where fanciful language is employed to express the extreme of passion, it is felt to be absurd, and is accordingly called rant and bombast: and where it is not used to express passion at all, but merely the quiet and normal state of the poet's mind, or of his characters, with regard to external nature; when it is considered, as it is by most of our modern poets, the staple of poetry, indeed poetic diction itself, so that the more numerous and the stranger conceits an author can cram into his verses, the finer poet he is; then, also, it is called rant and bombast, but of the most artificial, insincere, and (in every sense of the word) monstrous kind; the offspring of an effeminate nature-worship, without self-respect, without true manhood, because it exhibits the poet as the puppet of his own momentary sensations, and not as a man superior to nature, claiming his likeness to the Author of nature, by confessing and expressing the permanent laws of Nature, undisturbed by fleeting appearances without, or fleeting tempers within. Hence it is that, as in all insincere and effete times, the poetry of the day deals more and more with conceits, and less and less with true metaphors. In fact, hinc illæ lachrymæ. This is, after all, the primary symptom of disease in the public taste, which has set us on writing this review—that critics all round are crying: "An ill-constructed whole, no doubt; but full of beautiful passages"—the word "passages" turning out to mean, in plain English, conceits. The simplest distinction, perhaps, between an image and a conceit is this—that while both are analogies, the image is founded on an analogy between the essential properties of two things —the conceit on an analogy between its accidents. Images, therefore, whether metaphors or similes, deal with laws; conceits with private judgments. Images belong to the imagination, the power which sees things according to their real essence and inward life, and conceits to the fancy or phantasy, which only see things as they appear.

To give an example or two from the "Life Drama:"

> His heart holds a deep hope,
> As holds the wretched West the sunset's corse—
> Spit on, insulted by the brutal rains.
>
> The passion-panting sea
> Watches the unveiled beauty of the stars
> Like a great hungry soul.
>
> Great spirits,
> Who left upon the mountain-tops of Death
> A light that made them lovely.
>
> The moon,
> Arising from dark waves which plucked at her.

And hundreds, nay, thousands more in this book, whereof it must be said, that beautiful or not, in the eyes of the present generation—and many of them are put into very beautiful language, and refer to very beautiful natural objects—they are not beautiful really and in themselves, because they are mere conceits; the analogies in them are fortuitous, depending not on the nature of the things themselves, but on the private fancy of the writer, having no more real and logical coherence than a conundrum or a pun; in plain English, untrue, only allowable to Juliets or Othellos;

while their self-possession, almost their reason, is in temporary abeyance under the influence of joy or sorrow. Every one must feel the exquisite fitness of Juliet's "Gallop apace, ye fiery-footed steeds," etc., for one of her character, in her circumstances: every one, we trust, and Mr. Smith among the number, will some day feel the exquisite unfitness of using such conceits as we have just quoted, or any other, page after page, for all characters and chances. For the West is not wretched; the rains never were brutal yet, and do not insult the sun's corpse, being some millions of miles nearer us than the sun, but only have happened once to seem to do so in the poet's eyes. The sea does not pant with passion, does not hunger after the beauty of the stars; Death has no mountain-tops, or any property which can be compared thereto; and "the dark waves" —in that most beautiful conceit which follows, and which Mr. Smith has borrowed from Mr. Bailey, improving it marvellously nevertheless—do not "pluck at the moon," but only seem to do so. And what constitutes the beauty of this very conceit—far the best of those we have chosen—but that it looks so very like an image, so very like a law, from being so very common and customary an ocular deception to one standing on a low shore at night?

Or, again, in a passage which has been already often quoted as exquisite, and in its way is so:

> The bridegroom sea
> Is toying with the shore, his wedded bride;
> And in the fulness of his marriage joy
> He decorates her tawny brow with shells,
> Retires a pace, to see how fair she looks,
> Then proud, runs up to kiss her.

Exquisite? Yes; but only exquisitely pretty. It is untrue—a false explanation of the rush and recoil of the waves. We learn nothing by these lines; we gain no fresh analogy between the physical and the spiritual world, not even between two different parts of the physical world. If the poetry of this age has a peculiar mission, it is to declare that such an analogy exists throughout the two worlds; then let poetry declare it. Let it set forth a real intercommunion between man and nature, grounded on a communion between man and God, who made nature. Let it accept nature's laws as the laws of God. Truth, scientific truth, is the only real beauty. "Let God be true, and every man a liar."

Now, be it remembered that by far the greater proportion of this book consists of such thoughts as these; and that these are what are called its beauties; these are what young poets try more and more daily to invent—conceits, false analogies. Be it remembered, that the affectation of such conceits has always marked the decay and approaching death of a reigning school of poetry; that when, for instance, the primeval forest of the Elizabethan poets dwindled down into a barren scrub of Vaughans, and Cowleys, and Herberts, and Crashawes, this was the very form in which the deadly blight appeared. In vain did the poetasters, frightened now and then at their own nonsense, try to keep up the decaying dignity of poetry by drawing their conceits, as poetasters do now, from suns and galaxies, earthquakes, eclipses, and the portentous, and huge and gaudy in Nature; the lawlessness and irreverence for Nature, involved in the very worship of conceits, went on degrading the tone of the conceits themselves, till the very sense of true beauty and fitness seemed lost; and a pious and refined gentleman like George Herbert could actually dare to indite solemn conundrums to the Supreme Being, and believe that he was writing devout poetry, and "looking through nature up to nature's God," when he delivered himself thus in one of his least offensive poems (for the most sacred and most offensive of them we dare not quote, lest we incur the same blame which we have bestowed on Mr. Smith, and sing of Church festivals as—)

> Marrow of time, eternity in brief,
> Compendiums epitomised, the chief
> Contents, the indices, the title-pages
> Of all past, present, and succeeding ages,
> Sublimate graces, antedated glories;
> The cream of holiness.
> The inventories
> Of future blessedness,
> The florilegia of celestial stories,
> Spirit of Joys, the relishes and closes
> Of angels' music, pearls dissolved, roses
> Perfumed, sugar'd honeycombs.

That manner, happily for art, was silenced by the stern truth-loving common sense of the Puritans. Whatsoever else, in their crusade against shams, they were too hasty in sweeping away, they were right, at least, in sweeping away such a sham as that. And now, when a school has betaken itself to use the very same method in the cause of blasphemy, instead of in that of cant, the Pope himself, with his Index Prohibitus, might be a welcome guest, if he would but stop the noise, and compel our doting Muses to sit awhile in silence, and reconsider themselves.

In the meanwhile, poets write about poets, and poetry, and guiding the age, and curbing the world, and waking it, and thrilling it, and making it start, and weep, and tremble, and self-conceit only knows what else; and yet the age is not guided, or the world curbed, or thrilled, or waked, or anything else, by them. Why should it be? Curb and thrill the world? The world is just now a most practical world; and these men are utterly unpractical. The age is given up to physical science; these men disregard and outrage it in every page by their false analogies. If they intend, as they say, to link heaven and earth by preaching the analogy of matter and spirit, let them, in the name of common prudence, observe the laws of matter, about which the world does know something, and show their coincidence with the laws of spirit—if indeed they know anything about the said laws. Loose conceits, fancies of the private judgment, were excusable enough in the Elizabethan poets. In their day, nature was still unconquered by science; medieval superstitions still lingered in the minds of men; and the magical notions of nature which they had inherited from the Middle Age received a corroboration from those neoplatonist dreamers, whom they confounded with the true Greek philosophers. But, now that Bacon has spoken, and that Europe has obeyed him, surely, among the most practical, common sense, and scientific nation of the earth, severely scientific imagery, imagery drawn from the inner laws of nature, is necessary to touch the hearts of men. They know that the universe is not such as poets paint it; they know that these pretty thoughts are only pretty thoughts, springing from the caprice, the vanity, very often from the indigestion of the gentlemen who take the trouble to sing to them; and they listen, as they would to a band of street musicians, and give them sixpence for their tune, and go on with their work. The tune outside has nothing to do with the work inside. It will not help them to be wiser, abler, more valiant—certainly not more cheerful and hopeful men, and therefore they care no more for it than they do for an opera or a pantomime, if as much. Whereupon the poets get disgusted with the same hard-hearted prosaic world—which is trying to get its living like an industrious animal as it is—and demand homage—for what? For making a noise, pleasant or otherwise? For not being as other men are? For pleading "the eccentricities of genius" as an excuse for sitting like naughty children in the middle of the schoolroom floor, in everybody's way, shouting and playing on penny trumpets, and when begged to be quiet, that other people may learn their lessons, considering themselves insulted, and pleading "genius"? Genius!—hapless byword, which, like charity, covers nowadays the multitude of sins, all the seven deadly ones included! Is there any form of human folly which one has not heard excused by "He is a genius, you know—one must not judge him by common rules." Poor genius, to have come to this! To be, when confessed, not a reason for being more of a man than others, but an excuse for being less of a man, less amenable than the herd to the common laws of humanity, and therefore less able than they to comprehend its common duties, common temptations, common sins, common virtues, common destinies. Of old the wise singer did by virtue of feeling with all, and obeying with all, learn to see for all, to see eternal laws, eternal analogies, eternal consequences, and so became a seer, vates, prophet; but now he is become a genius, a poetical pharisee, a reviler of common laws and duties, the slave of his own private judgment, who prophesies out of his own heart, and hath seen nothing but only the appearances of things distorted and coloured by "genius." Heaven send the word, with many more, a speedy burial!

And what becomes of artistic form in the hands of such a school? Just what was to be expected. It is impossible to give outward form to that which is in its very nature formless, like doubt and discontent. For on such subjects thought itself is not defined; it has no limit, no self-coherence, not even method or organic law. And in a poem, as in all else, the body must be formed according to the law of the inner life; the utterance must be the expression, the outward and visible autotype of the spirit which animates it. But where the thought is defined by no limits, it cannot express itself in form, for form is that which has limits. Where it has no inward unity it cannot have any outward one. If the spirit be impatient of all moral rule, its utterance will be equally impatient of all artistic rule; and thus, as we are now beginning to discover from experience, the poetry of doubt will find itself unable to use those forms of verse which have been always held to be the highest—tragedy, epic, the ballad, and lastly, even the subjective lyrical ode. For they, too, to judge by every great lyric which remains to us, require a groundwork of consistent self-coherent belief; and they require also an appreciation of melody even more delicate, and a verbal polish even more complete than any other form of poetic utterance. But where there is no melody within, there will be no melody without. It is in vain to attempt the setting of spiritual discords to physical music. The mere practical patience and self-restraint requisite to work out rhythm when fixed on, will be wanting; nay, the fitting rhythm will never be found, the subject itself being arhythmic; and thus we shall have, or, rather, alas! do have, a wider and wider divorce of sound and sense, a greater and greater carelessness for polish, and for the charm of musical utterance, and watch the clear and spirit-stirring melodies of the older poets swept away by a deluge of half-metrical prose-run-mad, diffuse, unfinished, unmusical, to which any other metre than that in which it happens to have been written would have been equally appropriate, because all are equally inappropriate. Where men have nothing to sing, it is not of the slightest consequence how they sing it.

While poets persist in thinking and writing thus, it is in vain for them to talk loud about the poet's divine mission, as the prophet of mankind, the swayer of the universe, and so forth. Not that we believe the poet simply by virtue of being a singer to have any such power. While young gentlemen are talking about governing heaven and earth by verse, Wellingtons and Peels, Arkwrights and Stephensons, Frys, and Chisholms, are doing it by plain practical prose; and even of those who have moved and led the hearts of men by verse, every one, as far as we know, has produced his magical effects by poetry of the very opposite form to that which is now in fashion. What poet ever had more influence than Homer? What poet is more utterly antipodal to our modern schools? There are certain Hebrew psalms, too, which will be confessed, even by those who differ most from them, to have exercised some slight influence on human thought and action, and to be likely to exercise the same for some time to come. Are they any more like our modern poetic forms than they are like our modern poetic matter? Ay, even in our own time, what has been the form, what the temper, of all poetry, from Körner and Heine, which has made the German heart leap up, but simplicity, manhood, clearness, finished melody, the very opposite, in a word, of our new school? And to look at home, what is the modern poetry which lives on the lips and in the hearts of Englishmen, Scotchmen, Irishmen? It is not only simple in form and language, but much of it fitted, by a severe exercise of artistic patience, to tunes already existing. Who does not remember how the "Marseillaise" was born, or how Burns's "Scots wha ha' wi' Wallace bled," or the story of Moore's taking the old "Red Fox March," and giving it a new immortality as "Let Erin remember the days of old," while poor Emmett sprang up and cried, "Oh, that I had twenty thousand Irishmen marching to that tune!" So it is, even to this day, and let those who hanker after poetic fame take note of it; not a poem which is now really living but has gained its immortality by virtue of simplicity and positive faith.

Let the poets of the new school consider carefully Wolfe's "Sir John Moore," Campbell's "Hohenlinden," "Mariners of England," and "Rule Britannia," Hood's "Song of the Shirt" and "Bridge of Sighs," and then ask themselves, as men who would be poets: Were it not better to have written any one of those glorious lyrics than all which John Keats has left behind him? And let them be sure that, howsoever they may answer the question to themselves, the sound heart of the English people has already made its choice; and that when that beautiful "Hero and Leander," in which Hood has outrivalled the conceit-mongers at their own weapons, by virtue of the very terseness, clearness, and manliness which they neglect, has been gathered to the limbo of the Crashawes and Marinos, his "Song of the Shirt" and his "Bridge of Sighs" will be esteemed by great new English nations far beyond the seas, for what they are—two of the most noble lyric poems ever written by an English pen. If our poetasters talk with Wordsworth of the dignity and pathos of the commonest human things, they will find them there in perfection; if they talk about the cravings of the new time, they will find them there. If they want the truly sublime and the awful, they will find them there also. But they will find none of their own favourite concetti; hardly even a metaphor; no taint of this new poetic diction into which we have now fallen, after all our abuse of the far more manly and sincere "poetic diction" of the eighteenth century; they will find no loitering by the way to argue and moralise, and grumble at Providence, and show off the author's own genius and sensibility;

they will find, in short, two real works of art, earnest, melodious, self-forgetful, knowing clearly what they want to say, and saying it in the shortest, the simplest, the calmest, the most finished words. Saying it!—rather taught to say it. For if that "divine inspiration of poets," of which the poetasters make such rash and irreverent boastings, have indeed, as all ages have held, any reality corresponding to it, it will rather be bestowed on such works as these, appeals from unrighteous man to a righteous God, than on men whose only claim to celestial help seems to be that mere passionate sensibility, which our modern Draco once described when speaking of poor John Keats, as "an infinite hunger after all manner of pleasant things, crying to the universe: 'Oh that thou wert one great lump of sugar, that I might suck thee!'"

Our task is ended. We have given as plainly as we can our reasons for the opinion which this magazine has expressed several times already, that with the exception of Mr. Allingham, our young poets are a very hopeless generation, and will so continue unless they utterly repent and amend. If they do not choose to awaken themselves from within, all that is left for us is to hope that they may be awakened from without, or by some radical revulsion in public taste be shown their own real value and durability, and compelled to be true and manly under pain of being laughed at and forgotten. A general war might, amid all its inevitable horrors, sweep away at once the dyspeptic unbelief, the insincere bigotry, the effeminate frivolity which now paralyses our poetry as much as it does our action, and strike from England's heart a lightning flash of noble deeds, a thunder peal of noble song. Such a case is neither an impossible nor a far-fetched one; let us not doubt that by some other means if not by that, the immense volume of thought and power which is still among us will soon find its utterance, and justify itself to after ages by showing in harmonious and self-restrained poetry its kinship to the heroic and the beautiful of every age and clime. And till then, till the sunshine and the thaw shall come, and the spring flowers burst into bud and bloom, heralding a new golden year in the world's life, let us even be content with our pea-green and orange fungi; nay, even admire them as not without their own tawdry beauty, their clumsy fitness; for after all, they are products of nature, though only of her dyspepsia; and grow and breed—as indeed cutaneous disorders do—by an organic law of their own; fulfilling their little destiny, and then making, according to Professor Way, by no means bad manure. And so we take our leave of Mr. Alexander Smith, entreating him, if these pages meet his eye, to consider three things, namely, that in as far as he has written poetry, he is on the road to ruin by reason of following the worst possible models. That in as far as the prevailing taste has put these models before him, he is neither to take much blame to himself, nor to be in anywise disheartened for the future. That in as far as he shall utterly reverse his whole poetic method, whether in morals or in æsthetics, leave undone all that he has done, and do all that he has not done, he will become, what he evidently, by grace of God, can become if he will, namely, a lasting and a good poet.

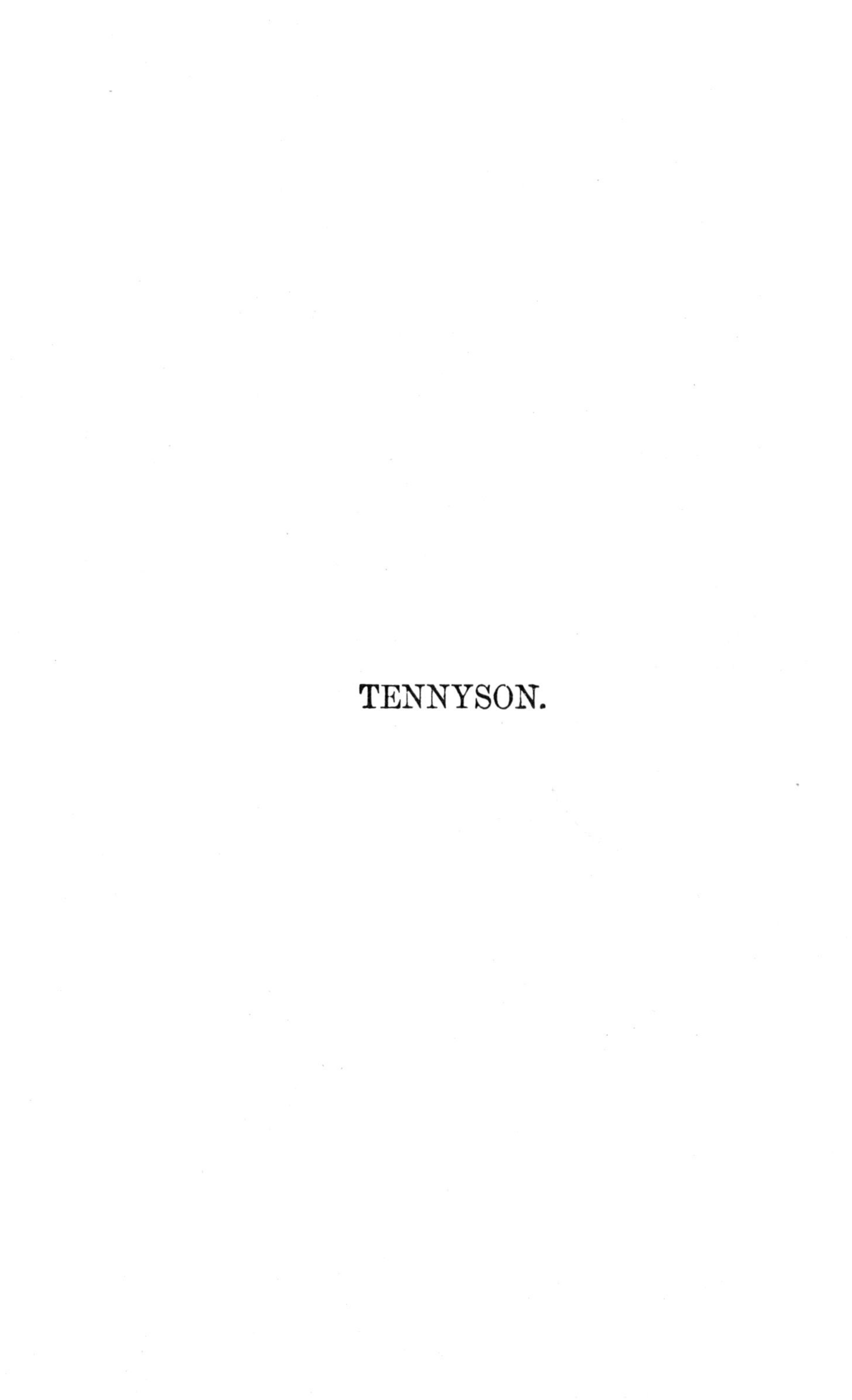

TENNYSON.

TENNYSON.*

CRITICS cannot in general be too punctilious in their respect for an incognito. If an author intended us to know his name, he would put it on his title-page. If he does not choose to do that, we have no more right to pry into his secret than we have to discuss his family affairs or open his letters. But every rule has its exceptional cases; and the book which stands first upon our list is surely such. All the world, somehow or other, knows the author. His name has been mentioned unhesitatingly by several reviews already, whether from private information, or from the certainty which every well-read person must feel that there is but one man in England possessed at once of poetic talent and artistic experience sufficient for so noble a creation. We hope, therefore, that we shall not be considered impertinent if we ignore an incognito which all England

* Fraser's Magazine, September, 1850.—"In Memoriam." Moxon, Dover Street. 1850.—"The Princess, a Medley:" by Alfred Tennyson. Third Edition. 1850.—"Poems:" by Alfred Tennyson. 1852.

has ignored before us, and attribute "In Memoriam" to the pen of the author of "The Princess."

Such a course will probably be the more useful one to our readers; for this last work of our only living great poet seems to us at once the culmination of all his efforts and the key to many difficulties in his former writings. Heaven forbid that we should say that it completes the circle of his powers. On the contrary, it gives us hope of broader effort in new fields of thought and forms of art. But it brings the development of his Muse and of his Creed to a positive and definite point. It enables us to claim one who has been hitherto regarded as belonging to a merely speculative and peirastic school as the willing and deliberate champion of vital christianity, and of an orthodoxy the more sincere because it has worked upward through the abyss of doubt; the more mighty for good because it justifies and consecrates the æsthetics and the philosophy of the present age. We are sure, moreover, that the author, whatever right reasons he may have had for concealing his own name, would have no quarrel against us for alluding to it, were he aware of the idolatry with which every utterance of his is regarded by the cultivated young men of our day, especially at the universities, and of the infinite service of which this "In Memoriam" may be to them, if they are taught by it that their superiors are not ashamed of faith, and that they will rise instead of falling, fulfil instead of denying the cravings of their hearts and intellects, if they will pass upwards with their teacher from the vague though noble expectations of "Locksley Hall," to the assured and everlasting facts of the proem to "In Memoriam" — in our eyes the noblest christian poem which England has produced for two centuries.

To explain our meaning, it will be necessary, perhaps, to go back to Mr. Tennyson's earlier writings, of which he is said to be somewhat ashamed now—a fastidiousness with which we will not quarrel; for it should be the rule of the poet, forgetting those things which are behind, to press on to those things which are before, and "to count not himself to have apprehended but——" no, we will not finish the quotation; let the readers of "In Memoriam" finish it for themselves, and see how, after all, the poet, if he would reach perfection, must be found by Him who found St. Paul of old. In the meantime, as a true poet must necessarily be in advance of his age, Mr. Tennyson's earlier poems, rather than these latter ones, coincide with the tastes and speculations of the young men of this day. And in proportion, we believe, as they thoroughly appreciate the distinctive peculiarities of those poems, will they be able to follow the author of them on his upward path.

Some of our readers, we would fain hope, remember as an era in their lives the first day on which they read those earlier poems; how, fifteen years ago, Mariana in the Moated Grange, "The Dying Swan," "The Lady of Shalott," came to them as revelations. They seemed to themselves to have found at last a poet who promised not only to combine the cunning melody of Moore, the rich fulness of Keats, and the simplicity of Wordsworth, but one who was introducing a method of observing nature different from that of all the three and yet succeeding in everything which they had attempted, often in vain. Both Keats and Moore had an eye for the beauty which lay in trivial and daily objects. But in both of them there was a want of deep religious reverence, which kept Moore playing gracefully upon the surface of phenomena without ever daring to dive into their laws or inner meaning; and made poor Keats fancy that he was rather to render nature poetical by bespangling her with florid ornament, than simply to confess that she was already, by the grace of God, far beyond the need of his paint and gilding. Even Wordsworth himself had not full faith in the great dicta which he laid down in his famous Introductory Essay. Deep as was his conviction that nature bore upon her simplest forms the finger-mark of God, he did not always dare simply to describe her as she was, and leave her to reveal her own mystery. We do not say this in depreciation of one who stands now far above human praise or blame. The wonder is, not that Wordsworth rose no higher, but that, considering the level on which his taste was formed, he had power to rise to the height above his age which he did attain. He did a mighty work. He has left the marks of his teaching upon every poet who has written verses worth reading for the last twenty years. The idea by which he conquered was, as Coleridge well sets forth, the very one which, in its practical results on his own poetry, procured him loud and deserved ridicule. This, which will be the root idea of the whole poetry of this generation, was the dignity of nature in all her manifestations, and not merely in those which may happen to suit the fastidiousness or Manichæism of any particular age.

He may have been at times fanatical on his idea, and have misused it, till it became self-contradictory, because he could not see the correlative truths which should have limited it. But it is by fanatics, by men of one great thought, that great works are done; and it is good for the time that a man arose in it of fearless honesty enough to write Peter Bell and the Idiot Boy, to shake all the old methods of nature-painting to their roots, and set every man seriously to ask himself what he meant, or whether he meant anything real, reverent, or honest, when he talked about "poetic diction," or "the beauties of nature." And after all, like all fanatics, Wordsworth was better than his own creed. As Coleridge thoroughly shows in the second volume of the "Biographia Literaria," and as may be seen nowhere more strikingly than in his grand posthumous work, his noblest poems and noblest stanzas are those in which his true poetic genius, unconsciously to himself, sets at naught his own pseudo-naturalist dogmas.

Now Mr. Tennyson, while fully adopting Wordsworth's principle from the very first, seemed by instinctive taste to have escaped the snares which had proved too subtle both for Keats and Wordsworth. Doubtless there are slight *niaiseries*, after the manner of both those poets, in the first editions of his earlier poems. He seems, like most other great artists, to have first tried imitations of various styles which already existed, before he learnt the art of incorporating them into his own, and learning from all his predecessors, without losing his own individual peculiarities. But there are descriptive passages in them also which neither Keats nor Wordsworth could have written, combining the honest sensuous observation which is common to them both, with a self-restrained simplicity which Keats did not live long enough to attain, and a stately and accurate melody, an earnest songfulness (to coin a word) which Wordsworth seldom attained, and from his inaccurate and uncertain ear, still seldomer preserved without the occurrence of a jar or a rattle, a false quantity, a false rapture, or a bathos. And above all, or rather beneath all—for we suspect that this has been throughout the very secret of Mr. Tennyson's power —there was a hush and a reverent awe, a sense of the mystery, the infinitude, the awfulness, as well as of the mere beauty of wayside things, which invested these poems as wholes with a peculiar richness, depth, and majesty of tone, beside which both Keats's and Wordsworth's methods of handling pastoral subjects looked like the colouring of Julio Romano or Watteau by the side of Correggio or Titian.

This deep simple faith in the divineness of Nature as she appears, which, in our eyes, is Mr. Tennyson's differentia, is really the natural accompaniment of a quality at first sight its very opposite, and for which he is often blamed by a prosaic world; namely, his subjective and transcendental mysticism. It is the mystic, after all, who will describe Nature most simply, because he sees most in her; because he is most ready to believe that she will reveal to others the same message which she has revealed to him. Men like Behmen, Novalis, and Fourier, who can soar into the inner cloud-world of man's spirit, even though they lose their way there, dazzled by excess of wonder—

men who, like Wordsworth, can give utterance to such subtle anthropologic wisdom as the "Ode on the Intimations of Immortality," will for that very reason most humbly and patiently "consider the lilies of the field, how they grow." And even so it is just because Mr. Tennyson is, far more than Wordsworth, mystical, and what an ignorant and money-getting generation, idolatrous of mere sensuous activity, calls "dreamy," that he has become the greatest naturalistic poet which England has seen for several centuries. The same faculty which enabled him to draw such subtle subjective pictures of womanhood as Adeline, Isabel, and Eleanor, enabled him to see, and therefore simply to describe, in one of the most distinctive and successful of his earlier poems, how

> The creeping mosses and clambering weeds,
> And the willow branches hoar and dank,
> And the wavy swell of the soughing reeds,
> And the wave-worn horns of the echoing bank,
> And the silvery marish flowers that throng
> The desolate creeks and pools among,
> Were flooded over with eddying song.

No doubt there are in the earlier poems exceptions to this style—attempts to adorn nature, and dazzle with a barbaric splendour akin to that of Keats—as, for instance, in the "Recollections of the Arabian Nights." But how cold and gaudy, in spite of individual beauties, is that poem by the side of either of the Marianas, and especially of the one in which the scenery is drawn, simply and faithfully, from those counties which the world considers the quintessence of the prosaic—the English fens.

Upon the middle of the night
  Waking she heard the night-fowl crow;
The cock sang out an hour ere light:
  From the dark fen the oxen's low
Came to her: without hope of change,
  In sleep she seemed to walk forlorn,
  Till cold winds woke the gray-eyed morn
About the lonely moated grange.

* * * *

About a stone-cast from the wall
  A sluice with blackened waters slept,
And o'er it many, round and small,
  The cluster'd marish-mosses crept.
Hard by a poplar shook alway,
  All silver-green with gnarled bark,
  For leagues no other tree did mark
The level waste, the rounding gray,

* * * *

Throughout all these exquisite lines occurs but one instance of what the vulgar call "poetic diction." All is simple description, in short and Saxon words, and yet who can deny the effect to be perfect—superior to any similar passage in Wordsworth? And why? Because the passage quoted, and indeed the whole poem, is perfect in what artists call tone—tone in the metre and in the sound of the words, as well as in the images and the feelings expressed. The weariness, the dreariness, the dark mysterious waste, exist alike within and without, in the slow monotonous pace of the metre and the words, as well as in the boundless fen, and the heart of her who, "without hope of change, in sleep did seem to walk forlorn."

The same faith in Nature, the same instinctive correctness in melody, springing from that correct insight into Nature, ran through the poems inspired by medieval legends. The very spirit of the old ballad writers, with their combinations of mysticism and objectivity, their freedom from any self-conscious attempt at reflective epithets or figures, runs through them all. We are never jarred in them, as we are in all the attempts at ballad-writing and ballad-restoring before Mr. Tennyson's time, by discordant touches of the reflective in thought, the picturesque in Nature, or the theatric in action. To illustrate our meaning, readers may remember the ballad of "Fair Emmeline," in Bishop Percy's "Reliques." The bishop confesses, if we mistake not, to have patched one end of the ballad. He need not have informed us of that fact, while such lines as these following meet our eyes:

> The Baron turned aside,
> And wiped away the rising tears
> He proudly strove to hide.

No old ballad writer would have used such a complicated concetto. Another, and even a worse instance is to be found in the difference between the old and new versions of the grand ballad of "Glasgerion." In the original, we hear how the elfin harper could

> Harp fish out of the water,
> And water out of a stone,
> And milk out of a maiden's breast
> That bairn had never none.

For which some benighted "restorer" substitutes—

> Oh, there was magic in his touch,
> And sorcery in his string!

No doubt there was. But while the new poetaster informs you of the abstract notion, the ancient poet gives you the concrete fact; as Mr. Tennyson has done with wonderful art in his exquisite "St. Agnes," where the saint's subjective mysticism appears only as embodied in objective pictures:

Break up the heavens, oh Lord! and far
  Through all yon starlight keen
Draw me, thy bride, a glittering star,
In raiment white and clean.

Sir Walter Scott's ballads fail just on the same point. Even Campbell cannot avoid an occasional false note of sentiment. In Mr. Tennyson alone, as we think, the spirit of the Middle Age is perfectly reflected; its delight, not in the "sublime and picturesque," but in the green leaves and spring flowers for their own sake—the spirit of Chaucer and of the "Robin Hood Garland"—the naturalism which revels as much in the hedgerow and garden as in Alps, and cataracts, and Italian skies, and the other strong stimulants to the faculty of admiration which the palled taste of an unhealthy age, from Keats and Byron down to Browning, has rushed abroad to seek. It is enough for Mr. Tennyson's truly English spirit to see how

On either side the river lie
Long fields of barley and of rye,
That clothe the wold and meet the sky;
And through the field the road runs by
    To many-tower'd Camelot.

Or how

> In the stormy east wind straining,
> The pale yellow woods were waning,
> The broad stream in his banks complaining,
> Heavily the low sky raining
> Over tower'd Camelot.

Give him but such scenery as that which he can see in every parish in England, and he will find it a fit scene for an ideal myth, subtler than a casuist's questionings, deep as the deepest heart of woman.

But in this earlier volume the poet has not yet arrived at the art of combining his new speculations on man with his new mode of viewing Nature. His objective pieces are too exclusively objective, his subjective too exclusively subjective; and where he deals with natural imagery in these latter, he is too apt, as in "Eleanore," to fall back upon the old and received method of poetic diction, though he never indulges in a commonplace or a stock epithet. But in the interval between 1830 and 1842 the needful interfusion of the two elements has taken place. And in "Locksley Hall" and the "Two Voices" we find the new doubts and questions of the time embodied naturally and organically, in his own method of simple natural expression. For instance, from the Search for Truth in the "Two Voices"—

> Cry, faint not, climb: the summits lope
> Beyond the furthest flights of hope,
> Wrapt in dense cloud from base to cope.
>
> Sometimes a little corner shines
> As over rainy mist inclines
> A gleaming crag with belts of pines.

"I will go forward," sayest thou;
"I shall not fail to find her now.
Look up, the fold is on her brow."

Or again, in "Locksley Hall," the poem which, as we think deservedly, has had most influence on the minds of the young men of our day:

Eager-hearted as a boy when first he leaves his father's field,
And at night along the dusky highway near and nearer drawn,
Sees in heaven the light of London flaring like a dreary dawn;
And his spirit leaps within him to be gone before him then,
Underneath the light he looks at, in among the throngs of men;
Men, my brothers, men the workers, ever reaping something new:
That which they have done but earnest of the things which they shall do:

and all the grand prophetic passage following, which is said, we know not how truly, to have won for the poet the respect of that great statesman whose loss all good men deplore.

In saying that "Locksley Hall" has deservedly had so great an influence over the minds of the young, we shall, we are afraid, have offended some who are accustomed to consider that poem as Werterian and unhealthy. But, in reality, the spirit of the poem is simply anti-Werterian. It is man rising out of sickness into health—not conquered by Werterism, but conquering his selfish sorrow, and the moral and intellectual paralysis which it produces, by faith and hope—faith in the progress of science and civilisation, hope in the final triumph of good. Doubtless, that is not the highest deliverance—not a permanent deliverance at all. Faith in God and hope in Christ alone can deliver a man once and for all from Werterism, or any other moral disease; that truth was reserved for "In Memoriam:" but as far as "Locksley Hall" goes, it is a step forward—a whole moral æon beyond Byron and Shelley; and a step, too, in the right direction, just because it is a step forward—because the path of deliverance is, as "Locksley Hall" sets forth, not backwards towards a fancied paradise of childhood—not backward to grope after an unconsciousness which is now impossible, an implicit faith which would be unworthy of the man, but forward on the road on which God has been leading him, carrying upward with him the aspirations of childhood, and the bitter experience of youth, to help the organised and trustful labour of manhood. There are, in fact, only two deliverances from Werterism possible in the nineteenth century; one is into Popery, and the other is—

> Forward, forward, let us range;
> Let the peoples spin for ever down the ringing grooves of change;
> Through the shadow of the world we sweep into the younger day:
> Better fifty years of Europe than a cycle of Cathay.

But such a combination of powers as Mr. Tennyson's naturally develop themselves into a high idyllic faculty; for it is the very essence of the idyl to set forth the poetry which lies in the simpler manifestations of Man and Nature; yet not explicitly, by a reflective moralising on them, as almost all our idyllists—Cowper, Gray, Crabbe, and Wordsworth—have been in the habit of doing, but implicitly, by investing them all with a rich and delightful tone of colouring, perfect grace of manner, perfect melody of rhythm, which, like a gorgeous summer atmosphere, shall glorify without altering the most trivial and homely sights. And it is this very power, as exhibited in the "Lord of Burleigh," "Audley Court," and the "Gardener's Daughter," which has made Mr. Tennyson, not merely the only English rival of Theocritus and Bion, but, in our opinion, as much their superior as modern England is superior to ancient Greece.

Yet in "The Princess," perhaps, Mr. Tennyson rises higher still. The idyllic manner alternates with the satiric, the pathetic, even the sublime, by such imperceptible gradations, and continual delicate variations of key, that the harmonious medley of his style becomes the fit outward expression of the bizarre and yet harmonious fairyland in which his fancy ranges. In this work, too, Mr. Tennyson shows himself more than ever the poet of the day. In it more than ever the old is interpenetrated with the new—the domestic and scientific with the ideal and sentimental. He dares, in every page, to make use of modern words and notions, from which the mingled clumsiness and archaism of his compeers shrinks, as unpoetical. Though, as we just said, his stage is an ideal fairyland, yet he has reached the ideal by the only true method—by bringing the Middle Age forward to the Present one, and not by ignoring the Present to fall back on a cold and galvanised Medievalism; and thus he makes his "Medley" a mirror of the nineteenth century, possessed of its own new art and science, its own new temptations and aspirations, and yet grounded on, and continually striving to reproduce, the forms and experiences of all past time. The idea, too, of "The Princess" is an essentially modern one. In every age women have been tempted, by the possession of superior beauty, intellect, or strength of will, to deny their own womanhood, and attempt to stand alone as men, whether on the ground of political intrigue, ascetic saintship, or philosophic pride. Cleopatra and St. Hedwiga, Madame de Staël and the Princess, are merely different manifestations of the same self-willed and proud longing of woman to unsex herself, and realise, single and self-sustained, some distorted and partial notion of her own as to what the "angelic life" should be. Cleopatra acted out the pagan ideal of an angel; St. Hedwiga, the medieval one; Madame de Staël hers, with the peculiar notions of her time as to what "spirituel" might mean; and in "The Princess" Mr. Tennyson has embodied the ideal of that nobler, wider, purer, yet equally fallacious, because equally unnatural, analogue, which we may meet too often up and down England now. He shows us the woman, when she takes her stand on the false masculine ground of intellect, working out her own moral punishment, by destroying in herself the tender heart of flesh: not even her vast purposes of philanthropy can preserve her, for they are built up, not on the womanhood which God has given her, but on her own self-will; they change, they fall, they become inconsistent, even as she does herself, till, at last, she loses all feminine sensibility; scornfully and stupidly she rejects and misunderstands the heart of man; and then falling from pride to sternness, from sternness to sheer inhumanity, she punishes sisterly love as a crime, robs the mother of her child, and becomes all but a vengeful fury, with all the peculiar faults of woman, and none of the peculiar excellences of man.

The poem being, as its title imports, a medley of jest and earnest, allows a metrical licence, of which we are often tempted to wish that its author had not availed himself; yet the most unmetrical and apparently careless passages flow with a grace, a lightness, a colloquial ease and frolic, which perhaps only heighten the effect of the serious parts, and serve as a foil to set off the unrivalled finish and melody of these latter. In these come out all Mr. Tennyson's instinctive choice of tone, his mastery of language, which always fits the right word to the right thing, and that word always the simplest one, and the perfect ear for melody which makes it superfluous to set to music poetry which, read by the veriest schoolboy, makes music of itself. The poem, we are glad to say, is so well known that it seems unnecessary to quote from it; yet there are here and there gems of sound and expression of which, however well our readers may know them, we cannot forbear reminding them again. For instance, the end of the idyl in book vii. beginning "Come down, O maid" (the whole of which is perhaps one of the most perfect fruits of the poet's genius):

> Myriads of rivulets hurrying through the lawn,
> The moan of doves in immemorial elms,
> And murmuring of innumerable bees.

Who, after three such lines, will talk of English as a harsh and clumsy language, and seek in the effeminate and monotonous Italian for expressive melody of sound? Who cannot hear in them the rapid rippling of the water, the stately calmness of the wood-dove's note, and, in the repetition of short syllables and soft liquids in the last line, the

Murmuring of innumerable bees?

Or again, what combination of richness with simplicity in such a passage as this:

Breathe upon my brows;
In that fine air I tremble, all the past
Melts mist-like into this bright hour, and this
I scarce believe, and all the rich to come
Reels, as the golden Autumn woodland reels
Athwart the smoke of burning leaves.

How Mr. Tennyson can have attained the prodigal fulness of thought and imagery which distinguishes this poem, and especially the last canto, without his style ever becoming overloaded, seldom even confused, is perhaps one of the greatest marvels of the whole production. The songs themselves, which have been inserted between the cantos in the last edition of the book, seem, perfect as they are, wasted and smothered among the surrounding fertility; till we discover that they stand there, not merely for the sake of their intrinsic beauty, but serve to call back the reader's mind, at every pause in the tale of the Princess's folly, to that very healthy ideal of womanhood which she has spurned.

At the end of the first canto, fresh from the description of the female college, with its professoresses, and hostleresses, and other utopian monsters, we turn the page, and—

> As through the land at eve we went,
> And pluck'd the ripen'd ears.
> We fell out, my wife and I,
> And kissed again with tears:
>
> And blessings on the falling-out
> That all the more endears,
> When we fall out with those we love,
> And kiss again with tears!
>
> For when we came where lies the child
> We lost in other years,
> There above the little grave,
> We kissed again with tears.

Between the next two cantos intervenes the well-known cradle-song, perhaps the best of all; and at the next interval is the equally well-known bugle-song, the idea of which is that of twin-labour and twin-fame, in a pair of lovers :

> Our echoes roll from soul to soul,
> And grow for ever and for ever.

In the next, the memory of wife and child inspirits the soldier in the field; in the next, the sight of the fallen hero's child opens the sluices of his widow's tears; and in the last, and perhaps the most beautiful of all, the poet has succeeded, in the new edition, in superadding a new form of emotion to a canto in which he seemed to have exhausted every resource of pathos which his subject allowed; and prepares us for the triumph of that art by which he makes us, after all, love the heroine whom he at first taught us to hate and despise, till we see that the naughtiness is after all one that must be kissed and not whipped out of her, and look on smiling while she repents, with Prince Harry of old, " not in sackcloth and ashes, but in new silk and old sack : "

Ask me no more : the moon may draw the sea ;
  The cloud may stoop from Heaven and take the shape,
  With fold to fold, of mountain or of cape ;
But, O too fond, when have I answered thee ?
  Ask me no more.

Ask me no more : what answer should I give ?
  I love not hollow cheek or faded eye :
  Yet, O my friend, I will not have thee die !
Ask me no more, lest I should bid thee live ;
  Ask me no more.

Ask me no more : thy fate and mine are seal'd :
  I strove against the stream and all in vain :
  Let the great river take me to the main :
No more, dear love, for at a touch I yield ;
  Ask me no more.

We now come to " In Memoriam ; " a collection of poems on a vast variety of subjects, but all united, as their name implies, to the memory of a departed friend. We know not whether to envy more—the poet the object of his admiration, or that object the monument which has been consecrated to his nobleness. For in this latest and highest volume, written at various intervals during a long series of years, all the poet's peculiar excellences, with all that he has acquired from others, seem to have been fused down into a perfect unity, and brought to bear on his subject with that care and finish which only a labour of love can inspire. We only now know the whole man, all his art, all his insight, all his faculty of discerning the *più nell' uno*, and the *uno nell' più*. As he says himself:

> My love has talked with rocks and trees,
> He finds on misty mountain-ground,
> His own vast shadow glory-crowned;
> He sees himself in all he sees.

Everything reminds him of the dead. Every joy or sorrow of man, every aspect of nature, from

> The forest crack'd, the waters curl'd,
> The cattle huddled on the lea.

> The thousand waves of wheat
> That ripple round the lonely grange.

In every place where in old days they had met and conversed; in every dark wrestling of the spirit with the doubts and fears of manhood, throughout the whole outward universe of Nature, and the whole inward universe of spirit, the soul of his dead friend broods—at first a memory shrouded in blank despair, then a living presence, a ministering spirit, answering doubts, calming fears, stirring up noble aspirations, utter humility, leading the poet upward, step by step, to faith, and peace, and hope. Not that there runs throughout the book a conscious or organic method. The poems seem often merely to be united by the identity of their metre, so exquisitely chosen, that while the major rhyme in the second and third lines of each stanza gives the solidity and self-restraint required by such deep themes, the mournful minor rhyme of each first and fourth line always leads the ear to expect something beyond, and enables the poet's thoughts to wander sadly on, from stanza to stanza and poem to poem, in an endless chain of

> Linkèd sweetness long drawn out.

There are records of risings and fallings again, of alternate cloud and sunshine, throughout the book; earnest and passionate, yet never bitter; humble, yet never abject; with a depth and vehemence of affection "passing the love of woman," yet without a taint of sentimentality; self-restrained and dignified, without ever narrowing into artificial coldness; altogether rivalling the sonnets of Shakespeare; and all knit together into one spiritual unity by the proem at the opening of the volume—in our eyes, the noblest English Christian poem which several centuries have seen.

We shall not quote the very poems which we should most wish to sink into men's hearts. Let each man find for himself those which suit him best, and meditate on them in silence. They are fit only to be read solemnly in our purest and most thoughtful moods, in the solitude of our chamber, or by the side of those we love, with thanks to the great heart who has taken courage to bestow on us the record of his own friendship, doubt, and triumph.

It has been often asked why Mr. Tennyson's great and varied powers had never been concentrated on one immortal work. The epic, the lyric, the idyllic faculties, perhaps the dramatic also, seemed to be all there, and yet all sundered, scattered about in small fragmentary poems. "In Memoriam," as we think, explains the paradox. Mr. Tennyson had been employed on higher, more truly divine, and yet more truly human work than either epos or drama. Within the unseen and alone truly Real world which underlies and explains this mere time-shadow, which men miscall the Real, he had been going down into the depths, and ascending into the heights, led, like Dante of old, by the guiding of a mighty spirit. And in this volume, the record of seventeen years, we have the result of those spiritual experiences in a form calculated, as we believe, to be a priceless benefit to many an earnest seeker in this generation, and perhaps to stir up some who are priding themselves on a cold dilettantism and barren epicurism, into something like a living faith and hope. Blessed and delightful it is to find, that even in these new ages the creeds which so many fancy to be at their last gasp, are still the final and highest succour, not merely of the peasant and the outcast, but of the subtle artist and the daring speculator. Blessed it is to find the most cunning poet of our day able to combine the complicated rhythm and melody of modern times with the old truths which gave heart to martyrs at the stake; and to see in the science and the history of the nineteenth century new and living fulfilments of the words which we learnt at our mother's knee. Blessed, thrice blessed, to find that hero-worship is not yet passed away; that the heart of man still beats young and fresh; that the old tales of David and Jonathan, Damon and Pythias, Socrates and Alcibiades, Shakespeare and his nameless friend, of "love passing the love of woman," ennobled by its own humility, deeper than death, and mightier than the grave, can still blossom out, if it be but in one heart here and there, to show men still how, sooner or later, "he that loveth knoweth God, for God is love."

BURNS AND HIS SCHOOL.

BURNS AND HIS SCHOOL.*

Four faces among the portraits of modern men, great or small, strike us as supremely beautiful; not merely in expression, but in the form and proportion and harmony of features: Shakespeare, Raffaelle, Goethe, Burns. One would expect it to be so; for the mind makes the body, not the body the mind; and the inward beauty seldom fails to express itself in the outward, as a visible sign of the invisible grace or disgrace of the wearer. Not that it is so always. A Paul, Apostle of the Gentiles, may be ordained to be "in presence weak, in speech contemptible," hampered by some thorn in the flesh—to interfere apparently with

* North British Review, No. XXXI.—1.—"Elliott's Poems." London, 1833.—2. "Poems of Robert Nicoll." Third Edition. Edinburgh, 1843.—3. "Life and Poems of John Bethune." London, 1841.—4. "Memoirs of Alexander Bethune." By W. M'Combie. Aberdeen, 1845.—5. "Rhymes and Recollections of a Handloom Weaver." By William Thom, of Inverury. Second Edition, London, 1845.—6. "The Purgatory of Suicides." By Thomas Cooper. London, 1845.—7. "The Book of Scottish Song." By Alexander Whitelaw. Edinburgh, 1848.

the success of his mission, perhaps for the same wise purpose of Providence which sent Socrates to the Athenians, the worshippers of physical beauty, in the ugliest of human bodies, that they, or rather those of them to whom eyes to see had been given, might learn that soul is after all independent of matter, and not its creature and its slave. But, in the generality of cases, physiognomy is a sound and faithful science, and tells us, if not, alas! what the man might have been, still what he has become. Yet even this former problem, what he might have been, may often be solved for us by youthful portraits, before sin and sorrow and weakness have had their will upon the features; and, therefore, when we spoke of these four beautiful faces, we alluded, in each case, to the earliest portraits of each genius which we could recollect. Placing them side by side, we must be allowed to demand for that of Robert Burns an honourable station among them. Of Shakespeare's we do not speak, for it seems to us to combine in itself the elements of all the other three; but of the rest, we question whether Burns be not, after all, if not the noblest, still the most lovable — the most like what we should wish that of a teacher of men to be. Raffaelle—the most striking portrait of him, perhaps, is the full-face pencil sketch by his own hand in the Taylor Gallery at Oxford—though without a taint of littleness or effeminacy, is soft, melancholy, formed entirely to receive and to elaborate in silence. His is a face to be kissed, not worshipped. Goethe, even in his earliest portraits, looks as if his expression depended too much on his own will. There is a self-conscious power, and purpose, and self-restraint, and all but scorn, upon those glorious lineaments, which might win worship, and did; but not love, except as the child of enthusiasm or of relationship. But Burns's face, to judge of it by the early portrait of him by Nasmyth, must have been a face like that of Joseph of old, of whom the Rabbis relate, that he was mobbed by the Egyptian ladies whenever he walked the streets. The magic of that countenance, making Burns at once tempter and tempted, may explain many a sad story. The features certainly are not perfectly regular; there is no superabundance of the charm of mere animal health in the outline or colour: but the marks of intellectual beauty in the face are of the highest order, capable of being but too triumphant among a people of deep thought and feeling. The lips, ripe, yet not coarse or loose, full of passion and the faculty of enjoyment, are parted, as if forced to speak by the inner fulness of the heart; the features are rounded, rich, and tender, and yet the bones show thought massively and manfully everywhere; the eyes laugh out upon you with boundless good humour and sweetness, with simple, eager, gentle surprise—a gleam as of the morning star, looking forth upon the wonder of a new-born world—altogether

> A station like the herald Mercury,
> New lighted on a heaven-kissing hill.

Bestow on such a man the wittiest and most winning eloquence—a rich flow of spirits and fulness of health and life—a deep sense of wonder and beauty in the earth and man—an instinct of the dynamic and supernatural laws which underlie and vivify this material universe and its appearances, healthy, yet irregular and unscientific, all but superstitious—turn him loose in any country in Europe, during the latter half of the eighteenth century, and it will not be difficult, alas! to cast his horoscope.

And what an age in which to be turned loose!—for loose he must go, to solve the problem of existence for himself. The grand simple old Scottish education which he got from his parents must prove narrow and unsatisfying for so rich and manifold a character; not because it was in itself imperfect; not because it did not contain implicitly all things necessary for his "salvation"—in every sense, all laws which he might require for his after-life guidance; but because it contained so much of them as yet only implicitly; because it was not yet conscious of its own breadth and depth, and power of satisfying the new doubts and cravings of such minds and such times as Burns's. It may be that Burns was the devoted victim by whose fall it was to be taught that it must awaken and expand and renew its youth in shapes equally sound, but more complex and scientific. But it had not done so then. And when Burns found himself gradually growing beyond his father's teaching in one direction, and tempted beyond it in another and a lower one, what was there in those times to take up his education at the point where it had been left unfinished? He saw around him in plenty animal good-nature and courage, barbaric honesty and hospitality—more, perhaps, than he would see now; for the upward progress into civilised excellences is sure to be balanced by some loss of savage ones—but reckless, shallow, above all, drunken. It was a hard-drinking, coarse, materialist age. The higher culture, of Scotland especially, was all but exclusively French—not a good kind, while Voltaire and Volney still remained unanswered, and "Les Liaisons Dangereuses" were accepted by all young gentlemen, and a great many young ladies who could read French, as the best account of the relation of the sexes.

Besides, the philosophy of that day, like its criticism, was altogether mechanical, nay, as it now seems, materialist in its ultimate and logical results. Criticism was outward, and of the form merely. The world was not believed to be already, and in itself, mysterious and supernatural, and the poet was not defined as the man who could see and proclaim that supernatural element. Before it was admired, it was to be raised above nature into the region of "the picturesque," or what not; and the poet was the man who gave it this factitious and superinduced beauty, by a certain "kompsologia" and "meteoroepeia," called "poetic diction," now happily becoming extinct, mainly, we believe, under the influence of Burns, although he himself thought it his duty to bedizen his verses therewith, and though it was destined to flourish for many a year more in the temple of the father of lies, like a jar of paper flowers on a Popish altar.

No wonder that in such a time, a genius like Burns should receive not only no guidance, but no finer appreciation. True; he was admired, petted, flattered; for that the man was wonderful no one could doubt. But we question whether he was understood; whether, if that very flowery and magniloquent style which we now consider his great failing had been away, he would not have been passed over by the many as a writer of vulgar doggrel. True, the old simple ballad-muse of Scotland still dropped a gem from her treasures, here and there, even in the eighteenth century itself—witness "Auld Robin Gray." But who suspected that they were gems, of which Scotland, fifty years afterwards, would be prouder and more greedy than of all the second-hand French culture which seemed to her then the highest earthly attainment? The Review of Burns in an early number of the "Edinburgh Review," said to be from the pen of the late Lord Jeffrey, shows, as clearly as anything can, the utterly inconsistent and bewildered feeling with which the world must have regarded such a phenomenon. Alas! there was inconsistency and bewilderment enough in the phenomenon itself, but that only made confusion worse confounded; the confusion was already there, even in the mind of the more practical literary men, who ought, one would have thought, also to have been the most deep-sighted. But no. The reviewer turns the strange thing over and over, and inside out—and some fifteen years after it has vanished out of the world, having said out its say and done all that it had to do, he still finds it too utterly abnormal to make up his mind about in any clear or consistent way, and gets thoroughly cross with it, and calls it hard names, because it will not fit into any established pigeon-hole or drawer of the then existing anthropological museum. Burns is "a literary prodigy," and yet it is "a derogation" to him to consider him as one. And that we find, not as we should have expected, because he possessed genius, which would have made success a matter of course in any rank, but because he was so well educated—"having acquired a competent knowledge of French, together with the elements of Latin and Geometry," and before he had composed a single stanza, was "far more intimately acquainted with Pope, Shakespeare, and Thomson, than nine-tenths of the youths who leave school for the university," etc. etc.—in short, because he was so well educated, that his becoming Robert Burns, the immortal poet, was a matter of course and necessity. And yet, a page or two on, the great reason why it was more easy for Robert Burns the cottar to become an original and vigorous poet, rather than for any one of "the herd of scholars and academical literati," who are depressed and discouraged by "perusing the most celebrated writers, and conversing with the most intelligent judges," is found to be, that "the literature and refinement of the age do not exist for a rustic and illiterate individual; and consequently the present time is to him what the rude times of old were to the vigorous writer who adorned them." In short the great reason of Robert Burns's success was that he did not possess that education the possession of which proves him to be no prodigy, though the review begins by calling him one, and coupling him with Stephen Duck and Thomas Dermody.

Now if the best critic of the age, writing fifteen years after Burns's death, found himself between the horns of such a dilemma—which indeed, like those of an old Arnee bull, meet at the points, and form a complete circle of contradictions—what must have been the bewilderment of lesser folk during the prodigy's very lifetime? what must, indeed, have been his own bewilderment at himself, however manfully he may have kept it down? No wonder that he was unguided, either by himself or by others. We do not blame them; him we must deeply blame; yet not as we ought to blame ourselves, did we yield in the least to those temptations under which Burns fell.

Biographies of Burns, and those good ones, according to the standard of biographies in these days, are said to exist; we cannot say that we have as yet cared to read them. There are several other biographies, even more important, to be read first, when they are written. Shakespeare has found as yet no biographer; has not even left behind him materials for a biography, such at least as are considered worth using. Indeed, we question whether such a biography would be of any use whatever to the world; for the man who cannot, by studying his dramas in some tolerably accurate chronological order, and using as a running accompaniment and closet commentary those awe-inspiring sonnets of his, attain to some clear notion of what sort of life William Shakespeare must have led, would not see him much the clearer for many folios of anecdote. For after all, the best biography of every sincere man is sure to be his own works; here he has set down, "transferred as in a figure," all that has happened to him, inward or outward, or rather, all which has formed him, produced a permanent effect upon his mind and heart; and knowing that, you know all you need know, and are content, being glad to escape the personality and gossip of names and places, and of dates even, except in as far as they enable you to place one step of his mental growth before or after another. Of the honest man this holds true always; and almost always of the dishonest man, the man of cant, affectation, hypocrisy; for even if he pretend in his novel or his poem to be what he is not, he still shows you thereby what he thinks he ought to have been, or at least what he thinks that the world thinks he ought to have been, and confesses to you, in the most naïve and confidential way, like one who talks in his sleep, what learning he has or has not had; what society he has or has not seen, and that in the very act of trying to prove the contrary. Nay, the smaller the man or woman, and the less worth deciphering his biography, the more surely will he show you, if you have eyes to see and time to look, what sort of people offended him twenty years ago; what meanness he would have liked "to indulge in," if he had dared, when young, and for what other meanness he relinquished it, as he grew up; of what periodical he stood in awe when he took pen in hand, and so forth. Whether his books treat of love or political economy, theology or geology, it is there, the history of the man legibly printed, for those who care to read it. In these poems and letters of Burns, we apprehend, is to be found a truer history than any anecdote can supply, of the things which happened to himself, and moreover of the most notable things which went on in Scotland between 1759 and 1796.

This latter assertion may seem startling, when we consider that we find in these poems no mention whatsoever of the discoveries of steamboats and spinning-jennies, the rise of the great manufacturing cities, the revolution in Scottish agriculture, or even in Scottish metaphysics. But after all, the history of a nation is the history of the men, and not of the things thereof; and the history of those men is the history of their hearts, and not of their purses, or even of their heads; and the history of one man who has felt in himself the heart experiences of his generation, and anticipated many belonging to the next generation, is so far the collective history of that generation, and of much —no man can say how much—of the next generation; and such a man, bearing within his single soul two generations of working-men, we take Robert Burns to have been; and his poems, as such, a contemporaneous history of Scotland, the equal to which we are not likely to see written for this generation, or several to come.

Such a man sent out into such an age, would naturally have a hard and a confused battle to fight, would probably, unless he fell under the guidance of some master-mind, end se ipso minor, stunted and sadly deformed, as Burns did. His works are after all only the disjecta membra poetæ; full of hints of a great might-have-been. Hints of the keenest and most dramatic appreciation of human action and thought. Hints of an unbounded fancy, playing gracefully in the excess of its strength, with the vastest images, as in that robe of the Scottish Muse, in which

> Deep lights and shades, bold mingling, threw
> A lustre grand,
> And seem'd to my astonished view
> A well-known land.

The image, and the next few stanzas which dilate

it, might be a translation from Dante's "Paradiso," so broad, terse, vivid, the painter's touch. Hints, too, of a humour, which, like that of Shakespeare, rises at times by sheer depth of insight into the sublime; as when

> Hornie did the Laigh Kirk watch
> Just like a winking baudrons.

Hints of a power of verbal wit, which, had it been sharpened in such a perpetual word-battle as that amid which Shakespeare lived from the age of twenty, might have rivalled Shakespeare's own; which even now asserts its force by a hundred little never-to-be-forgotten phrases scattered through his poems, which stick, like barbed arrows, in the memory of every reader. And as for his tenderness—the quality without which all other poetic excellence is barren—it gushes forth toward every creature, animate and inanimate, with one exception, namely, the hypocrite, ever alike "spiacente a Dio e ai nemici sui;" and therefore intolerable to Robert Burns's honesty, whether he be fighting for or against the cause of right. Again we say, there are evidences of a versatile and manifold faculty in this man, which, with a stronger will and a larger education, might have placed him as an equal by the side of those great names which we mentioned together with his at the commencement of this article.

But one thing Burns wanted; and of that one thing his age helped to deprive him—the education which comes by reverence. Looking round in such a time, with his keen power of insight, his keen sense of humour, what was there to worship? Lord Jeffrey, or whosoever was the author of the review in the "Edinburgh," says disparagingly, that Burns had as much education as Shakespeare. So he very probably had, if education mean book-learning. Nay, more, of the practical education of the fireside, the sober, industrious, God-fearing education, and "drawing out" of the manhood, by act and example, Burns may have had more under his good father than Shakespeare under his; though the family life of the small English burgher in Elizabeth's time would have generally presented, as we suspect, the very same aspect of staid manfulness and godliness which a Scotch farmer's did fifty years ago. But let that be as it may, Burns was not born into an Elizabethan age. He did not see around him Raleighs and Sidneys, Cecils and Hookers, Drakes and Frobishers, Spensers and Jonsons, Southamptons and Willoughbys, with an Elizabeth, guiding and moulding the great whole, a crowned Titaness, terrible, and strong, and wise—a woman who, whether right or wrong, bowed the proudest, if not to love, yet still to obey.

That was the secret of Shakespeare's power. Heroic himself, he was born into an age of heroes. You see it in his works. Not a play but gives patent evidence that to him all forms of human magnanimity were common and wayside flowers — among the humours of men which he and Ben Jonson used to wander forth together to observe. And thus he could give living action and speech to the ancient noblenesses of Rome and the Middle Age; for he had walked and conversed with them, unchanged in everything but in the dress. Had he known Greek literature he could have recalled to imperishable life such men as Cimon and Aristides, such deeds as Marathon and Salamis. For had we not had our own Salamis acted within a few years of his birth; and were not the heroes of it still walking among men? It was surely this continual presence of "men of worship," this atmosphere of admiration and respect and trust, in which Shakespeare must have lived, which tamed down the wild selfwill of the deer-stealing fugitive from Stratford, into the calm large-eyed philosopher, tolerant and loving, and full of faith in a species made in the likeness of God. Not so with Burns. One feels painfully in his poems the want of great characters; and still more painfully that he has not drawn them, simply because they were not there to draw. That he has a true eye for what is noble, when he sees it, let his "Lament for Glencairn" testify, and the stanzas in his "Vision," in which, with a high-bred grace which many a courtly poet of his day might have envied, he alludes to one and another Scottish worthy of his time. There is no vein of saucy and envious "banausia" in the man; even in his most graceless sneer, his fault—if fault it be—is, that he cannot and will not pretend to respect that which he knows to be unworthy of respect. He sees around him and above him, as well as below him, an average of men and things dishonest, sensual, ungodly, shallow, ridiculous by reason of their own lusts and passions, and he will not apply to the shams of dignity and worth, the words which were meant for their realities. After all, he does but say what every one round him was feeling and thinking;

but he said it; and hypocritical respectability shrank shrieking from the mirror of her own inner heart. But it was all the wórse for him. In the sins of others he saw an excuse for his own. Losing respect for and faith in his brother-men, he lost, as a matter of course, respect for himself, faith in himself. The hypocrisy which persecutes in the name of law, whether political or moral, while in private it transgresses the very law which is for ever on its tongue, is turned by his passionate and sorely-tempted character into a too easy excuse for disbelieving in the obligation of any law whatsoever. He ceases to worship, and therefore to be himself worshipful—and we know the rest.

"He might have still worshipped God?" He might, and surely amid all his sins, doubts, and confusions, the remembrance of the old faith learned at his parent's knee, does haunt him still as a beautiful regret—and sometimes, in his bitterest hours, shine out before his poor broken heart as an everlasting Pharos, lighting him homewards after all. Whether he reached that home or not, none on earth can tell. But his writings show, if anything can, that the vestal-fire of conscience still burned within, though choked again and again with bitter ashes and foul smoke. Consider the time in which he lived, when it was "as with the people, so with the priest," and the grand old life-tree of the Scottish Kirk, now green and vigorous with fresh leaves and flowers, was all crusted with foul scurf and moss, and seemed to have ceased growing, and to be crumbling down into decay; consider the terrible contradiction between faith and practice which must have met the eyes of the man, before he could write with the same pen—and one as honestly as the other—"The Cottar's Saturday Night," and "Holy Willie's Prayer." But those times are past, and the men who acted in them gone to another tribunal. Let the dead bury their dead; and, in the meantime, instead of cursing the misguided genius, let us consider whether we have not also something for which to thank him; whether, as competent judges of him aver from their own experience, those very seeming blasphemies of his have not produced more good than evil; whether, though "a savour of death unto death," to conceited and rebellious spirits, they may not have helped to open the eyes of the wise to the extent to which the general eighteenth-century rottenness had infected Scotland, and to make intolerable a state of things which ought to have been intolerable, even if Burns had never written.

We are not attacking the reviewer, far less the "Edinburgh Review," which some years after this not only made the amende honorable to Burns, but showed a frank impartiality only too rare in the reviews of these days, by publishing in its pages the noble article on Burns which has since appeared separately in Mr. Carlyle's "Miscellanies." We only wish to show, from the reviewer's own words, the element in which Burns had to work, the judges before whom he had to plead, and the change which, as we think, very much by the influence of his own poems, has passed upon the minds of men. How few are there who would pen now about him such a sentence as this: "He is" (that is, was, having gone to his account fifteen years before) "perpetually making a parade of his own inflammability and imprudence, and talking with much self-complacency and exultation of the offence he has occasioned to the sober and correct part of mankind"—a very small part of mankind, one would have thought, in the British Isles at least, about the end of the last century. But, it was the fashion then, as usual, to substitute the praise of virtues for the practice of them; and three-bottle and ten-tumbler men had a very good right, of course, to admire sobriety and correctness, and to denounce any two-bottle and six-tumbler man who was not ashamed to confess in print the weaknesses which they confessed only by word of mouth. Just, and yet not just. True, Burns does make a parade of his thoughtlessness, and worse; but why? because he gloried in it? He must be a very skin-deep critic who cannot see, even in the most insolent of those blameworthy utterances, an inward shame and self-reproach, which if any man had ever felt in himself, he would be in nowise inclined to laugh at it in others. Why, it is the very shame which wrings those poems out of him. They are the attempt of the strong man fettered to laugh at his own consciousness of slavery—to deny the existence of his chains—to pretend to himself that he likes them. To us, some of those wildest "Rob the Ranter" bursts of blackguardism are most deeply mournful, hardly needing that the sympathies which they stir up should be heightened by the little scraps of prayer and bitter repentance, which lie up and down among their uglier brethren, the disjecta membra of a great "De Profundis," perhaps not all unheard. These latter pieces are most significant. The very doggrel of them, the total absence of any attempt at ornament in diction or polish in metre, is proof complete of their deep heart-wrung sincerity. They are like the wail of a lost child, rather than the remorse of a Titan. The heart of the man was so young to the last; the boy-vein in him, as perhaps in all great poets, beating on through manhood for good and for evil. No! there was parade there, as of the lost woman, who tries to hide her self-disgust by staring you out of countenance, but of complacency and exultation none.

On one point, namely politics, Burns's higher sympathies seem to have been awakened. It had been better for him, in a worldly point of view, that they had not. In an intellectual, and even in a moral point of view, far worse. A fellow-feeling with the French Revolution, in the mind of a young man of that day, was a sign of moral health, which we should have been sorry to miss in him. Unable to foresee the outcome of the great struggle, having lost faith in those everlasting truths, religious and political, which it was madly setting at naught, what could it appear to him but an awakening from the dead, a return to young and genial health, a purifying thunderstorm. Such was his dream, the dream of thousands more, and not so wrong a one after all. For that, since that fearful outburst of the nether pit, all Europe has arisen and awakened into manifold and beautiful new life, who can deny? We are not what we were, but better, or rather, with boundless means of being better if we will. We have entered a fresh era of time for good and evil; the fact is patent in every sermon we hear, in every book we read, in every invention, even the most paltry, which we see registered. Shall we think hardly of the man who saw the dawn of our own day, and welcomed it cheerfully and hopefully, even though he fancied the mist-spectres to be elements of the true sunrise, and knew not—and who knows?—the purposes of Him whose paths are in the great deep, and His ways past finding out? At least, the greater part of his influence on the times which have followed him, is to be ascribed to that very "Radicalism" which in the eyes of the respectable around him, had sealed his doom, and consigned him to ignoble oblivion. It has been, with the working men who read him, a passport for the rest of his writings; it has allured them to listen to him, when he spoke of high and holy things, which but for him, they might have long ago tossed away as worthless, in the recklessness of ignorance and discontent. They could trust his "Cottar's Saturday Night;" they could believe that he spoke from his heart, when in deep anguish he cries to the God whom he had forgotten, while they would have turned with a distrustful sneer from the sermon of the sleek and comfortable minister, who in their eyes, however humbly born, had deserted his class, and gone over to the camp of the enemy, and the flesh-pots of Egypt.

After the time of Burns, as was to be expected, Scottish song multiplies itself tenfold. The nation becomes awakened to the treasures of its own old literature, and attempts, what after all, alas! is but a revival; and like most revivals, not altogether a successful one. Of the twelve hundred songs contained in Mr. Whitelaw's excellent collection, whereof more than a hundred and fifty are either wholly or partly

Burns's, the small proportion written before him are decidedly far superior in value to those written after him; a discouraging fact, though not difficult to explain, if we consider the great social changes which have been proceeding, the sterner subjects of thought which have been arising, during the last half-century. True song requires for its atmosphere a state rather of careless Arcadian prosperity, than of struggle and doubt, of earnest looking forward to an unknown future, and pardonable regret for a dying past; and in that state the mind of the masses, throughout North Britain, has been weltering confusedly for the last few years. The new and more complex era into which we are passing has not yet sufficiently opened itself to be sung about; men hardly know what it is, much less what it will be; and while they are hard at work creating it, they have no breath to spare in talking of it. One thing they do see and feel, painfully enough at times, namely, that the old Scottish pastoral life is passing away, before the combined influence of manufactures and the large-farm system; to be replaced, doubtless, hereafter, by something better, but in the meanwhile dragging down with it in its decay but too much that can ill be spared of that old society which inspired Ramsay and Burns. Hence the later Scottish song-writers seldom really sing; their proses want the unconscious lilt and flash of their old models; they will hardly go (the true test of a song) without music. The true test, we say again, of a song. Who needs music, however fitting and beautiful the accustomed air may happen to be, to "Roy's Wife of Aldivalloch," or "The Bride cam' out o' the byre," or either of the casts of "The Flowers of the Forest," or to "Auld Lang Syne" itself? They bubble right up out of the heart, and by virtue of their inner and unconscious melody, which all that is true to the heart has in it, shape themselves into a song, and are not shaped by any notes whatsoever. So with many, most indeed, of Burns's; and a few of Allan Cunningham's; the "Wet sheet and a flowing sail," for instance. But the great majority of these later songs seem, if the truth is to be spoken, inspirations at second hand, of people writing about things which they would like to feel, and which they ought to feel, because others used to feel them in old times; but which they do not feel as their forefathers felt—a sort of poetical Tractarianism, in short. Their metre betrays them, as well as their words; in both they are continually wandering, unconsciously to themselves, into the elegiac—except when on one subject, whereon the muse of Scotia still warbles at first hand, and from the depths of her heart—namely, alas! the barley bree: and yet never, even on this beloved theme, has she risen again to the height of Burns's bacchanalian songs.

But when sober, there is a sadness about the Scottish muse nowadays—as perhaps there ought to be—and the utterances of hers which ring the truest are laments. We question whether in all Mr. Whitelaw's collection there is a single modern poem (placing Burns as the transition point between the old and new) which rises so high, or pierces so deep, with all its pastoral simplicity, as Smibert's "Widow's Lament."

> Afore the Lammas tide
>   Had dwin'd the birken tree,
> In a' our water-side,
>   Nae wife was blest like me:

A kind gudeman, and twa
  Sweet bairns were round me here;
But they're a' ta'en awa',
  Sin' the fa' o' the year.

Sair trouble cam' our gate,
  And made me, when it cam',
A bird without a mate,
  A ewe without a lamb.
Our hay was yet to maw,
  And our corn was yet to shear;
When they a' dwined awa',
  In the fa' o' the year.

I daurna look a-field,
  For aye I trow to see,
The form that was a bield
  To my wee bairns and me.
But wind, and weet, and snaw,
  They never mair can fear,
Sin' they a' got the ca',
  In the fa' o' the year.

Aft on the hill at e'ens,
  I see him 'mang the ferns,
The lover o' my teens,
  The father o' my bairns:
For there his plaid I saw,
  As gloamin' aye drew near—
But my a's now awa',
  Sin' the fa' o' the year.

Our bonnie rigs theirsel',
  Reca' my waes to mind,
Our puir dumb beasties tell
  O' a' that I ha'e tyned;
For whae our wheat will saw,
  And whae our sheep will shear,
Sin' my a' gaed awa',
  In the fa' o' the year?

My heart is growing cauld,
  And will be caulder still,
And sair sair in the fauld,
  Will be the winter's chill;
For peats were yet to ca',
  Our sheep they were to smear,
When my a' dwined awa',
  In the fa' o' the year.

I ettle whiles to spin,
  But wee wee patterin' feet,
Come rinnin' out and in,
  And then I first maun greet:
I ken its fancy a'
  And faster rows the tear,
That my a' dwined awa',
  In the fa' o' the year.

Be kind, O heav'n abune!
  To ane sae wae and lane,
An' tak' her hamewards sune,
  In pity o' her mane:
Lang ere the March winds blaw,
  May she, far far frae here,
Meet them a' that's awa',
  Sin' the fa' o' the year.

It seems strange why the man who could write this, who shows, in the minor key of metre, which he has so skilfully chosen, such an instinct for the true music of words, could not have written much more. And yet, perhaps, we have ourselves given the reason already. There was not much more to sing about. The fashion of imitating old Jacobite songs is past, the mine now being exhausted, to the great comfort of sincerity and common sense. The peasantry, whose courtship, rich in animal health, yet not over pure and refined, Allan

Ramsay sang a hundred years ago, are learning to think, and act, and emigrate, as well as to make love. The age of Theocritus and Bion has given place to—shall we say the age of the Cæsars, or the irruption of the barbarians?—and the love-singers of the North are beginning to feel, that if that passion is to retain any longer its rightful place in their popular poetry, it must be spoken of henceforth in words as lofty and refined as those in which the most educated and the most gifted speak of it. Hence, in the transition between the old animalism and the new spiritualism, a jumble of the two elements, not always felicitous; attempts at ambitious description, after Burns's worst manner; at subjective sentiment, after the worst manner of the world in general; and yet, all the while, a consciousness that there was something worth keeping in the simple objective style of the old school, without which the new thoughtfulness would be hollow, and barren, and windy; and so the two are patched together, "new cloth into an old garment, making the rent worse." Accordingly, these new songs are universally troubled with the disease of epithets. Ryan's exquisite "Lass wi' the Bonny Blue Een," is utterly spoiled by two offences of this kind.

> She'll steal out to meet her loved Donald again,

and—

> The world's false and vanishing scene;

as Allan Cunningham's still more exquisite "Lass of Preston Mill" is by one subjective figure:

> Six hills are woolly with my sheep,
> Six vales are lowing with my kye.

Burns doubtless committed the same fault again and again; but in his time it was the fashion; and the older models (for models they are and will remain for ever) had not been studied and analysed as they have been since. Burns, indeed, actually spoiled one or two of his own songs by altering them from their first cast to suit the sentimental taste of his time. The first version, for instance, of the "Banks and Braes o' Bonnie Doon," is far superior to the second and more popular one, because it dares to go without epithets. Compare the second stanza of each:

Thou'lt break my heart, thou bonnie bird,
  That sings upon the bough;
Thou minds me o' the happy days
  When my fause love was true.

* * * *

Thou'lt break my heart, thou warbling bird,
  That wantons through the flowery thorn;
Thou minds me o' departed joys,
  Departed never to return.

What is said in the latter stanza which has not been said in the former, and said more dramatically, more as the images would really present themselves to the speaker's mind? It would be enough for him that the bird was bonnie, and singing; and his very sorrow would lead him to analyse and describe as little as possible a thing which so painfully contrasted with his own feelings; whether the thorn was flowery or not, would not have mattered to him, unless he had some distinct association with the thorn-flowers, in which case he would have brought out the image full and separate, and not merely thrown it in as a make-weight to "thorn"—and this is the great reason why epithets are, nine times out of ten, mistakes in song and ballad poetry; he never would have thought of "departed" before he thought of "joys." A very little consideration of the actual processes of thought in such a case, will show the truth of our observation, and the instinctive wisdom of the older song-writers, in putting the epithet as often as possible after the noun, instead of before it, even at the expense of grammar. They are bad things at all times in song poetry, these epithets; and, accordingly, we find that the best German writers, like Uhland and Heine, get rid of them as much as possible, and succeed thereby, every word striking and ringing down with full force, no cushion of an epithet intruding between the reader's brain-anvil and the poet's hammer to break the blow. In Uhland's "Three Burschen," if we recollect right, there are but two epithets, and those of the simplest descriptive kind: "Thy fair daughter" and a "black pall." Were there more, we question whether the poet would have succeeded, as he has done, in making our flesh creep as he leads us on from line to line and verse to verse. So Tennyson, the greatest of our living poets, eschews as much as possible, in his later writings, these same epithets, except in cases where they are themselves objective and pictorial—in short, the very things which he wants you to look at, as, for instance:

> And into silver arrows break
> The sailing moon in creek and cove.

This is fair enough; but, indeed, after laying down our rule, we must confess that it is very difficult to keep always true to it, in a language which does not, like the Latin and German, allow us to put our adjectives very much where we choose. Nevertheless, whether we can avoid it or not, every time we place before the noun an epithet which, like "departed joys," relates to our consciousness concerning the object, and not merely to the object itself; or an epithet which, like "flowery thorn," gives us, before we get to the object itself, those accidents of the object which we only discern by a second look, by analysis and reflection—(for the thorn, if in the flower, would look to us, at the first glance, not "flowery," but "white," "snowy," or what you will which expresses colour, and not scientific fact)—every time, we repeat, this is done, the poet descends from the objective and dramatic domain of song, into the subjective and reflective one of elegy.

But the field in which Burns's influence has been, as was to be expected, most important and most widely felt, is in the poems of working men. He first proved that it was possible to become a poet and a cultivated man, without deserting his class, either in station or in sympathies; nay, that the healthiest and noblest elements of a lowly-born poet's mind might be, perhaps must be, the very feelings and thoughts which he brought up with him from below, not those which he received from above, in the course of his artificial culture. From the example of Burns, therefore, many a working man, who would otherwise have "died and given no sign," has taken courage, and spoken out the thought within him, in verse or prose, not always wisely and well, but in all cases, as it seems to us, in the belief that he had a sort of divine right to speak and be heard, since Burns had broken down the artificial ice-wall of centuries, and asserted, by act as well as song, that "a man's a man for a' that." Almost every volume of working men's poetry which we have read, seems to re-echo poor Nicoll's spirited, though somewhat over-strained address to the Scottish genius:

This is the natal day of him
  Who, born in want and poverty,
Burst from his fetters and arose,
  The freest of the free.

Arose to tell the watching earth
  What lowly men could feel and do,
To show that mighty heaven-like souls
  In cottage hamlets grew.

Burns! thou hast given us a name
  To shield us from the taunts of scorn:
The plant that creeps amid the soil
  A glorious flower has borne.

Before the proudest of the earth
  We stand with an uplifted brow;
Like us, thou wast a toil-worn man,
  And we are noble now!

The critic, looking calmly on, may indeed question whether this new fashion of verse-writing among working men has been always conducive to their own happiness. As for absolute success as poets, that was not to be expected of one in a hundred, so that we must not be disappointed if among the volumes of working men's poetry, of which we give a list at the head of our article, only two should be found, on perusal, to contain any writing of a very high order, although these volumes form a very small portion of the verses which have been written, during the last forty years, by men engaged in the rudest and most monotonous toil. To every man so writing, the art, doubtless, is an ennobling one. The habit of expressing thought in verse not only indicates culture, but is a culture in itself of a very high order. It teaches the writer to think tersely and definitely; it evokes in him the humanising sense of grace and melody, not merely by enticing him to study good models, but by the very act of composition. It gives him a vent for sorrows, doubts, and aspirations, which might otherwise fret and canker within, breeding, as they too often do in the utterly dumb English peasant, self-devouring meditation, dogged melancholy, and fierce fanaticism. And if the effect of verse-writing had stopped there, all had been well; but bad models have had their effect, as well as good ones, on the half-tutored taste of the working men, and engendered in them but too often a fondness for frothy magniloquence and ferocious raving, neither morally nor æsthetically profitable to themselves or their readers. There are excuses for the fault; the young of all ranks naturally enough mistake noise for awfulness, and violence for strength; and there is generally but too much, in the biographies of these working poets, to explain, if not to excuse, a vein of bitterness, which they certainly did not learn from their master, Burns. The two poets who have done them most harm, in teaching the evil trick of cursing and swearing, are Shelley and the Corn-Law Rhymer; and one can well imagine how seducing two such models must be, to men struggling to utter their own complaints. Of Shelley this is not the place to speak. But of the Corn-Law Rhymer we may say here, that howsoever he may have been indebted to Burns's example for the notion of writing at all, he has profited very little by Burns's own poems. Instead of the genial loving tone of the great Scotchman, we find in Elliott a tone of deliberate savageness, all the more ugly, because evidently intentional. He tries to curse; "he delights" —may we be forgiven if we misjudge the man—"in cursing;" he makes a science of it; he defiles, of malice prepense, the loveliest and sweetest thoughts and scenes (and he can be most sweet) by giving some sudden sickening revulsion to his reader's feelings; and he does it generally with a power which makes it at once as painful to the calmer reader as alluring to those who are struggling with the same temptations as the poet. Now and then, his trick drags him down into sheer fustian and bombast; but not always. There is a terrible Dantean vividness of imagination about him, perhaps unequalled in England, in his generation. His poems are like his countenance, coarse and ungoverned, yet with an intensity of eye, a rugged massiveness of feature, which would be grand but for the seeming deficiency of love and of humour—love's twin and inseparable brother. Therefore it is, that although single passages may be found in his writings, of which Milton himself need not have been ashamed, his efforts at dramatic poetry are utter failures, dark, monstrous, unrelieved by any really human vein of feeling or character. As in feature, so in mind, he has not even the delicate and graceful organisation which made up in Milton for the want of tenderness, and so enabled him to write, if not a drama, yet still the sweetest of masques and idyls.

Rather belonging to the same school than to that of Burns, though never degrading itself by Elliott's ferocity, is that extraordinary poem, "The Purgatory of Suicides," by Thomas Cooper. As he is still in the prime of life, and capable of doing more and better than he yet has done, we will not comment on it as freely as we have on Elliott, except to regret a similar want of softness and sweetness, and also of a clearness and logical connection of thought, in which Elliott seldom fails, except when cursing. The imagination is hardly as vivid as Elliott's, though the fancy and invention, the polish of the style, and the indications of profound thought on all subjects within the poet's reach, are superior in every way to those of the Corn-Law Rhymer; and when we consider that the man who wrote it had to gather his huge store of classic and historic anecdote while earning his living, first as a shoemaker, and then as a Wesleyan country preacher, we can only praise and excuse, and hope that the day may come when talents of so high an order will find some healthier channel for their energies than that in which they now are flowing.

Our readers may wonder at not seeing the Ettrick Shepherd's poems among the list at the head of the article. It seems to us, however, that we have done right in omitting them. Doubtless, he too was awakened into song by the example of Burns; but he seems to us to owe little to his great predecessor, beyond the general consciousness that there was a virgin field of poetry in Scotch scenery, manners, and legends —a debt which Walter Scott himself probably owed to the Ayrshire peasant just as much as Hogg did. Indeed, we perhaps are right in saying, that had Burns not lived, neither Wilson, Galt, Allan Cunningham, or the crowd of lesser writers who have found material for their fancy in Scotch peculiarities, would have written as they have. The three first names, Wilson's above all, must have been in any case distinguished; yet it is surely no derogation to some of the most exquisite rural sketches in "Christopher North's Recreations," to claim them as the intellectual foster-children of "The Cottar's Saturday Night." In this respect, certainly, the Ettrick Shepherd has a place in Burns's school, and, in our own opinion, one which has been very much overrated. But the deeper elements of Burns's mind, those which have especially endeared him to the working man, reappear very little, or not at all, in Hogg. He left his class too much below him; became too much of the mere æsthetic prodigy, and member of a literary clique; frittered away his great talents in brilliant talk and insincere Jacobite songs, and, in fine, worked no deliverance on the earth. It is sad to have to say this: but we had it forced upon us painfully enough a few days ago, when re-reading "Kilmeny." There may be beautiful passages in it; but it is not coherent, not natural, not honest. It is throughout an affectation of the Manichæan sentimental-sublime, which God never yet put into the heart of any brawny, long-headed, practical Borderer, and which he therefore probably put into his own head, or, as we call it, affected, for the time being; a method of poetry writing which comes forth out of nothing, and into nothing must return.

This is unfortunate, perhaps, for the world; for we question whether a man of talents in anywise to be compared with those of the Ettrick Shepherd has followed in the footsteps of Burns. Poor Tannahill, whose sad story is but too well known, perished early, at the age of thirty-six, leaving behind him a good many pretty love-songs of no great intrinsic value, if the specimens of them given in Mr. Whitelaw's collection are to be accepted as the best. Like all Burns's successors, including even Walter Scott and Hogg, we have but to compare him with his original to see how altogether unrivalled on his own ground the Ayrshire farmer was. In one feature only Tannahill's poems, and those later than him, except where pedantically archaist, like many of Motherwell's, are an improvement on Burns: namely, in the more easy and complete interfusion of the two dialects, the Norse Scotch and the Romanesque English, which Allan Ramsay attempted in vain to unite; while Burns, though not succeeding by any means perfectly, welded them together into something of continuity and harmony—thus doing for the language of his own country very much what Chaucer did for that of England—a happy union, in the opinion of those who, as we do, look on the vernacular Norse Scotch as no barbaric dialect, but as an independent tongue, possessing a copiousness, melody, terseness, and picturesqueness which makes it, both in prose and verse, a far better vehicle than the popular English for many forms of thought.

Perhaps the young peasant who most expressly stands out as the pupil and successor of Burns, is Robert Nicoll. He is a lesser poet, doubtless, than his master, and a lesser man, if the size and number of his capabilities be looked at; but he is a greater man, in that, from the beginning to the end of his career, he seems to have kept that very wholeness of heart and head which poor Burns lost. Nicoll's story is, mutatis mutandis, that of the Bethunes, and many a noble young Scotsman more. Parents holding a farm between Perth and Dunkeld, they and theirs before them for generations inhabitants of the neighbourhood, "decent, honest, God-fearing people." The farm is lost by reverses, and manfully Robert Nicoll's father becomes a day-labourer on the fields which he lately rented: and there begins, for the boy, from his earliest recollections, a life of steady sturdy drudgery. But they must have been grand old folk, these parents, and in no wise addicted to wringing their hands over "the great might-have-been." Like true Scots Bible lovers, they do believe in a God, and in a will of God, underlying, absolute, loving, and believe that the might-have-been ought not to have been, simply because it has not been; and so they put their shoulders to the new collar patiently, cheerfully, hopefully, and teach the boys to do the same. The mother especially, as so many great men's mothers do, stands out large and heroic, from the time when, the farm being gone, she, "the ardent book-woman," finds her time too precious to be spent in reading, and sets little Robert to read to her as she works—what a picture!—to the last sad day, when, wanting money to come up to Leeds to see her dying darling, she "shore for the siller," rather than borrow it. And her son's life is like her own—a most pure, joyous, valiant little epic. Robert does not even take to work as something beyond himself, uninteresting and painful, which, however, must be done courageously: he lives in it, enjoys it as his proper element, one which is no more a burden and an exertion to him than the rush of the strid is to the trout who plays and feels in it day and night, unconscious of the amount of muscular strength which he puts forth in merely keeping his place in the stream. Whether carrying "Kenilworth" in his plaid to the woods, to read while herding, or selling currants and whisky as the Perth storekeeper's apprentice, or keeping his little circulating library in Dundee, tormenting his pure heart with the thought of the twenty pounds which his mother has borrowed wherewith to start him, or editing *The Leeds Times*, or lying on his early deathbed, just as life seems to be opening clear and broad before him, he

> Bates not a jot of heart or hope,

but steers right onward, singing over his work, without bluster or self-gratulation, for very joy at having work to do. There is a keen practical insight about him, rarely combined, in these days, with his single-minded determination to do good in his generation. His eye is single, and his whole body full of light.

It would indeed (writes the grocer's boy, encouraging his despondent and somewhat Werterean friend) be hangman's work to write articles one day to be forgotten to-morrow, if that were all; but you forget the comfort—the repayment. If one prejudice is overthrown, one error rendered untenable; if but one step in advance be the consequence of your articles and mine—the consequences of the labour of all true men—are we not deeply repaid?

Or again, in a right noble letter to his noble mother:

That money of R.'s hangs like a millstone about my neck. If I had paid it, I would never borrow again from mortal man. But do not mistake me, mother; I am not one of those men who faint and falter in the great battle of life. God has given me too strong a heart for that. I look upon earth as a place where every man is set to struggle and to work, that he may be made humble and pure-hearted, and fit for that better land for which earth is a preparation—to which earth is the gate. . . . . If men would but consider how little of real evil there is in all the ills of which they are so much afraid—poverty included—there would be more virtue and happiness, and less world and Mammon-worship on earth than is. I think, mother, that to me has been given talent; and if so, that talent was given to make it useful to man.

And yet there is a quiet self-respect about him withal:

In my short course through life (says he in confidence to a friend at one-and-twenty), I have never feared an enemy, or failed a friend; and I live in the hope I never shall. For the rest, I have written my heart in my poems; and rude and unfinished and hasty as they are, it can be read there.

* * * * *

From seven years of age to this very hour, I have been dependent only on my own head and hands for everything—for very bread. Long years ago—ay, even in childhood—adversity made me think, and feel, and suffer; and would pride allow me, I could tell the world many a deep tragedy enacted in the heart of a poor, forgotten, uncared-for boy.

. . . . But I thank God, that though I felt and suffered, the scathing blast neither blunted my perceptions of natural and moral beauty, nor, by withering the affections of my heart, made me a selfish man. Often when I look back I wonder how I bore the burden—how I did not end the evil day at once and for ever.

Such is the man, in his normal state; and as was to be expected, God's blessing rests on him. Whatever he sets his hand to succeeds. Within a few weeks of his taking the editorship of *The Leeds Times* its circulation begins to rise rapidly, as was to be expected with an honest man to guide it. For Nicoll's political creed, though perhaps neither very deep nor wide, lies clear and single before him, as everything else which he does. He believes naturally enough in ultra-Radicalism according to the fashions of the Reform Bill era. That is the right thing; and for that he will work day and night, body and soul, and if needs be, die. There, in the editor's den at Leeds, he "begins to see the truth of what you told me about the world's unworthiness; but stop a little. I am not sad as yet. . . . If I am hindered from feeling the soul of poetry among woods and fields, I yet trust I am struggling for something worth prizing—something of which I am not ashamed, and need not be. If there be aught on earth worth aspiring to, it is the lot of him who is enabled to do something for his miserable and suffering fellow-men; and this you and I will try to do at least."

His friend is put to work a ministerial paper, with orders "not to be rash, but to elevate the population gradually;" and finding those orders to imply a considerable leaning towards the By-ends, Lukewarm, and

Facing-both-ways school, kicks over the traces, wisely, in Nicoll's eyes, and breaks loose.

> Keep up your spirits (says honest Nicoll). You are higher at this moment in my estimation, in your own, and that of every honest man, than you ever were before. Tait's advice was just such as I should have expected of him; honest as honesty itself. You must never again accept a paper but where you can tell the whole truth without fear or favour. . . . . Tell E. (the broken-loose editor's lady-love), from me to estimate as she ought the nobility and determination of the man who has dared to act as you have done. Prudent men will say that you are hasty: but you have done right, whatever may be the consequences.

This is the spirit of Robert Nicoll; the spirit which is the fruit of early purity and self-restraint, of living "on bread-and-cheese and water," that he may buy books; of walking out to the Inch of Perth at four o'clock on summer mornings, to write and read in peace before he returns to the currants and the whisky. The nervous simplicity of the man come out, in the very nervous simplicity of the prose he writes; and though there be nothing very new or elevated in it, or indeed in his poems themselves, we call on our readers to admire a phenomenon so rare, in the "upper classes" at least, in these days, and taking a lesson from the peasant's son, rejoice with us that "a man is born into the world."

For Nicoll, as few do, practises what he preaches. It seems to him, once on a time, right and necessary that Sir William Molesworth should be returned for Leeds; and Nicoll having so determined, "throws himself, body and soul, into the contest, with such ardour, that his wife afterwards said (and we can well believe it) that if Sir William had failed, Robert would have died on the instant!"—why not? Having once made up his mind that that was the just and right thing, the thing which was absolutely good for Leeds, and the human beings who lived in it, was it not a thing to die for, even if it had been but the election of a new beadle? The advanced sentry is set to guard some obscure worthless dike-end—obscure and worthless in itself, but to him a centre of infinite duty. True, the fate of the camp does not depend on its being taken; if the enemy round it, there are plenty behind to blow them out again. But that is no reason whatsoever why he, before any odds, should throw his musket over his shoulder, and retreat gracefully to the lines. He was set there to stand by that, whether dike-end or representation of Leeds; that is the right thing for him; and for that right he will fight, and if he be killed, die. So have all brave men felt, and so have all brave deeds been done, since man walked the earth. It is because that spirit, the spirit of faith, has died out among us, that so few brave deeds are done now, except on battle-fields and in hovels, whereof none but God and the angels know.

So the man prospers. Several years of honourable and self-restraining love bring him a wife, beautiful, loving, worshipping his talents; a help meet for him, such as God will send at times to those whom he loves. Kind men meet and love and help him—"The Johnstones, Mr. Tait, William and Mary Howitt;" Sir William Molesworth, hearing of his last illness, sends him unsolicited fifty pounds, which, as we understand it, Nicoll accepts without foolish bluster about independence. Why not?—man should help man, and be helped by him. Would he not have done as much for Sir William? Nothing to us proves Nicoll's heart-wholeness more than the way in which he talks of his benefactors, in a tone of simple gratitude and affection, without fawning and without vapouring. The man has too much self-respect to consider himself lowered by accepting a favour.

But he must go after all. The editor's den at Leeds is not the place for lungs bred on Perthshire breezes; and work rises before him, huger and heavier as he goes on, till he drops under the ever-increasing load. He will not believe it at first. In sweet childlike playful letters, he tells his mother that it is nothing. It has done him good—"opened the grave before his eyes, and taught him to think of death." "He trusts that he has not borne this, and suffered, and thought in vain." This too, he hopes, is to be a fresh lesson-page of experience for his work. Alas! a few months more of bitter suffering, and of generous kindness and love from all around him—and it is over with him at the age of twenty-three. Shall we regret him?—shall we not rather believe that God knew best; and considering the unhealthy moral atmosphere of the second-class press, and the strange confused ways into which old ultra-Radicalism, finding itself too narrow for the new problems of the day, has stumbled and floundered during the last fifteen years, believe that he might have been a worse man had he been a longer-lived one, and thank heaven that "the righteous is taken away from the evil to come?"

As it is, he ends as he began. The first poem in his book is "The Ha' Bible;" and the last, written a few days before his death, is still the death-song of a man—without fear, without repining, without boasting, blessing and loving the earth which he leaves, yet with a clear joyful eye upwards and outwards and homewards. And so ends his little epic, as we called it. May Scotland see many such another!

The actual poetic value of his verses is not first-rate by any means. He is far inferior to Burns in range of subject, as he is in humour and pathos. Indeed, there is very little of these latter qualities in him anywhere—rather playfulness, flashes of childlike fun, as in "The Provost," and "Bonnie Bessie Lee." But he has attained a mastery over English, a simplicity and quiet which Burns never did; and also, we need not say, a moral purity. His "Poems illustrative of the Scotch peasantry" are charming throughout—alive and bright with touches of real humanity, and sympathy with characters apparently antipodal to his own.

His more earnest poems are somewhat tainted with that cardinal fault of his school, of which he steered so clear in prose—fine words; yet he never, like the Corn-Law Rhymer, falls a cursing. He is evidently not a good hater even of "priests and kings, and aristocrats, and superstition;" or perhaps he worked all that froth safely over and off in debating-club speeches and leading articles, and left us, in these poems, the genuine metheglin of his inner heart, sweet, clear, and strong; for there is no form of lovable or right thing which this man has come across, which he does not seem to have appreciated. Besides pure love and the beauties of nature—those on which every man of poetic power, and a great many of none, as a matter of course, have a word to say—he can feel for and with the drunken beggar, and the warriors of the ruined manor-house, and the monks of the abbey, and the old mailed Normans with their "priest with cross and counted beads in the little Saxon chapel"—things which a Radical editor might have been excused for passing by with a sneer.

His verses to his wife are a delicious little glimpse of Eden; and his "People's Anthem" rises into somewhat of true grandeur by virtue of simplicity:

Lord, from Thy blessed throne,
Sorrow look down upon!
God save the Poor!
Teach them true liberty—
Make them from tyrants free—
Let their homes happy be!
God save the Poor!

The arms of wicked men
Do Thou with might restrain—
God save the Poor!
Raise Thou their lowliness—
Succour Thou their distress—
Thou whom the meanest bless!
God save the Poor!

Give them stanch honesty—
Let their pride manly be—
God save the Poor!
Help them to hold the right;
Give them both truth and might,
Lord of all LIFE and LIGHT!
God save the Poor!

And so we leave Robert Nicoll, with the parting remark, that if the "Poems illustrative of the feelings of the intelligent and religious among the working-classes of Scotland" be fair samples of that which they profess to be, Scotland may thank God, that in spite of temporary manufacturing rot-heaps, she is still whole at heart; and that the influence of her great peasant poet, though it may seem at first likely to be adverse to Christianity, has helped, as we have already hinted, to purify and not to taint; to destroy the fungus, but not to touch the heart, of the grand old Covenant-kirk life-tree.

Still sweeter, and, alas! still sadder, is the story of the two Bethunes. If Nicoll's life, as we have said, be a solitary melody, and short though triumphant strain of work-music, theirs is a harmony and true concert of fellow-joys, fellow-sorrows, fellow-drudgery, fellow-authorship, mutual throughout, lovely in their joint-life, and in their deaths not far divided. Alexander survives his brother John only long enough to write his "Memoirs," and then follows; and we have his story given us by Mr. M'Combie, in a simple unassuming little volume—not to be read without many thoughts, perhaps not rightly without tears. Mr. M'Combie has been wise enough not to attempt panegyric. He is all but prolix in details, filling up some half of his volume with letters of preternatural length from Alexander to his publishers and critics, and from the said publishers and critics to Alexander, altogether of an unromantic and business-like cast, but entirely successful in doing that which a book should do—namely, in showing the world that here was a man of like passions with ourselves, who bore from boyhood to the grave hunger, cold, wet, rags, brutalising and health-destroying toil, and all the storms of the world, the flesh, and the devil, and conquered them every one.

Alexander is set at fourteen to throw earth out of a ditch so deep, that it requires the full strength of a grown man, and loses flesh and health under the exertion; he is twice blown up with his own blast in quarrying, and left for dead, recovers slowly, maimed and scarred, with the loss of an eye. John, when not thirteen, is set to stone-breaking on the roads during intense cold, and has to keep himself from being frost-bitten and heart-broken by monkey gambols; takes to the weaving trade, and having helped his family by the most desperate economy to save ten pounds wherewith to buy looms, begins to work them, with his brother as an apprentice, and finds the whole outlay rendered useless the very same year by the failures of 1825–26. So the two return to day-labour at fourteenpence a-day. John, in a struggle to do task-work honestly, over-exerts himself, and ruins his digestion for life. Next year he is set in November to clean out a watercourse knee-deep in water; then to take marl from a pit; and then to drain standing water off a swamp during an intense December frost; and finds himself laid down with a three months' cough, and all but sleepless illness, laying the foundation of the consumption which destroyed him. But the two brothers will not give in. Poetry they will write; and they write it to the best of their powers, on scraps of paper, after the drudgery of the day, in a cabin pervious to every shower, teaching themselves the right spelling of the words from some "Christian Remembrancer" or other—apparently not our meek and unbiassed contemporary of that name; and all this without neglecting their work a day or even an hour, when the weather permitted—the "only thing which tempted them to fret," being—hear it, readers, and perpend!—"the being kept at home by rain and snow." Then an additional malady (apparently some calculous one) comes on John, and stops by him for the six remaining years of his life. Yet between 1826 and 1832, John had saved fourteen pounds out of his miserable earnings, to be expended to the last farthing on his brother's recovery from the second quarry accident. Surely the devil is trying hard to spoil these men. But no. They are made perfect by sufferings. In the house with one long narrow room, and a small vacant space at the end of it, lighted by a single pane of glass, they write and write untiring, during the long summer evenings, poetry, "Tales of the Scottish Peasant Life," which at last bring them in somewhat; and a work on practical economy, which is bepraised and corrected by kind critics in Edinburgh, and at last published—without a sale. Perhaps one cause of its failure might be found in those very corrections. There were too many violent political allusions in it, complains their good Mentor of Edinburgh; and persuades them, seemingly the most meek and teachable of heroes, to omit them; though Alexander, while submitting, pleads fairly enough for retaining them, in a passage which we will give, as a specimen of the sort of English possible to be acquired by a Scotch day-labourer, self-educated, all but the rudiments of reading and writing, and a few lectures on popular poetry from "a young student of Aberdeen," now the Rev. Mr. Adamson, who must look back on the friendship which he bore these two young men as one of the noblest pages in his life.

Talk to the many of religion, and they will put on a long face, confess that it is a thing of the greatest importance to all —and go away and forget the whole. Talk to them of education; they will readily acknowledge that it's "a braw thing to be weel learned," and begin a lamentation, which is only shorter than the lamentations of Jeremiah because they cannot make it as long, on the ignorance of the age in which they live; but they neither stir hand nor foot in the matter. But speak to them of politics, and their excited countenances and kindling eye show in a moment how deeply they are interested. Politics are therefore an important feature, and an almost indispensable element in such a work as mine. Had it consisted solely of exhortations to industry and rules of economy, it would have been dismissed with an "Ou ay, it's braw for him to crack that way: but if he were whaur we are, 'deed he wad just hae to do as we do." But by mixing up the science with politics, and giving it an occasional political impetus, a different result may be reasonably expected. In these days no man can be considered a patriot or friend of the poor, who is not also a politician.

It is amusing, by-the-bye, to see how the world changes its codes of respectability, and how, what is anathema in one generation, becomes trite orthodoxy in the next. The political sins in the work were, that "my brother had attacked the corn-laws with some severity; and I have attempted to level a battery against that sort of servile homage which the poor pay to the rich!"

There is no use pursuing the story much farther.

They again save a little money, and need it; for the estate on which they have lived from childhood changing hands, they are, with their aged father, expelled from the dear old dog-kennel to find house-room where they can. Why not?—"it was not in the bond." The house did not belong to them; nothing of it, at least, which could be specified in any known lease. True, there may have been associations: but what associations can men be expected to cultivate on fourteenpence a-day? So they must forth, with their two aged parents, and build with their own hands a new house elsewhere, having saved some thirty pounds from the sale of their writings. The house, as we understand, stands to this day—hereafter to become a sort of artisan's caaba and pilgrim's station, only second to Burns's grave. That, at least, it will become, whenever the meaning of the words "worth" and "worship" shall become rightly understood among us.

For what are these men, if they are not heroes and saints? Not of the Popish sort, abject and effeminate, but of the true, human, evangelic sort, masculine and grand—like the figures in Raffaelle's Cartoons compared with those of Fra Bartolomeo. Not from superstition, not from selfish prudence, but from devotion to their aged parents, and the righteous dread of dependence, they die voluntary celibates, although their writings show that they, too, could have loved as nobly as they did all other things. The extreme of endurance, self-restraint, of "conquest of the flesh," outward as well as inward, is the life-long lot of these men; and they go through it. They have their share of injustice, tyranny, disappointment; one by one each bright boy's dream of success and renown is scourged out of their minds, and sternly and lovingly their Father in heaven teaches them the lesson of all lessons. By what hours of misery and blank despair that faith was purchased, we can only guess; the simple strong men give us the result, but never dream of sitting down and analysing the process for the world's amusement or their own glorification. We question, indeed, whether they could have told us; whether the mere fact of a man's being able to dissect himself, in public or in private, is not proof-patent that he is no man, but only a shell of a man, with works inside, which can of course be exhibited and taken to pieces—a rather more difficult matter with flesh and blood. If we believe that God is educating, the when, the where, and the how are not only unimportant, but, considering who is the teacher, unfathomable to us, and it is enough to be able to believe with John Bethune that the Lord of all things is influencing us through all things; whether sacraments, or sabbaths, or sun-gleams, or showers—all things are ours, for all are His, and we are His, and He is ours—and for the rest, to say with the same John Bethune:

Oh God of glory! thou hast treasured up
  For me my little portion of distress;
But with each draught—in every bitter cup
  Thy hand hath mixed, to make its soreness less,
Some cordial drop, for which thy name I bless,
And offer up my mite of thankfulness.
  Thou hast chastised my frame with dire disease,
Long, obdurate, and painful; and thy hand
  Hath wrung cold sweat-drops from my brow; for these
I thank thee too. Though pangs at thy command
Have compassed me about, still, with the blow,
Patience sustained my soul amid its woe.

Of the actual literary merit of these men's writings there is less to be said. However extraordinary, considering the circumstances under which they were written, may be the polish and melody of John's verse, or the genuine spiritual health, deep death-and-devil-defying earnestness, and shrewd practical wisdom, which shines through all that either brother writes, they do not possess any of that fertile originality, which alone would have enabled them, as it did Burns, to compete with the literary savants, who, though for the most part of inferior genius, have the help of information and appliances, from which they were shut out. Judging them, as the true critic, like the true moralist, is bound to do, "according to what they had, not according to what they had not," they are men who, with average advantages, might have been famous in their day. God thought it better for them to "hide them in his tabernacle from the strife of tongues;" and—seldom believed truism—He knows best. Alexander shall not, according to his early dreams, "earn nine hundred pounds by writing a book, like Burns," even though his ideal method of spending be to buy all the boys in the parish "new shoes with iron tackets and heels," and send them home with shillings for their mothers, and feed their fathers on wheat bread and milk, with tea and bannocks for Sabbath-days, and build a house for the poor old toil-stiffened man whom he once saw draining the hill field, "with a yard full of gooseberries, and an apple-tree!"—not that, nor even, as the world judges, better than that, shall he be allowed to do. The poor, for whom he writes his "Practical Economy," shall not even care to read it; and he shall go down to the grave a failure and a lost thing in the eyes of men: but not in the eyes of grand God-fearing old Alison Christie, his mother, as he brings her, scrap by scrap, the proofs of their dead idol's poems, which she has prayed to be spared just to see once in print, and, when the last half-sheet is read, loses her sight for ever—not in her eyes, nor in those of God who saw him, in the cold winter mornings, wearing John's clothes, to warm them for the dying man before he got up.

His grief at his brother's death is inconsolable. He feels for the first time in his life, what a lot is his—for he feels for the first time that—

> Parent and friend and brother gone,
> I stand upon the earth alone.

Four years he lingers; friends begin to arise from one quarter and another, but he, not altogether wisely or well, refuses all pecuniary help. At last Mr. Hugh Miller recommends him to be editor of a projected "Non-Intrusion" paper in Dumfries, with a salary, to him boundless, of 100*l.* a-year. Too late! The iron has entered too deeply into his soul; in a few weeks more he is lying in his brother's grave—"Lovely and pleasant in their lives, and in their deaths not divided."

"William Thom of Inverury" is a poet altogether of the same school. His "Rhymes and Recollections of a Handloom Weaver" are superior to those of either Nicoll or the Bethunes, the little love-songs in the volume reminding us of Burns's best manner, and the two languages in which he writes being better amalgamated, as it seems to us, than in any Scotch song-writer. Moreover, there is a terseness, strength, and grace about some of these little songs, which would put to shame many a volume of vague and windy verse, which the press sees yearly sent forth by men, who, instead of working at the loom, have been pampered from their childhood with all the means and appliances of good taste and classic cultivation. We have room only for one specimen of his verse, not the most highly finished, but of a beauty which can speak for itself.

DREAMINGS OF THE BEREAVED.

The morning breaks bonny o'er mountain and stream,
An' troubles the hallowed breath of my dream.
The gowd light of morning is sweet to the e'e,
But ghost-gathering midnight, thou'rt dearer to me.
The dull common world then sinks from my sight,
And fairer creations arise to the night;
When drowsy oppression has sleep-sealed my e'e,
Then bright are the visions awakened to me!

Oh, come, spirit-mother! discourse of the hours
My young bosom beat all its beating to yours,
When heart-woven wishes in soft counsel fell
On ears—how unheedful, proved sorrow might tell!
That deathless affection nae sorrow could break;
When all else forsook me, ye would na forsake;
Then come, oh my mother! come often to me,
An' soon an' for ever I'll come unto thee!

An' then, shrouded loveliness! soul-winning Jean,
How cold was thy hand on my bosom yestreen!
'Twas kind—for the love that your e'e kindled there
Will burn, ay an' burn, till that breast beat nae mair—
Our bairnies sleep round me, oh bless ye their sleep!
Your ain dark-eyed Willie will wauken and weep!
But blythe through his weepin', he'll tell me how you,
His heaven-hamed mammie, was dauting his brow.

Though dark be our dwellin', our happin' tho' bare,
And night closes round us in cauldness and care,
Affection will warm us—and bright are the beams
That halo our hame in yon dear land o' dreams:
Then weel may I welcome the night's deathly reign,
Wi' souls of the dearest I mingle me then;
The gowd light of morning is lightless to me,
But, oh for the night with its ghost revelrie!

But even more interesting than the poems themselves, is the autobiographical account prefixed, with its vivid sketches of factory life in Aberdeen, of the old regime of 1770; when "four days did the weaver's work—Sunday, Monday, Tuesday, were of course jubilee. Lawn frills gorged (?) freely from under the wrists of his fine blue gilt-buttoned coat. He dusted his head with white flour on Sunday, smirked and wore a cane; walked in clean slippers on Monday; Tuesday heard him talk war bravado, quote Volney, and get drunk: weaving commenced gradually on Wednesday. Then were little children pirn-fillers, and such were taught to steal warily past the gate-keeper, concealing the bottle. These wee smugglers had a drop for their services, over and above their chances of profiting by the elegant and edifying discussions uttered in their hearing. Infidelity was then getting fashionable." But by the time Thom enters on his seventeen years' weaving, in 1814, the Nemesis has come. "Wages are six shillings a-week where they had been forty; but the weaver of forty shillings, with money instead of wit, had bequeathed his vices to the weaver of six shillings, with wit instead of money." The introduction of machinery works evil rather than good, on account of the reckless way in which it is used, and the reckless material which it uses. "Vacancies in the factory, daily made, were daily filled by male and female workers; often queer enough people, and from all parts —none too coarse for using. The pickpocket, trained to the loom six months in Bridewell, came forth a journeyman weaver; and his precious experiences were infused into the common moral puddle, and in due time did their work." No wonder that "the distinctive character of all sunk away. Man became less manly—woman unlovely and rude." No wonder that the factory, like too many more, though a thriving concern to its owners, becomes "a prime nursery of vice and sorrow." "Virtue perished utterly within its walls, and was dreamed of no more; or, if remembered at all, only in a deep and woful sense of self-debasement—a struggling to forget, where it was hopeless to obtain." But to us, almost the most interesting passage in his book, and certainly the one which bears most directly on the general purpose of this article, is one in which he speaks of the effects of song on himself and his fellow factory-workers.

Moore was doing all he could for love-sick boys and girls, yet they had never enough! Nearer and dearer to hearts like ours was the Ettrick Shepherd, then in his full tide of song and story; but nearer and dearer still than he, or any living songster, was our ill-fated fellow-craftsman Tannahill. Poor weaver chiel! what we owe to you!—your "Braes of Balquidder," and "Yon Burnside," and "Gloomy Winter," and the "Minstrel's" wailing ditty, and the noble "Gleneiffer." Oh! how they did ring above the rattle of a thousand shuttles! Let me again proclaim the debt which we owe to these song spirits, as they walked in melody from loom to loom, ministering to the low-hearted; and when the breast was filled with everything but hope and happiness, let only break out the healthy and vigorous chorus, "A man's a man for a' that," and the fagged weaver brightens up. . . . . Who dare measure the restraining influences of these very songs? To us they were all instead of sermons. Had one of us been bold enough to enter a church, he must have been ejected for the sake of decency. His forlorn and curiously patched habiliments would have contested the point of attraction with the ordinary eloquence of that period. Church bells rang not for us. Poets were indeed our priests: but for those, the last relic of moral existence would have passed away. Song was the dewdrop which gathered during the long dark night of despondency, and was sure to glitter in the very first blink of the sun. You might have seen "Auld Robin Gray" wet the eyes that could be tearless amid cold and hunger, and weariness and pain. Surely, surely, then there was to that heart one passage left.

Making all allowance for natural and pardonable high-colouring, we recommend this most weighty and significant passage to the attention of all readers, and draw an argumentum à fortiori, from the high estimation in which Thom holds those very songs of Tannahill's, of which we just now spoke somewhat depreciatingly, for the extreme importance which we attach to popular poetry, as an agent of incalculable power in moulding the minds of nations.

The popular poetry of Germany has held that great nation together, united and heart-whole for centuries, in spite of every disadvantage of internal division, and the bad influence of foreign taste; and the greatest of their poets have not thought it beneath them to add their contributions, and their very best, to the common treasure, meant not only for the luxurious and learned, but for the workman and the child at school. In Great Britain, on the contrary, the people have been left to form their own tastes, and choose their own modes of utterance, with great results, both for good and evil; and there has sprung up before the new impulse which Burns gave to popular poetry, a considerable literature —considerable not only from its truth and real artistic merit, but far more so from its being addressed principally to the working classes. Even more important is this people's literature question, in our eyes, than the more palpable factors of the education question, about which we now hear such ado. It does seem to us, that to take every possible precaution about the spiritual truth which children are taught in school, and then leave to chance the more impressive and abiding teaching which popular literature, songs especially, give them out of doors, is as great a *niaiserie* as that of the Tractarians who insisted on getting into the pulpit in their surplices, as a sign that the clergy only had the right of preaching to the people, while they forgot that, by means of a free press (of the licence of which they, too, were not slack to avail themselves), every penny-a-liner was preaching to the people daily, and would do so, maugre their surplices, to the end of time. The man who makes the people's songs is a true popular preacher. Whatsoever, true or false, he sends forth, will not be carried home, as a sermon often is, merely in heads, to be forgotten before the week is out: it will ring in the ears, and cling round the imagination, and follow the pupil to the workshop, and the tavern, and the fireside; even to the deathbed, such power is in the magic of rhyme. The emigrant, deep in Australian forests, may take down Chalmers's sermons on Sabbath evenings from the scanty shelf: but the songs of Burns have been haunting his lips, and cheering his heart, and moulding him, unconsciously to himself, in clearing and in pasture all the weary week. True, if he be what a Scotchman should be, more than one old Hebrew psalm has brought its message to him during these week-days; but there are feelings of his nature on which those psalms, not from defect, but from their very purpose, do not touch: how is he to express them, but in the songs which echo them? These will keep alive, and intensify in him, and in the children who learn them from his lips, all which is like themselves. Is it, we ask again, to be left to chance what sort of songs these shall be?

As for poetry written for the working classes by the upper, such attempts at it as we yet have seen, may be considered nil. The upper must learn to know more of the lower, and to make the lower know more of them—a frankness of which we honestly believe they will never have to repent. Moreover, they must read Burns a little more, and cavaliers and Jacobites a little less. As it is, their efforts have been as yet exactly in that direction which would most safely secure the blessings of undisturbed obscurity. Whether "secular" or "spiritual," they have thought proper to adopt a certain Tommy-good-child tone, which, whether to Glasgow artisans or Dorsetshire labourers, or indeed for any human being who is "grinding among the iron facts of life," is, to say the least, nauseous; and the only use of their poematicula has been to demonstrate practically the existence of a great and fearful gulf between those who have, and those who have not, in thought as well as in purse, which must be, in the former article at least, bridged over as soon as possible, if we are to remain one people much longer. The attempts at verse for children are somewhat more successful—a certain little "Moral Songs" especially, said to emanate from the Tractarian School, yet full of a health, spirit, and wild sweetness, which makes its authoress, in our eyes, "wiser than her teachers." But this is our way. We are too apt to be afraid of the men, and take to the children as our *pis-aller,* covering our despair of dealing with the majority, the adult population, in a pompous display of machinery for influencing that very small fraction, the children. "Oh, but the destinies of the empire depend on the rising generation! Who has told us so? —how do we know that they do not depend on the risen generation? Who are likely to do more work during our lifetime, for good and evil,—those who are now between fifteen and five-and-forty, or those who are between five and fifteen? Yet for those former, the many, and the working, and the powerful, all we seem to be inclined to do is to parody Scripture, and say: "He that is unjust, let him be unjust still; and he that is filthy, let him be filthy still."

Not that we ask any one to sit down, and, out of mere benevolence, to write songs for the people. Wooden out of a wooden birthplace, would such go forth, to feed fires, not spirits. But if any man shall read these pages, to whom God has given a truly poetic temperament, a gallant heart, a melodious ear, a quick and sympathetic eye for all forms of human joy, and sorrow, and humour, and grandeur; an insight which can discern the outlines of the butterfly, when clothed in the roughest and most rugged chrysalis-hide; if the teachers of his heart and purposes, and not merely of his taste and sentiments, have been the great songs of his own and of every land and age; if he can see in the divine poetry of David and Solomon, of Isaiah and Jeremiah, and, above all, in the parables of Him who spake as never man spake, the models and elemental laws of a people's poetry, alike according to the will of God and the heart of man; if he can welcome gallantly and hopefully the future, and yet know that it must be, unless it would be a monster and a machine, the loving and obedient child of the past; if he can speak of the subjects which alone will interest the many, on love, marriage, the sorrows of the poor, their hopes, political and social, their wrongs, as well as their sins and duties; and that with a fervour and passion akin to the spirit of Burns and Elliott, yet with more calmness, more purity, more wisdom, and therefore with more hope, as one who stands upon a vantage-ground of education and culture, sympathising none the less with those who struggle behind him in the valley of the shadow of death, yet seeing from the mountain peaks the coming dawn, invisible as yet to them: then let that man think it no fall, but rather a noble rise, to leave awhile the barren glacier ranges of pure art, for the fertile gardens of practical and popular song, and write for the many, and with the many, in words such as they can understand; remembering that that which is simplest is always deepest; that the many contain in themselves the few; and that when he speaks to the wanderer and the drudge, he speaks to the elemental and primeval man, and in him speaks to all who have risen out of him. Let him try, undiscouraged by inevitable failures; and if at last he succeeds in giving vent to one song which will cheer hard-worn hearts at the loom and the forge, or wake one pauper's heart with the hope that his children are destined not to die as he died, or recall, amid Canadian forests or Australian sheep-walks, one thrill of love for the old country, her liberties, and her laws, and her religion, to the settler's heart—let that man know that he has earned a higher place among the spirits of the wise and good, by doing, in spite of the unpleasantness of self-denial, the duty which lay nearest him, than if he had outrivalled Goethe on his own classic ground, and made all the cultivated and the comfortable of the earth desert, for the exquisite creations of his fancy, Faust, and Tasso, and Iphigenie.

THE POETRY OF
SACRED AND LEGENDARY ART.

THE POETRY OF SACRED AND LEGENDARY ART.*

MUCH attention has been excitea this year by the alleged fulfilment of a prophecy that the Papal power was to receive its death-blow—in temporal matters, at least—during the past year 1848. For ourselves, we have no more faith in Mr. Fleming, the obsolete author, who has so suddenly revived in the public esteem, than we have in many other interpreters of prophecy. Their shallow and bigoted views of past history are enough to damp our faith in their discernment of the future. It does seem that people ought to understand what has been, before they predict what will be. History is "the track of God's footsteps through time;" it is in His dealings with our forefathers that we may expect to find the laws by which He will deal with us. Not that Mr. Fleming's conjecture must be false; among a thousand guesses there ought surely to be one right one. And it is almost impossible for earnest men to

* Fraser's Magazine, March, 1849.—"Sacred and Legendary Art." By Mrs. Jameson. 2 vols. London. 1848. Longman and Co.

bend their whole minds, however clumsily, to one branch of study without arriving at some truth or other. The interpreters of prophecy therefore, like all other interpreters, have our best wishes, though not our sanguine hopes. But, in the meantime, there are surely signs of the approaching ruin of Popery, more certain than any speculations on the mystic numbers of the Revelation. We should point to recent books—not to books which merely expose Rome, that has been done long ago, usque ad nauseam—but to books which do her justice: to Mr. Maitland's "Dark Ages;" Lord Lindsay's "Christian Art;" and last, but not least, to the very charming work of Mrs. Jameson, whose title heads this review. In them, and in a host of similar works in Germany, which Dr. Wiseman's party hail as signs of coming triumph, we fancy we see the death-warrant of Romanism; because they prove that Rome has nearly done her work—that the Protestants are learning the lesson for the sake of which Providence has so long borne with that monstrous system. When Popery has no more truth to teach us, but not till then, will it vanish away into its native night.

We entreat Protestant readers not to be alarmed at us. We have not the slightest tendency toward the stimulants of Popery, either in their Roman unmixed state, or in their diluted Oxford form. We are, with all humility, more Protestant than Protestantism itself; our fastidious nostril, more sensitive of Jesuits than even those of the author of "Hawkstone," has led us at moments to fancy that we scent indulgences in Conduit-street Chapel, and discern inquisitors in Exeter Hall itself. Seriously, none believe more firmly than ourselves that the cause of Protestantism is the cause of liberty, of civilisation, of truth; the cause of man and God. And because we think Mrs. Jameson's book especially Protestant, both in manner and intention, and likely to do service to the good cause, we are setting to work herein to praise and recommend it. For the time, we think, for calling Popery ill names is past; though to abstain is certainly sometimes a sore restraint for English spirits, as Mrs. Jameson herself, we suspect, has found; but Romanism has been exposed and refuted triumphantly, every month for centuries, and yet the Romish nations are not converted; and too many English families of late have found, by sad experience, that such arguments as are in vogue are powerless to dissuade the young from rushing headlong into the very superstitions which they have been taught from their childhood to deride. The truth is, Protestantism may well cry: "Save me from my friends!" We have attacked Rome too often on shallow grounds, and finding our arguments weak, have found it necessary to overstate them. We have got angry, and caught up the first weapon which came to hand, and have only cut our own fingers. We have very nearly burnt the Church of England over our heads, in our hurry to make a bonfire of the Pope. We have been too proud to make ourselves acquainted with the very tenets which we exposed, and have made a merit of reading no Popish books but such as we were sure would give us a handle for attack, and not even them without the precaution of getting into a safe passion beforehand. We have dealt in exaggerations, in special pleadings, in vile and reckless imputations of motive, in suppressions of all palliating facts. We have outraged the common feelings of humanity by remaining blind to the virtues of noble and holy men because they were Papists, as if a good deed was not good in Italy as well as in England. We have talked as if God had doomed to hopeless vileness in this world and reprobation in the next millions of Christian people, simply because they were born of Romish and not of Protestant fathers. And we have our reward; we have fared like the old woman who would not tell the children what a well was for fear they should fall into one. We see educated and pious Englishmen joining the Romish communion simply from ignorance of Rome, and have no talisman wherewith to disenchant them. Our medicines produce no effect on them, and all we can do is, like quacks, to increase the dose. Of course, if ten boxes of Morison's pills have killed a man, it only proves that—he ought to have taken twelve of them. We are jesting, but, as an Ulster Orangeman would say, "it is in good Protestant earnest."

In the meantime some of the deepest cravings of the human heart have been left utterly unsatisfied. And be it remembered, that such universal cravings are more than fancies; they are indications of deep spiritual wants, which, unless we supply them with the good food which God has made for them, will supply themselves with poison—indications of spiritual faculties, which it is as wicked to stunt or distort by mis-education as it is to maim our own limbs or stupefy our understanding. Our humanity is an awful and divine gift; our business is to educate it throughout—God alone must judge which part of it shall preponderate over the rest. But in the last generation—and, alas! in this also—little or no proper care has been taken of the love for all which is romantic, marvellous, heroic, which exists in every ingenuous child. Schoolboys, indeed, might, if they chose, in play-hours, gloat over the "Seven Champions of Christendom," or Lemprière's gods and goddesses; girls might, perhaps, be allowed to devour by stealth a few fairy tales, or the "Arabian Nights;" but it was only by connivance that their longings were satisfied from the scraps of Moslemism, Paganism—anywhere but from Christianity. Protestantism had nothing to do with the imagination—in fact, it was a question whether reasonable people had any; whether the devil was not the original maker of that troublesome faculty in man, woman, and child. Poetry itself was, with most parents, a dram, to be given, like Dalby's Carminative, as a *pis-aller*, when children could not possibly be kept quiet by Miss Edgeworth or Mrs. Mangnall. Then, as the children grew up, and began to know something of history and art, two still higher cravings began to seize on many of them, if they were at all of deep and earnest character: a desire to associate with religion their new love for the beautiful, and a reverence for antiquity; a wish to find some bond of union between themselves and the fifteen centuries of Christianity which elapsed before the Reformation. They applied to Protestant teachers and Protestant books, and received too often the answer that the Gospel had nothing to do with art—art was either Pagan or Popish; and as for the centuries before the Reformation, they and all in them belonged utterly to darkness and the pit. As for the heroes of early Christianity, they were madmen or humbugs; their legends, devilish and filthy puerilities. They went to the artists and literary men, and received the same answer. The medieval writers were fools. Classical art was the only art; all painters before the age of Raphael superstitious bunglers. To be sure, as Fuseli said, Christianity had helped art a little; but then it was the Christianity of Julio and Leone—in short, of the worst age of Popery.

These falsehoods have worked out their own punishment. The young are examining for themselves, and finding that we have deceived them, a revulsion in their feelings has taken place, similar to that which took place in Germany some half-century ago. They are reading the histories of the Middle Ages, and if we call them barbarous—they will grant it, and then quote instances of individual heroism and piety, which they defy us or any honest man not to admire. They are reading the old legends, and when we call them superstitious—they grant it, and then produce passages in which the highest doctrines of Christianity are embodied in the most pathetic and noble stories. They are looking for themselves at the ante-Raphaellic artists, and when we tell them that Fra Angelico's pictures are weak, affected, ill-drawn, ill-coloured—they grant it, and then ask us if we can deny the sweetness, the purity, the rapt devotion, the saintly virtue, which shines forth from his faces. They ask us how beautiful and holy words or figures can be inspired by an evil spirit. They ask us why they are to deny the excellence of tales and pictures which make men more pure and humble, more earnest and noble. They tell us truly that all beauty is God's stamp, and that all beauty ought to be consecrated to his service. And then they ask us: "If Protestantism denies that she can consecrate the beautiful, how can you wonder if we love the Romanism which can? You say that Popery created these glorious schools of art; how can you wonder if, like Overbeck, "we take the faith for the sake of the art which it inspired?"

To all which, be it true or false (and it is both), are we to answer merely by shutting our eyes and ears tight, and yelling "No Popery!" or are we to say boldly to them: "We confess ourselves in fault; we sympathise with your longings; we confess that Protestantism has not satisfied them; but we assert that the only cause is, that Protestantism has not been true to herself; that Art, like every other product of the free human spirit, is her domain and not Popery's; that these legends, these pictures, are beautiful just in as far as they contain in them the germs of those eternal truths about man, nature, and God, which the Reformation delivered from bondage; that you can admire them, and yet remain thorough Protestants; and more, that unless you do remain Protestants, you will never enter into their full beauty and significance, because you will lose sight of those very facts and ideas from which they derive all their healthy power over you?

These thoughts are not our own; they are uttered all over England, thank God! just now, by many voices and in many forms; if they had been boldly spoken during the last fifteen years, many a noble spirit, we believe, might have remained in the Church of its fathers which has now taken refuge in Romanism from the fruits of miseducation. One great reason why Romanism has been suffered to drag on its existence is, we humbly think, that it might force us at last to say this: We have been long learning the lesson; till we have learnt it thoroughly Romanism will exist, and we shall never be safe from its allurements.

These thoughts may help to explain our opening sentences, as well as the extreme pleasure with which we hail the appearance of Mrs. Jameson's work.

The authoress has been struck, during her examination of the works of Christian artists, with the extreme ignorance which prevails in England on the subjects which they portray.

We have had (she says, in an introduction, every word of which we recommend as replete with the truest Christian philosophy)—

Inquiries into the Principles of Taste, treatises on the Sublime and Beautiful, Anecdotes of Painting, and we abound in antiquarian essays on disputed pictures and mutilated statues; but up to a late period any inquiry into the true spirit and significance of works of art, as connected with the history of religion and civilisation, would have appeared ridiculous or, perhaps, dangerous. We should have had another cry of "No Popery!" and Acts of Parliament prohibiting the importation of saints and Madonnas.—P. xxi.

And what should we have gained by it, but more ignorance of the excuses for Popery, and, therefore, of its real dangers? If Protestantism be the truth, knowledge of whatsoever kind can only further it. We have found it so in the case of classical literature. Why should we strain at a gnat and swallow a camel? Our boys have not taken to worshipping Jupiter and Juno by reading about them. We never feared that they would. We knew that we should not make them pagans by teaching them justly to admire the poetry, the philosophy, the personal virtues of pagans. And, in fact, the few who since the revival of letters have deserted Christianity for what they called philosophic heathenism, have in almost every case sympathised, not with the excellences, but with the worst vices of the Greek and Roman. They have been men like Leo X. or the Medici, who, ready to be profligates under any religion, found in heathenism only an excuse for their darling sins. The same will be the fruits of a real understanding of the medieval religion. It will only endanger those who carried already the danger in themselves, and would have fallen into some other snare if this had been away. Why should we fancy that Protestantism, like the Romanism which it opposes, is a plant that will not bear the light, and can only be protected at the expense of the knowledge of facts? Why will we forget the great spiritual law which Mrs. Jameson and others in these days are fully recognising, that "we cannot safely combat the errors of any man or system without first giving them full credit for whatever excellences they may retain"? Such a course is the true fruit of that free spirit of Protestantism which ought to delight in recognising good to whatever party it may belong; which asserts that every good gift and perfect gift comes directly from above, and not through the channel of particular formularies or priesthoods; which, because it loves faith and virtue, for their own sakes, and not as mere parts of a "Catholic system," can recognise them and delight in them wherever it finds them.

Upon these creations of ancient art (as Mrs. Jameson says) we cannot look as those did for whom they were created; we cannot annihilate the centuries which lie between us and them; we cannot in simplicity of heart, forget the artist in the image he has placed before us, nor supply what may be deficient in his work through a reverentially excited fancy. We are critical, not credulous. We no longer accept this polytheistic form of Christianity; and there is little danger, I suppose, of our falling again into the strange excesses of superstition to which it led. But if I have not much sympathy with modern imitations of medieval art, still less can I sympathise with that narrow puritanical jealousy which holds the monuments of a real and earnest faith in contempt: all that God has permitted to exist once in the past should be considered as the possession of the present; sacred for example or warning, and held as the foundation on which to build up what is better and purer.—Introd. p. xx.

Mrs. Jameson here speaks in the name of a large and rapidly-increasing class. The craving for religious art, of which we spoke above, is spreading far and wide; even in dissenting chapels we see occasional attempts at architectural splendour, which would have been considered twenty years ago heretical or idolatrous. And yet with all this there is, as Mrs. Jameson says, a curious ignorance with regard to the subject of medieval art, even though it has now become a reigning fashion among us.

We have learned, perhaps, after running through half the galleries and churches in Europe, to distinguish a few of the attributes and characteristic figures which meet us at every turn, yet without any clear idea of their meaning, derivation, or relative propriety. The palm of victory, we know, designates the martyr, triumphant in death. We so far emulate the critical sagacity of the gardener in "Zeluco," that we have learned to distinguish St. Laurence by his gridiron, and St. Catherine by her wheel. We are not at a loss to recognise the Magdalene's "loose hair and lifted eye," even when without her skull and her vase of ointment. We learn to know St. Francis by his brown habit, and shaven crown, and wasted ardent features; but how do we distinguish him from St. Anthony, or St. Dominick? As for St. George and the Dragon —from the St. George of the Louvre—Raphael's—who sits his horse with the elegant tranquillity of one assured of celestial aid, down to him "who swings on a sign-post at mine hostess's door"—he is our familiar acquaintance. But who is that lovely being in the first blush of youth, who, bearing aloft the symbolic cross, stands with one foot on the vanquished dragon? "That is a copy after Raphael." And who is that majestic creature holding her palm-branch, while the unicorn crouches at her feet? "That is the famous Moretto at Vienna." Are we satisfied? Not in the least! but we try to look wiser and pass on.

In the old times, the painters of these legendary scenes and subjects could always reckon securely on certain associations and certain sympathies in the minds of the spectators. We have outgrown these associations, we repudiate these sympathies. We have taken these works from their consecrated localities, in which they once held each their dedicated place, and we have hung them in our drawing-rooms and our dressing-rooms, over our pianos and our sideboards, and now what do they say to us? That Magdalene weeping amid her hair, who once spoke comfort to the soul of the fallen sinner, —that Sebastian, arrow-pierced, whose upward ardent glance, spoke of courage and hope to the tyrant-ridden serf—that poor tortured slave to whose aid St. Mark comes sweeping down from above—can they speak to us of nothing save flowing lines, and correct drawing, and gorgeous colour? Must we be told that one is a Titian, the other a Guido, the third a Tintoret, before we dare to melt into compassion or admiration? or the moment we refer to their ancient religious signification and influence, must it be with disdain or with pity? This, as it appears to me, is to take not a rational, but rather a most irrational, as well as a most irreverent, view of the question: it is to confine the pleasure and improvement to be derived from works of art within very narrow bounds; it is to seal up a fountain of the richest poetry, and to shut out a thousand ennobling and inspiring thoughts. Happily there is a growing appreciation of these larger principles of criticism as applied to the study of art. People look at the pictures which hang round their walls, and have an awakening suspicion that there is more in them than meets the eye—more than mere connoisseurship can interpret; and that they have another, a deeper significance than has been dreamed of by picture dealers and picture collectors, or even picture critics.—Introd. xxiii.

On these grounds Mrs. Jameson treats of the Poetry of Sacred and Legendary Art. Her first volume contains a general sketch of the legends connected with angels, with the scriptural personages, and the primitive fathers. Her second, the histories of most of "those sainted personages who lived, or are supposed to have lived, in the first ages of Christianity, and whose real history, founded on fact or tradition, has been so disfigured by poetical embroidery that they have in some sort the air of ideal beings." Each story is followed by a series of short but brilliant criticisms on those pictures in which the story has been embodied by painters of various schools and periods, and illustrated by numerous spirited etchings and woodcuts, which add greatly to the value and intelligibility of the work. A future volume is promised which shall contain the "legends of the monastic orders, and the history of the Franciscans and the Dominicans, considered merely in their connection with the revival and the development of the fine arts in the thirteenth and fourteenth centuries"—a work which, if it equal the one before us, will doubtless be hailed by those conversant with that wonderful phase of human history as a valuable addition to our psychologic and æsthetic literature.

We ought to petition, also, for a volume which should contain the life of the Saviour, and the legends of the Virgin Mary; though this latter subject, we are afraid, will be too difficult for even Mrs. Jameson's tact and delicacy to make tolerable to English readers, so thoroughly has the Virgin Mary, as especial patroness of purity, been intermixed in her legends with every form of prudish and prurient foulmindedness.*

The authoress has wisely abstained from all controversial matters. In her preface she begs that it may be clearly understood, "that she has taken throughout the æsthetic and not the religious view of these productions of art; which, in as far as they are informed with a true and earnest feeling, and steeped in that beauty which emanates from Genius inspired by Faith, may cease to be religion, but cannot cease to be poetry; and as poetry only," she says, "I have considered them." In a word, Mrs. Jameson has done for them what schoolmasters and schoolboys, bishops and Royal Academicians, have been doing for centuries, by Greek plays and Greek statues, without having incurred, as

* Since this was written, Mrs. Jameson's volume on the Legends of the Madonna has succeeded excellently in giving us, if not a complete, yet still a readable and modest picture of medieval Mariolatry.

we said above, the slightest suspicion of wanting to worship heathen gods and goddesses.

Not that she views these stories with the cold unbelieving eye of a Goethe, merely as studies of "artistic effect;" she often transgresses her rule of impartiality, and just where we should wish her to do so. Her geniality cannot avoid an occasional burst of feeling, such as concludes her notice of the stories about the Magdalene and the other "beatified penitents."

> Poets have sung, and moralists and sages have taught, that for the frail woman there was nothing left but to die; or if more remained for her to suffer, there was at least nothing left for her to be or do—no choice between sackcloth and ashes and the livery of sin. The beatified penitents of the early Christian Church spoke another lesson—spoke divinely of hope for the fallen, hope without self-abasement or defiance. We, in these days, acknowledge no such saints; we have even done our best to dethrone Mary Magdalene; but we have martyrs—"by the pang without the palm"—and one, at least, among these who has not died without lifting up a voice of eloquent and solemn warning; who has borne her palm on earth, and whose starry crown may be seen on high even now amid the constellations of Genius.—Vol. ii. p. 386.

To whom the authoress may allude in this touching passage our simplicity cannot guess in the least. We may, therefore, without the suspicion of partiality, say to the noble spirit of purity, compassion, and true liberality which breathes throughout this whole chapter, "Go on and conquer."

Nor again can Mrs. Jameson's English honesty avoid an occasional slip of delicate sarcasm; for instance, in the story of St. Filomena, a brand-new saint, whose discovery at Rome, in 1802, produced there an excitement which we should suspect was very much wanted, which we recommend to all our readers as an instance of the state into which the virtues of honesty and common sense seem to have fallen in the Eternal City—of humbugs.

No doubt there are many such cases of imposture among the list of saints and martyrs; yet, granting all which have been exposed, and more, there still remains a list of authentic stories, sadder and stranger than any romance of man's invention, to read which without deep sympathy and admiration our hearts must be callous or bigoted indeed. As Mrs. Jameson herself well says (vol. ii. p. 137):

> When in the daily service of our Church we repeat these words of the sublime hymn ("The noble army of martyrs praise Thee!"), I wonder sometimes whether it be with a full appreciation of their meaning? whether we do really reflect on all that this noble army of martyrs has conquered for us? Did they indeed glorify God through their courage, and seal their faith in their Redeemer with their blood? And if it be so, how is it that we Christians have learned to look coldly upon the effigies of those who sowed the seed of the harvest which we have reaped?—Sanguis martyrum semen Christianorum! We may admit that the reverence paid to them in former days was unreasonable and excessive; that credulity and ignorance have in many instances falsified the actions imputed to them; that enthusiasm has magnified their numbers beyond all belief; that when the communion with martyrs was associated with the presence of their material remains, the passion for relics led to a thousand abuses, and the belief in their intercession to a thousand superstitions. But why, in uprooting the false, uproot also the beautiful and the true?

Thoroughly and practically convinced as we are of the truth of these words, it gave us some pain when, in the work of a very worthy person, "The Church in the Catacombs," by Dr. Maitland (not the author of "The Dark Ages"), we found, as far as we could perceive, a wish "to advance the Protestant cause," by throwing general doubt on the old martyrologies and their monuments in the Roman catacombs. If we shall have judged hastily, we shall be ready to apologise. None, as we have said before, more firmly believe that the Protestant cause is the good cause; none are more reverentially inclined toward all honest critical investigations, more anxious to see all truth, the Bible itself, sifted and tested in every possible method; but we must protest against what certainly seems too contemptuous a rejection of a mass of historic evidence hitherto undoubted, except by the school of Voltaire; and of the hasty denial of the meaning of Christian and martyrologic symbols, as well known to antiquaries as Stonehenge or Magna Charta.

At the same time, Dr. Maitland's book seems the work of a righteous and earnest man, and it is not its object, but its method, of which we complain. The whole question of martyrology, a far more important one than historians generally fancy, requires a thorough investigation, critical and historical; it has to be done, and especially just now. The Germans, the civil engineers of the intellectual world, ought to do it for us, and no doubt will. But those who undertake it must bring to the work, not only impartiality, but enthusiasm; it is the spirit only, after all, which can quicken the eye, which can free the understanding from the idols of laziness, prejudice, and hasty induction. To talk philosophically of such matters a man must love them; he must set to work with a Christian sympathy, and a manly admiration for those old spiritual heroes to whose virtue and endurance Europe owes it that she is not now a den of heathen savages. He must be ready to assume everything about them to be true which is neither absurd, immoral, nor unsupported by the same amount of evidence which he would require for any other historic fact. And, just because this very tone of mind—enthusiastic but not idolatrous, discriminating but not captious—runs through Mrs. Jameson's work, we hail it with especial pleasure, as a fresh move in a truly philosophic and Christian direction. Indeed, for that branch of the subject which she has taken in hand, not the history, but the poetry of legends and of the art which they awakened, she derives a peculiar fitness, not merely from her own literary talents and acquaintance with continental art, but also from the very fact of her being an English wife and mother. Women ought, perhaps, always to make the best critics—at once more quicksighted, more tasteful, more sympathetic than ourselves, whose proper business is creation. Perhaps in Utopia they will take the reviewer's business entirely off our hands, as they are said to be doing already, by-the-bye, in one leading periodical. But of all critics an English matron ought to be the best—open as she should be, by her womanhood, to all tender and admiring sympathies, accustomed by her Protestant education to unsullied purity of thought, and inheriting from her race, not only freedom of mind and reverence for antiquity, but the far higher birthright of English honesty.

And such a genial and honest spirit, we think, runs through this book.

Another difficult task, perhaps the most difficult of all, the authoress has well performed. We mean the handling of stories whose facts she partly or wholly disbelieves, while she admires and loves their spirit and moral; or doctrines, to pronounce on whose truth or falsehood is beyond her subject. This difficulty Mr. Newman, in the "Lives of the English Saints," edited and partly written by him, turned with wonderful astuteness to the advantage of Romanism; but others, more honest, have not been so victorious. Witness the painfully uncertain impression left by some parts of one or two of those masterly articles on Romish heroes which appeared in the "Quarterly Review;" an uncertainty which we have the fullest reason to believe was most foreign to the reviewer's mind and conscience. Even Mr. Macaulay's brilliant history here and there falls into the same snare. No one but those who have tried it can be aware of the extreme difficulty of preventing the dramatic historian from degenerating into an apologist or heating into a sneerer; or understand the ease with which an earnest author, in a case like the present, becomes frantically reckless, under the certainty that, say what he will, he will be called a Jesuit by the Protestants, an Infidel by the Papists, a Pantheist by the Ultra-High-Church, and a Rogue by all three.

Now, we certainly shall not say that Mrs. Jameson is greater than the writers just mentioned; but we must say, that female tact and deep devotional feeling cut the Gordian knot which has puzzled more cunning heads.

Not that Mrs. Jameson is faultless; we want something yet, in the telling of a Christian fairy-tale, and know not what we want: but never were legends narrated with more discernment and simplicity than these.

As an instance, take the legend of St. Dorothea (vol. ii. p. 184), which is especially one of those stories of "sainted personages who," as Mrs. Jameson says, "lived, or are supposed to have lived, in the first ages of Christianity: and whose real history, founded on fact or tradition, has been so disguised by poetical embroidery, that they have in some sort the air of ideal beings;" and which may, therefore, be taken as a complete test of the authoress's tact and honesty:

In the province of Cappadocia and in the city of Cæsarea, dwelt a noble virgin, whose name was Dorothea. In the whole city there was none to be compared to her in beauty and grace of person. She was a Christian, and served God day and night with prayers, with fasting, and with alms.

The governor of the city, by name Sapritius (or Fabricius), was a very terrible persecutor of the Christians, and hearing of the maiden, and of her great beauty, he ordered her to be brought before him. She came, with her mantle folded on her bosom, and her eyes meekly cast down. The governor asked "Who art thou?" and she replied: "I am Dorothea, a virgin, and a servant of Jesus Christ." He said: "Thou must serve our gods, or die." She answered mildly: "Be it so; the sooner shall I stand in the presence of Him whom I most desire to behold." Then the governor asked her: "Whom meanest thou?" She replied: "I mean the Son of God, Christ, mine espoused! his dwelling is paradise; by his side are joys eternal; and in his garden grow celestial fruits and roses that never fade." Then Sapritius, overcome by her eloquence and beauty, ordered her to be carried back to her dungeon. And he sent to her two sisters, whose names were Calista and Christeta, who had once been Christians, but who, from terror of the torments with which they were threatened, had renounced their faith in Christ. To these women the governor promised large rewards if they would induce Dorothea to follow their evil example; and they, nothing doubting of success, boldly undertook the task. The result, however, was far different; for Dorothea, full of courage and constancy, reproved them as one having authority, and drew such a picture of the joys they had forfeited through their falsehood and cowardice, that they fell at her feet, saying: "O blessed Dorothea, pray for us, that, through thy intercession, our sins may be forgiven and our penitence accepted!" And she did so. And when they had left the dungeon they proclaimed aloud that they were servants of Christ.

Then the governor, furious, commanded that they should be burned, and that Dorothea should witness their torments. And she stood by, bravely encouraging them, and saying: "O my sisters, fear not! suffer to the end! for these transient pangs shall be followed by the joys of eternal life!" Thus they died: and Dorothea herself was condemned to be tortured cruelly, and then beheaded. The first part of her sentence she endured with invincible fortitude. She was then led forth to death; and, as she went, a young man, a lawyer of the city named Theophilus, who had been present when she was first brought before the governor, called to her mockingly: "Ha! fair maiden, goest thou to join thy bridegroom? Send me, I pray thee, of the fruits and flowers of that same garden of which thou hast spoken: I would fain taste of them!" And Dorothea looking on him inclined her head with a gentle smile, and said: "Thy request, O Theophilus, is granted!" Whereat he laughed aloud with his companions; but she went on cheerfully to death.

When she came to the place of execution, she knelt down and prayed; and suddenly appeared at her side a beautiful boy, with hair bright as sunbeams:

> A smooth-faced glorious thing,
> With thousand blessings dancing in his eyes.

In his hand he held a basket containing three apples, and three fresh-gathered and fragrant roses. She said to him: "Carry these to Theophilus; say that Dorothea hath sent them, and that I go before him to the garden whence they came, and await him there." With these words she bent her neck, and received the death-stroke.

Meantime the angel (for it was an angel) went to seek Theophilus, and found him still laughing in merry mood over the idea of the promised gift. The angel placed before him the basket of celestial fruit and flowers, saying: "Dorothea sends thee this," and vanished. What words can express the wonder of Theophilus? Struck by the prodigy operated in his favour, his heart melted within him; he tasted of the celestial fruit, and a new life was his; he proclaimed himself a servant of Christ, and, following the example of Dorothea, suffered with like constancy in the cause of truth, and obtained the crown of martyrdom.

We have chosen this legend just because it is in itself as superstitious and fantastic as any in the book. We happen to hold the dream of "The Spiritual Marriage," as there set forth, in especial abhorrence, and we have no doubt Mrs. Jameson does so also. We are well aware of the pernicious effect which this doctrine has exercised on matrimonial purity among the southern nations; that by making chastity synonymous with celibacy, it degraded married faithfulness into a restriction which there were penalties for breaking, but no rewards for keeping. We see clearly enough the cowardice, the shortsightedness, of fancying that man can insure the safety of his soul by fleeing from the world—in plain English, deserting the post to which God has called him, like the monks and nuns of old. We believe that the numbers of the early martyrs have been exaggerated. We believe that they were like ourselves, imperfect and inconsistent human beings; that, on the showing of the legends and fathers themselves, their testimony for the truth was too often impaired by superstition, fanaticism, or passion. But granting all this, we must still say, in the words of one who cannot be suspected of Romanising—the great Dr. Arnold—

> Divide the sum total of reported martyrs by twenty; by fifty, if you will; after all, you have a number of persons of all ages and sexes suffering cruel torments and deaths for conscience' sake, and for Christ's; and by their sufferings, manifestly with God's blessing, insuring the triumph of Christ's Gospel. Neither do I think that we consider the excellence of this martyr spirit half enough.

Indeed we do not. Let all the abatements mentioned above, and more, be granted; yet, even then, when we remember that the world from which Jerome or Anthony fled was even worse than that denounced by Juvenal and Persius—that the nuptials which, as legends say, were often offered the virgin martyrs as alternatives for death, were such as employed the foul pens of Petronius and Martial—that the tyrants whom they spurned were such as live in the pages of Suetonius, and the Augustæ Historiæ Scriptores—that the gods whom they were commanded to worship, the rites in which they were to join, were those over which Ovid and Apuleius had gloated, which Lucian had held up to the contempt of heathendom itself—that the tortures which they preferred to apostacy and to foul crimes were, by the confessions of the heathens themselves, too horrible for pen to tell—it does raise a flush of indignation to hear some sleek bigot-sceptic, bred up in the safety and luxury of modern England, among Habeas Corpus Acts and endowed churches, trying from his warm fireside to sneer away the awful responsibilities and the heroic fortitude of valiant men and tender girls, to whose piety and courage he owes the very enlightenment, the very civilisation, of which he boasts.

It is an error, doubtless, and a fearful one, to worship even such as them. But the error, when it arose, was at worst the caricature of a blessed truth. Even for the sinful, surely it was better to admire holiness than to worship their own sin. Shame on those who, calling themselves Christians, repine that a Cecilia or a Magdalen replaced an Isis and a Venus; or who can fancy that they are serving Protestantism by tracing malevolent likenesses between even the idolatry of a saint and the idolatry of a devil! True, there was idolatry in both, as gross in one as the other. And what wonder? What wonder if, amid a world of courtesans, the nun was worshipped? At least God allowed it; and will man be wiser than God? "The times of that ignorance He winked at." The lie that was in it He did not interfere to punish. He did more; He let it work out, as all lies will, their own punishment. We may see that in the miserable century which preceded the glorious Reformation; we may see it in the present state of Spain and Italy. The crust of lies, we say, punished itself; to the germ of truth within it we partly owe that we are Christian men this day.

But granting, or rather boldly asserting all this, and smiling as much as we choose at the tale of St. Dorothea's celestial basket, is it not absolutely, and in spite of all, an exquisite story? Is it likely to make people better or worse? We might believe the whole of it, and yet we need not, therefore, turn idolaters and worship sweet Dorothea for a goddess. But if, as we trust in God is the case, we are too wise to believe it all —if even we see no reason (and there is not much) for believing one single word of it—yet still we ask, Is it not an exquisite story? Is there not heroism in it greater than of all the Ajaxes and Achilles who ever blustered on this earth? Is there not power greater than of kings—God's strength made perfect in woman's weakness? Tender forgiveness, the Saviour's own likeness; glimpses, brilliant and true at the core, however distorted and miscoloured, of that spiritual world where the wicked cease from troubling, where the meek alone shall inherit the earth, where, as Protestants too believe, all that is spotless and beautiful in nature as well as in man shall bloom for ever perfect?

It is especially in her descriptions of paintings that Mrs. Jameson's great talents are displayed. Nowhere do we recollect criticisms more genial, brilliant, picturesque than those which are scattered through these pages. Often they have deeper merits, and descend to those fundamental laws of beauty and of religion by which all Christian art must ultimately be tested. Mrs. Jameson has certainly a powerful inductive faculty; she comprehends at once the idea* and central

* We are sorry to see, however, that Mrs. Jameson has been so far untrue to her own faculty as to join in the common mistake of naming Raphael's well-known cartoon at Hampton Court, "Elymas the Sorcerer struck Blind." On the supposition that this is its subject, its method of arrangement is quite unworthy of the rest, as the action would be split into the opposite corners of the picture, and the post of honour in the centre occupied by a figure of secondary importance; besides, the picture would lose its significance as one of this great series on "Religious Conviction and Conversion." But,

law of a work of art, and sketches it in a few vivid and masterly touches; and really, to use a hack quotation honestly for once, "in thoughts which breathe, and words which burn." As an instance, we must be allowed to quote at length this charming passage on angel paintings, so valuable does it seem not only as information, but as a specimen of what criticism should be:

On the revival of art, we find the Byzantine idea of angels everywhere prevailing. The angels in Cimabue's famous "Virgin and Child enthroned" are grand creatures, rather stern, but this arose, I think, from his inability to express beauty. The colossal angels at Assisi, solemn sceptred kingly forms, all alike in action and attitude, appeared to me magnificent.

In the angels of Giotto we see the commencement of a softer grace and a purer taste, further developed by some of his scholars. Benozzo Gozzoli and Orcagna have left in the Campo Santo examples of the most graceful and fanciful treatment. Of Benozzo's angels in the Ricardi Palace I have spoken at length. His master, Angelico (worthy the name !), never reached the same power of expressing the rapturous rejoicing of celestial beings, but his conception of the angelic nature remains unapproached, unapproachable: it is only his, for it was the gentle, passionless, refined nature of the recluse which stamped itself there. Angelico's angels are unearthly, not so much in form as in sentiment; and superhuman, not in

strange to say, Raphael has all the while especially guarded against this very error, by labelling the picture with a description of its subject. Directly under the central figure is written, "Sergius Paulus, Proconsul, embraces the Christian faith at the preaching of Paul." Taking which simple hint, and looking at the face of the proconsul (himself a miracle of psychology) as the centre to which all is to be referred, the whole composition, down to the minutest details, arranges itself at once in that marvellous unity which is Raphael's especial glory.

power but in purity. In other hands, any imitation of his soft ethereal grace would become feeble and insipid. With their long robes falling round their feet, and drooping many-coloured wings, they seem not to fly or to walk, but to float along, "smooth sliding without step." Blessed blessed creatures! love us, only love us! for we dare not task your soft serene beatitude, by asking you to help us!

There is more sympathy with humanity in Francia's angels: they look as if they could weep as well as love and sing.

* * * * *

Correggio's angels are grand and lovely, but they are like children enlarged and sublimated, not like spirits taking the form of children; where they smile it is truly—as Annibal Caracci expresses it—con una naturalezza et simplicità che innamora e sforza a ridere con loro: but the smile in many of Correggio's angel heads has something sublime and spiritual, as well as simple and natural.

And Titian's angels impress me in a similar manner—I mean those in the glorious "Assumption" at Venice—with their childish forms and features, but an expression caught from beholding the face of "our Father that is in heaven:" it is glorified in fancy. I remember standing before this picture, contemplating those lovely spirits, one after another, until a thrill came over me like that which I felt when Mendelssohn played the organ—I became music while I listened. The face of one of those angels is to the face of a child just what that of the Virgin in the same picture is compared with the fairest of the daughters of earth: it is not here superiority of beauty, but mind, and music, and love kneaded, as it were, into form and colour.

But Raphael, excelling in all things, is here excellent above all; his angels combine in a higher degree than any other, the various faculties and attributes in which the fancy loves to clothe these pure, immortal, beatified creatures. The angels of Giotti, of Benozzo, of Fiesole, are, if not female, feminine; those of Filippo Lippi and of Andrea, masculine; but you cannot say of those of Raphael, that they are masculine or feminine. The idea of sex is wholly lost in the blending of power, intelligence, and grace. In his early pictures, grace is the predominant characteristic, as in the dancing and singing angels in his "Coronation of the Virgin." In his later pictures the sentiment in his ministering angels is more spiritual, more dignified. As a perfect example of grand and poetical feeling, I may cite the angels as "Regents of the Planets," in the Capella Chigiana. The cupola represents in a circle the creation of the solar system, according to the theological and astronomical (or rather astrological) notions which then prevailed—a hundred years before "the starry Galileo and his woes." In the centre is the Creator; around, in eight compartments, we have, first, the angel of the celestial sphere, who seems to be listening to the divine mandate: "Let there be light in the firmament of heaven;" then follow in their order, the Sun, the Moon, Mercury, Venus, Mars, Jupiter, and Saturn. The name of each planet is expressed by its mythological representative; the Sun by Apollo, the Moon by Diana: and over each presides a grand colossal-winged spirit, seated or reclining on a portion of the zodiac as on a throne. I have selected two angels to give an idea of this peculiar and poetical treatment. The union of the theological and the mythological attributes is in the classical taste of the time, and quite Miltonic. In Raphael's child-angels, the expression of power and intelligence, as well as innocence, is quite wonderful; for instance, look at the two angel-boys, in the Dresden Madonna di San Sisto, and the angels, or celestial genii, who bear along the Almighty when he appears to Noah. No one has expressed like Raphael the action of flight, except perhaps Rembrandt. The angel who descends to crown Santa Felicità cleaves the air with the action of a swallow: and the angel in Rembrandt's Tobit soars like a lark with upward motion, spurning the earth.

Michael Angelo rarely gave wings to his angels; I scarcely recollect an instance, except the angel in the "Annunciation:" and his exaggerated human forms, his colossal creatures, in which the idea of power is conveyed through attitude and muscular action, are, to my taste, worse than unpleasing. My admiration for this wonderful man is so profound that I can afford to say this. His angels are superhuman, but hardly angelic: and while in Raphael's angels we do not feel the want of wings, we feel while looking at those of Michael Angelo that not even the "sail-broad vans" with which Satan laboured through the surging abyss of chaos could suffice to lift those Titanic forms from earth, and sustain them in mid-air. The group of angels over the "Last Judgment," flinging their mighty limbs about, and those that surround the descending figure of Christ in the "Conversion of St. Paul," may be referred to here as characteristic examples. The angels, blowing their trumpets, puff and strain like so many troopers. Surely this is not angelic: there may be power—great, imaginative, and artistic power—exhibited in the conception of form, but in the beings themselves there is more of effort than of power: serenity, tranquillity, beatitude, ethereal purity, spiritual grace, are out of the question.

In this passage we may remark an excellence in Mrs. Jameson's mode of thought which has become lately somewhat rare. We mean a freedom from that bigoted and fantastic habit of mind which leads nowadays the worshippers of high art to exalt the early schools to the disadvantage of all others, and to talk as if Christian painting had expired with Perugino. We were much struck with our authoress's power of finding spiritual truth and beauty in Titian's "Assumption," one of the very pictures in which the "high-art" party are wont to see nothing but "coarseness" and "earthliness" of conception. She, having, we suppose, a more acute as well as a more healthy eye for the beautiful and the spiritual, and therefore able to perceive its slightest traces wherever they exist, sees in those "earthly" faces of the great masters, "an expression caught from beholding the face of our Father that is in heaven." The face of one of those "angels," she continues, "is to the face of a child just what that of the Virgin in the same picture is compared with the fairest of the daughters of earth:

it is not here superiority of beauty, but mind, and music, and love, kneaded, as it were, into form and colour."

Mrs. Jameson acknowledges her great obligations to M. Rio; and all students of art must be thankful to him for the taste, learning, and earnest religious feeling which he has expended on the history of the earlier schools of painting. An honest man, doubtless, he is; but it does not follow, alas! in this piecemeal world, that he should write an honest book. And his bigotry stands in painful contrast to the genial and comprehensive spirit by which Mrs. Jameson seems able to appreciate the specific beauties of all schools and masters. M. Rio's theory (and he is the spokesman of a large party) is, unless we much misjudge him, this—that the ante-Raphaelic is the only Christian art; and that all the excellences of these early painters came from their Romanism; all their faults from his two great bugbears—Byzantinism and Paganism. In his eyes, the Byzantine idea of art was Manichean; in which we fully coincide, but add, that the idea of the early Italian painters was almost equally so: and that almost all in them that was not Manichean they owe not to their Romanism or their asceticism, but to their healthy layman's common sense, and to the influence of that very classical art which they are said to have been pious enough to despise. Bigoted and ascetic Romanists have been, in all ages, in a hurry to call people Manicheans, all the more fiercely because their own consciences must have hinted to them that they were somewhat Manichean themselves. When a man suspects his own honesty, he is, of course, inclined to prove himself blameless by shouting the loudest against the dishonesty of others. Now M. Rio sees clearly and philosophically enough what is the root of Manicheanism—the denial that that which is natural, beautiful, human, belongs to God. He imputes it justly to those Byzantine artists who fancied it carnal to attribute beauty to the Saviour or to the Virgin Mary, and tried to prove their own spirituality by representing their sacred personages in the extreme of ugliness and emaciation, though some of the specimens of their painting which Mrs. Jameson gives proves that this abhorrence of beauty was not so universal as M. Rio would have us believe. We agree with him that this absurdity was learned from them by earlier and semi-barbarous Italian artists, that these latter rapidly escaped from it, and began rightly to embody their conceptions in beautiful forms; and yet we must urge against them, too, the charge of Manicheanism, and of a spiritual eclecticism also, far deeper and more pernicious than the mere outward eclecticism of manner which has drawn down hard names on the school of the Caracci.

For an eclectic, if it mean anything, means this—one who, in any branch of art or science, refuses to acknowledge Bacon's great law, "that nature is only conquered by obeying her;" who will not take a full and reverent view of the whole mass of facts with which he has to deal, and from them deducing the fundamental laws of his subject, obey them whithersoever they may lead; but who picks and chooses out of them just so many as may be pleasant to his private taste, and then constructs a partial system which differs from the essential ideas of nature, in proportion to the number of facts which he has determined to discard. And such a course was pursued in the art by the ascetic painters between the time of Giotto and Raphael. Their idea of beauty was a partial and a Manichean one; in their adoration for a fictitious "angelic nature," made up from all which is negative in humanity, they were prone to despise all by which man is brought in contact with this earth—the beauties of sex, of strength, of activity, of grandeur of form; all, that is, in which Greek art excels: their ideal of beauty was altogether effeminate. They prudishly despised the anatomic study of the human figure, of landscape and chiaroscuro. Spiritual expression with them was everything; but it was only the expression of the passive spiritual faculties of innocence, devotion, meekness, resignation —all good, but not the whole of humanity. Not that they could be quite consistent in their theory. They were forced to paint their very angels as human beings; and a standard of human beauty they had to find somewhere; and they found one, strange to say, exactly like that of the old Pagan statues (wings and all—for the wings of Christian angels are copied exactly from those of Greek Genii), and only differing in that ascetic and emasculate tone, which was peculiar to themselves. Here is a dilemma which the worshippers of high art have slurred over. Where did Angelico de Fiesole get the idea of beauty which dictated his exquisite angels? We shall not, I suppose, agree with those who attribute it to direct inspiration, and speak of it as the reward of the prayer and fasting by which the good monk used to prepare himself for painting.

Must we then confess that he borrowed his beauties from the faces of the prettiest nuns with whom he was acquainted? That would be sad naturalism; and sad eclecticism too, considering that he must have seen among his Italian sisters a great many beauties of a very different type from that which he has chosen to copy; though, we suppose, of God's making equally with that of his favourites. Or did he, in spite of himself, steal a side-glance now and then at some of the unrivalled antique statues of his country, and copy on the sly any feature or proportion in them which was emasculate enough to be worked into his pictures? That, too, is likely enough; nay, it is certain. We are perfectly astonished how any draughtsman, at least how such a critic as M. Rio, can look at the early Italian painters without tracing everywhere in them the classic touch, the peculiar tendency to mathematic curves in the outlines, which is the distinctive peculiarity of Greek art. Is not Giotto, the father of Italian art, full of it in every line? Is not Perugino? Is not the angel of Lorenzo Credi in Mrs. Jameson's woodcut? Is not Francia, except just where he is stiff, and soft, and clumsy? Is not Fra Angelico himself? Is it not just the absence of this Greek tendency to mathematical forms in the German painters before Albert Dürer, which makes the specific difference, evident to every boy, between the drawing of the Teutonic and Italian schools?

But if so, what becomes of the theory which calls Pagan art by all manner of hard names? which dates the downfall of Christian art from the moment when painters first lent an eye to its pernicious seductions?

How can those escape the charge of eclecticism, who, without going to the root-idea of Greek art, filched from its outside just as much as suited their purpose? And how, lastly, can M. Rio's school of critics escape the charge of Manichean contempt for God's world and man, not as ascetics have fancied him, but as God has made him, when they think it a sufficient condemnation of a picture to call it naturalistic; when they talk and act about art as if the domain of the beautiful were the devil's kingdom, from which some few species of form and elements were to be stolen by Christian painters, and twisted from their original evil destination into the service of religion?

On the other hand, we owe much to those early ascetic painters; their works are a possession for ever. No future school of religious art will be able to rise to eminence without taking full cognisance of them, and learning from them their secret. They taught artists, and priests, and laymen too, that beauty is only worthy of admiration when it is the outward sacrament of the beauty of the soul within; they helped to deliver men from that idolatry to merely animal strength and loveliness into which they were in danger of falling in ferocious ages, and among the relics of Roman luxury; they asserted the superiority of the spirit over the flesh; according to their light, they were faithful preachers of the great Christian truth, that devoted faith, and not fierce self-will, is man's glory. Well did their pictures tell to brutal peasant, and to still more brutal warrior, that God's might was best shown forth, not in the elephantine pride of a Hercules, or the Titanic struggles of a Laocoon, but in the weakness of martyred women, and of warriors who were content meekly to endure shame and death, for the sake of Him who conquered by sufferings, and bore all human weaknesses; who "was led as a lamb to the slaughter, and, like a sheep dumb before the shearer, opened not his mouth."

We must conclude with a few words on one point on which we differ somewhat from Mrs. Jameson—the allegoric origin of certain legendary stories. She calls the story of the fiend, under the form of a dragon, devouring St. Margaret, and then bursting at the sign of the cross while the saint escaped unhurt, "another form of the familiar allegory—the power of Sin overcome by the power of the Cross."

And again, vol. ii. p. 4:

> The legend of St. George came to us from the East; where, under various forms, as Apollo and the Python, as Bellerophon and the Chimæra, as Perseus and the Sea-monster, we see perpetually recurring the mythic allegory by which was figured the conquest achieved by beneficent Power over the tyranny of Wickedness, and which reappears in Christian art in the legends of St. Michael and half a hundred other saints.

To us these stories seem to have had by no means an allegorical, but rather a strictly historic foundation; and our reasons for this opinion may possibly interest some readers.

Allegory, strictly so called, is the offspring of an advanced, and not of a semi-barbarous state of society. Its home is in the East—not the East of barbarous Pontine countries peopled by men of our own race, where the legend of St. George is allowed to have sprung up, but of the civilised, metaphysical, dark-haired races of Egypt, Syria, and Hindostan. The "objectivity" of the Gothic mind has never had any sympathy with it. The Teutonic races, like the earlier Greeks, before they were tinctured with Eastern thought, had always wanted historic facts, dates, names, and places. They even found it necessary to import their saints; to locate Mary Magdalene at Marseilles, Joseph of Arimathea at Glastonbury, the three Magi at Cologne, before they could thoroughly love or understand them. Englishmen especially cannot write allegories. John Bunyan alone succeeded tolerably, but only because his characters and language were such as he had encountered daily at every fireside and in every meeting-house. But Spenser wandered perpetually away, or rather, rose up from his plan into mere dramatic narrative. His work and other English allegories, are hardly allegoric at all, but rather symbolic; spiritual laws in them are not expressed by arbitrary ciphers, but embodied in imaginary examples, sufficiently startling or simple to form a plain key to other and deeper instances of the same law. They are analogous to those symbolic devotional pictures in which the Madonna and saints of all ages are grouped together with the painter's own contemporaries—no allegories at all, but the plain embodiment of a fact in which the artist believed; not only "the communion of all saints," but also their habit of assisting, often in visible form, the Christians of his own time.

These distinctions may seem over-subtle, but our meaning will surely be plain to anyone who will compare "The Faërie Queen," or the legend of St. George, with the Gnostic or Hindoo reveries, and the fantastic and truly Eastern interpretation of Scripture, which the European monks borrowed from Egypt. Our opinion is, that in the old legends the moral did not create the story, but the story the moral; and that the story had generally a nucleus of fact within all its distortions and exaggerations. This holds good of the Odinic and Grecian myths; all are now more or less inclined to believe that the deities of Zeus's or Odin's dynasties were real conquerors or civilisers of flesh and blood, like the Manco Capac of the Peruvians, and that it was around records of their real victories over barbarous aborigines, and over the brute powers of nature, that extravagant myths grew up, till more civilised generations began to say: "These tales must have some meaning—they must be either allegories or nonsense;" and then fancied that in the remaining thread of fact they found a clue to the mystic sense of the whole.

Such, we suspect, has been the history of St. George and the Dragon, as well as of Apollo and the Python. It is very hard to have to give up the dear old dragon who haunted our nursery dreams, especially when there is no reason for it. We have no patience with antiquaries who tell us that the dragons who guarded princesses were merely "the winding walls or moats of their castles." What use then, pray, was there in the famous nether garment with which Regnar Lodbrog (shaggy-trousers) choked the dragon who guarded his lady-love? And Regnar was a real piece of flesh and blood, as King Ælla and our Saxon forefathers found to their cost; his awful death-dirge, and the effect which it produced, are well known to historians. We cannot give up Regnar's trousers, for we suspect the key to the whole dragon-question is in the pocket of them.

Seriously, Why should not these dragons have been simply what the Greek word dragon means—what the earliest romances, the Norse myths, and the superstitions of the peasantry in many parts of England to this day assert them to have been—"mighty worms," huge snakes? All will agree that the Python, the representative in the old world of the Boa-constrictor of the new, lingered in the Homeric age, if not later, both in Greece and in Italy. It existed on the opposite coast of Africa (where it is now extinct) in the time of Regulus; we believe, from the traditions of all nations, that it existed to a far later date in more remote and barbarous parts of Europe. There is every reason to suppose that it still lingered in England after the invasion of the Cymri—say not earlier than B.C. 600—for it was among them an object of worship; and we question whether they would have been likely to have adored a foreign animal, and, as at Abury, built enormous temples in imitation of its windings, and called them by its name.

The only answer to these traditions has as yet been, that no reptile of that bulk is known in cold climates. Yet the Python still lingers in the Hungarian marshes. A few years ago a huge snake, as large as the Pythons of Hindostan, spread havoc among the flocks and terror among the peasantry. Had it been Ariosto's "Orc," an à priori argument from science would have had weight. A marsupiate sea-monster is horribly unorthodox; and the dragon, too, has doubtless been made a monster of, but most unjustly: his legs have been patched on by crocodile-slaying crusaders, while his wings—where did they come from? From the traditions of "flying serpents," which have so strangely haunted the deserts of Upper Egypt from the time of the old Hebrew prophets, and which may not, after all, be such lies as folk fancy. How scientific prigs shook with laughter at the notion of a flying dragon! till one day geology revealed to them, in the Pterodactylus, that a real flying dragon, on the model of Carlo Crivelli's in Mrs. Jameson's book, with wings before and legs behind, only more monstrous than that, and than all the dreams of Seba and Aldrovandus (though some of theirs, to be sure, have seven heads), got its living once on a time in this very island of England! But such is the way of this wise world! When Le Vaillant, in the last century, assured the Parisians that he had shot a giraffe at the Cape, he was politely informed that the giraffe was fabulous, extinct—in short, that he lied; and now, behold! the respectable old unicorn (and good Tories ought to rejoice to hear it) has been discovered at last by a German naturalist, Von Müller, in Abyssinia, just where our fathers told us to look for it! And why should we not find the flying serpent too? The interior of Africa is as yet an unknown world of wonders; and we may yet discover there, for aught we know, the descendants of the very satyr who chatted with St. Anthony.

No doubt the discovery of huge fossil animals, as Mrs. Jameson says, on the high authority of Professor Owen, may have modified our ancestors' notions of dragons: but in the old serpent worship we believe the real explanation of these stories is to be found. There is no doubt that human victims, and even young maidens, were offered to these snake-gods; even the sunny mythology of Greece retains horrible traces of such customs, which lingered in Arcadia, the mountain fastness of the old and conquered race. Similar cruelties existed among the Mexicans; and there are but too many traces of it throughout the history of heathendom.

The same superstition may, as the legends assert, have lingered on, or been at least revived during the later ages of the empire, in remote provinces, left in their primeval barbarism, at the same time that they were brutalised by the fiendish exhibitions of the Circus, which the Roman governors found it their interest to introduce everywhere. Thus the serpent became naturally regarded as the manifestation of the evil spirit by Christians as well as by the old Hebrews; thus, also, it became the presiding genius of the malaria and fever which arose from the fens haunted by it—a superstition which gave rise to the theory that the tales of Hercules and the Hydra, Apollo and the mud-Python, St. George and the Dragon, were sanitary-reform allegories, and the monsters whose poisonous breath destroyed cattle and young maidens only typhus and consumption. We see no reason why early Christian heroes should not have actually met with such snake-gods, and felt themselves bound, like Southey's Madoc, or Daniel in the old rabbinical story, whose truth has never been disproved, to destroy the monsters at all risk. We see no reason, either, why their righteous daring may not have been crowned with victory; and suspect that on such events were gradually built up the dragon-slaying legends which charmed all Europe, and grew in extravagances and absurdities, till they began to degenerate into the bombast of the "Seven Champions," and expired in the immortal ballad of the "Dragon of Wantley," in which More of More Hall, on the morning of his battle with the monster, invoked the saints no more, but—

> To make him strong and mighty—
> He drank by the tale
> Six pots of ale
> And a quart of aqua-vitæ.

So ended the sublime sport of dragon-slaying. Its only remnant may now be seen in Borneo, whither that noble Christian man, Bishop Macdougall, took out the other day a six-chambered rifle, on the ground that "while the alligators ate his school-children at Sarawak, it was his duty as a bishop to shoot the alligators."

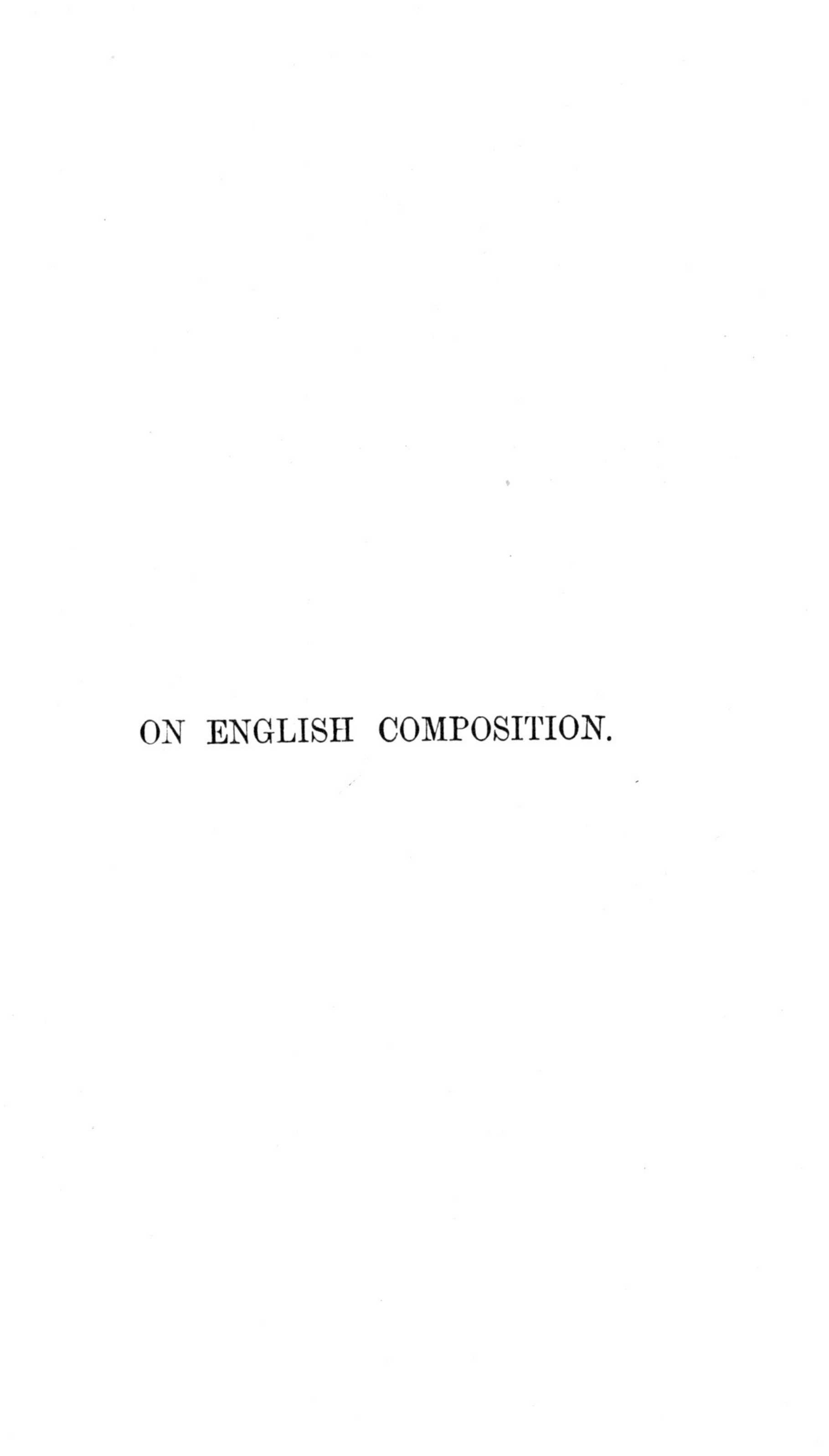

ON ENGLISH COMPOSITION.

ON ENGLISH COMPOSITION.

Introductory Lectures given at Queen's College, London, 1848.

An introductory lecture on English composition is, I think, as much needed as one on any other subject taught in this College. For in the first place, I am not sure whether we all mean the same thing when we speak of English composition; and in the next place, I believe that pupils themselves are very often best able to tell their teachers what sort of instruction they require. I purpose therefore to-day, not only to explain freely my intentions with regard to this course of lectures, but to ask you to explain freely your own wants.

I must suppose, however, that the ladies who attend here wish to be taught how to write English better. Now the art of writing English is, I should say, the art of speaking English, and speech may be used for any one of three purposes: to conceal thought, as the French diplomatist defined its use; to conceal the want of thought, as the majority of popular writers and orators seem nowadays to employ it; or, again, to express thought, which would seem to have been the original destination of the gift of language. I am therefore, I suppose, in duty bound to take for granted that you come here to be taught to express your thoughts better.

The whole matter then will very much depend on what thoughts you have to express. For the form of the symbol must depend on the form of the thing symbolised, as the medal does upon its die; and thus style and language are the sacraments of thoughts, the outward and visible signs of the inward and spiritual grace, or want of grace, in the writer. And even where language is employed to conceal either thought, or want thereof, it generally tells a truer tale than it was meant to do. Out of the abundance of the heart the mouth must speak, and the hollowness or foolishness of the spirit will show itself, in spite of all cunning sleights, in unconscious peculiarities or defects of style.

Hence I say style, as the expression of thought, will depend entirely on what there is within to be expressed, on the character of the writer's mind and heart. We all allow this implicitly in the epithets which we apply to different styles. We talk of a vigorous, a soft, a weak, a frigid, an obscure style, not meaning that the words and sentences in themselves are vigorous, soft, weak, or even obscure (for the words and their arrangement may be simple enough all the while). No, you speak of the quality of the thoughts conveyed in the words; that a style is powerful, because the writer is feeling and thinking strongly and clearly; weak or frigid, because his feelings on the subject have been weak or cold;

obscure to you, because his thoughts have been obscure to himself—because, in short, he has not clearly imagined to himself the notion which he wishes to embody. The meaning of the very words "expression" and "composition," prove the truth of my assertion. Expression is literally the pressing out into palpable form that which is already within us, and composition, in the same way, is the composing or putting together of materials already existing—the form and method of the composition depend mainly on the form and quality of the materials. You cannot compose a rope of sand, or a round globe of square stones—and my friend Mr. Strettell will tell you, in his lectures on grammar, that words are just as stubborn and intractable materials as sand or stone, and that we cannot alter their meaning or value a single shade, for they derive that meaning from a higher fountain than the soul of man, from the Word of God, the fount of utterance, who inspires all true and noble thought and speech—who vindicated language as His own gift, and man's invention, in that miracle of the day of Pentecost. And I am bound to follow up Mr. Strettell's teaching by telling you that what holds true of words, and of their grammatic and logical composition, holds true also of their æsthetic and artistic composition, of style, of rhythm, of poetry, and oratory. Every principle of these which is true and good, that is, which produces beauty, is to be taken as an inspiration from above, as depending not on the will of man but of God; not on any abstract rules, of pedant's invention, but on the eternal necessities and harmony, on the being of God Himself.

These may seem lofty words, but I do not think they are likely to make us lofty-minded. I think that the belief of them will tend to make us all more reverent and earnest in examining the utterances of others, more simple and truthful in giving vent to our own, fearing equally all prejudiced and hasty criticism, all self-willed mannerism, all display of fine words, as sins against the divine dignity of language. From these assertions I think we may conclude what is the true method of studying style. The critical examination of good authors, looking at language as an inspiration, and its laws as things independent of us, eternal and divine, we must search into them as we would into any other set of facts, in nature, or the Bible, by patient induction. We must not be content with any traditional maxims, or abstract rules, such as have been put forth in Blair and Lord Kaimes, for these are merely worked out by the head, and can give us no insight into the magic which touches the heart. All abstract rules of criticism, indeed, are very barren. We may read whole folios of them without getting one step farther than we were at first, viz. that what is beautiful is beautiful. Indeed, these abstract rules generally tend to narrow our notions of what is beautiful, in their attempt to explain spiritual things by the carnal understanding. All they do is to explain them away, and so those who depend on them are tempted to deny the beauty of every thing which cannot be thus analysed and explained away, according to the established rule and method. I shall have to point out this again to you, when we come to speak of the Pope and Johnson school of critics, and the way in which they wrote whole folios on Shakespeare, without ever penetrating a single step deeper towards the secret of his sublimity. It was just this idolatry of abstract rules which made Johnson call Bishop Percy's invaluable collection of ancient ballads "stuff and nonsense." It was this which made Voltaire talk of "Hamlet" as the ravings of a drunken savage, because forsooth it could not be crammed into the artificial rules of French tragedy. It is this which, even at this day, makes some men of highly-cultivated taste declare that they can see no poetry in the writings of Mr. Tennyson; the cause, little as they are aware of it, simply being that neither his excellences nor his faults are after the model of the Etonian classical school which reigned in England fifty years ago. When these critics speak of that with which they sympathise they are admirable. They become childish only when they resolve to bind all by maxims which may suit themselves.

We must then, I think, absolutely eschew any abstract rules as starting-points. What rules we may require, we must neither borrow nor invent, but discover, during the course of our reading. We must take passages whose power and beauty is universally acknowledged, and try by reverently and patiently dissecting them to see into the secret of their charm, to see why and how they are the best possible expressions of the author's mind. Then for the wider laws of art, we may proceed to examine whole works, single elegies, essays, and dramas.

In carrying out all this, it will be safest, as always, to follow the course of nature, and begin where God begins with us. For as every one of us is truly a microcosm, a whole miniature world within ourselves, so is the history of each individual more or less the history of the whole human race, and there are few of us but pass through the same course of intellectual growth, through which the whole English nation has passed, with an exactness and perfection proportionate, of course, to the richness and vigour of each person's character. Now as in the nation, so in the individual, poetry springs up before prose. Look at the history of English literature, how completely it is the history of our own childhood and adolescence, in its successive fashions. First, fairy tales—then ballads of adventure, love, and war—then a new tinge of foreign thought and feeling, generally French, as it was with the English nation in the twelfth and thirteenth centuries—then elegiac and reflective poetry—then classic art begins to influence our ripening youth, as it did the youth of our nation in the sixteenth century, and delight in dramatic poetry follows as a natural consequence—and last, but not least, as the fruit of all these changes, a vigorous and matured prose. For indeed, as elocution is the highest melody, so is true prose the highest poetry. Consider how in an air, the melody is limited to a few arbitrary notes, and recurs at arbitrary periods, while the more scientific the melody becomes, the more numerous and nearly allied are the notes employed, and the more complex and uncertain is their recurrence—in short, the nearer does the melody of the air approach to the melody of elocution, in which the notes of the voice ought continually to be passing into each other, by imperceptible gradations, and their recurrence to depend entirely on the emotions conveyed in the subject words. Just so, poetry employs a confined and arbitrary metre, and a periodic recurrence of sounds which disappear gradually in its higher forms of the ode and the drama, till the poetry at last passes into prose, a free and ever-shifting flow of every imaginable rhythm and metre, determined by no arbitrary rules, but only by the spiritual intent of the subject. The same will hold good of whole prose compositions, when compared with whole poems.

Prose then is highest. To write a perfect prose must be your ultimate object in attending these lectures; but we must walk before we can run, and walk with leading-strings before we can walk alone, and such leading-strings are verse and rhyme. Some tradition of this is still kept up in the practice of making boys write Latin and Greek verses at school, which is of real service to the intellect, even when most carelessly employed, and which, when earnestly carried out, is one great cause of the public school and University man's superiority in style to most self-educated authors. And why should women's writings be in any respect inferior to that of men, if they are only willing to follow out the same method of self-education?

Do not fancy, when I say that we must learn poetry before we learn prose, that I am only advancing a paradox; mere talking is no more prose than mere rhyme is poetry. Monsieur Jourdain, in Molière's comedy, makes, I suspect, a very great mistake, when he tells his master: "If that means prose, I've been talking prose all my life." I fancy the good man had been no more talking prose, than an awkward country boy has been really walking all his life, because he has been contriving somehow to put one leg before the other. To see what walking is, we must look at the perfectly-drilled soldier, or at the perfectly-accomplished lady, who has been taught to dance in order that she may know how to walk. Dancing has been well called the poetry of motion; but the tender grace, the easy dignity in every gesture of daily life which the perfect dancer exhibits answers exactly to that highly-organised prose which ought to be the offspring of a critical acquaintance with poetry. Milton's matchless prose style, for instance, grows naturally from his matchless power over rhyme and metre. Practice in versification might be unnecessary if we were all born world-geniuses; so would practice in dancing, if every lady had the figure of a Venus and the garden of Eden for a playground. But even the ancient Greeks amid every advantage of climate, dress, and physical beauty, considered a thorough instruction in all athletic and graceful exercises as indispensably necessary, not only to a boy's but also to a girl's education, and in like manner, I think the exquisite models of prose with which English literature abounds will not supersede the necessity of a careful training in versification, nay, will rather make such a training all the more requisite for those who wish to imitate such excellence. Pray understand me, by using the word "imitate," I do not mean that I wish you to ape the style of any favourite author. Your aim will not be to write like this man or that woman, but to write like yourselves, being of course responsible for what yourselves are like. Do not be afraid to let the peculiarities of your different characters show yourselves in your styles. Your prose may be the rougher for it, but it will be at least honest; and all mannerism is dishonesty, an attempt to gain beauty at the expense of truthful expression which invariably defeats its own ends, and produces an unpleasing effect, so necessarily one are truth and beauty. So far then from wishing to foster in you any artificial mannerism, mannerism is that foul enchanter from whom, above all others, I am sworn "en preux chevalier" to deliver you. As Professor Maurice warned me when I undertook this lectureship, my object in teaching you about "styles" should be that you may have no style at all. But mannerism can be only avoided by the most thorough practice and knowledge. Half-educated writers are always mannerists; while, as the ancient canon says, "the perfection of art is to conceal art"—to depart from uncultivated and therefore defective nature, to rise again through art to a more organised and therefore more simple naturalness. Just as, to carry on the analogy which I employed just now, it is only the perfect dancer who arrives at that height of art at which her movements seem dictated not by conscious science, but unconscious nature.

I do hope then that the study, and still more the practice of versification, may produce in you the same good effects which they do in young men; that they may give you a habit of portioning out your thoughts distinctly and authentically in a more simple, condensed, and expressive style; that they may teach you what elevation of language, what class of sounds, what flow of words may best suit your tone of thought and feeling, that they may prevent in you that tendency to monotonous repetition, and vain wordiness, which is the bosom sin of most uneducated prose writers, not only of the ladies of the nineteenth century, but of the Middle Age monks, who, having in general no poetry on which to form their taste, except the effeminate and bombastic productions of the dying Roman empire, fell into a certain washy prolixity, which has made monk Latin a byword, and puts one sadly in mind of what is too truly called "young ladies' English."

I should like then to begin with two or three of the early ballads, and carefully analyse them with you. I am convinced that in them we may discover many of the great primary laws of composition, as well as the secrets of sublimity and pathos in their very simplest manifestations. It may be that there are some here to whom the study of old ballads may be a little distasteful, who are in an age when the only poetry which has charms is the subjective and self-conscious "poetry of the heart"—to whom a stanza of "Childe Harolde" may seem worth all the ballads that ever were written: but let me remind them that woman is by her sex an educator, that every one here must expect, ay hope, to be employed at some time or other in training the minds of children; then let me ask them to recall the years in which objective poems, those which dealt with events, ballads, fairy tales, down to nursery rhymes, were their favourite intellectual food, and let me ask them whether it will not be worth while, for the sake of the children whom they may hereafter influence, to bestow a little thought on this earlier form of verse.

I must add too, that without some understanding of these same ballads, we shall never arrive at a critical appreciation of Shakespeare. For the English drama springs from an intermarriage between this same ballad poetry, the poetry of incidents, and that subjective elegiac poetry which deals with the feelings and consciousnesses of man. They are the two poles, by whose union our drama is formed, and some critical knowledge of both of them will be, as I said, necessary before we can study it.

After the ballads, we ought, I think, to know a little about the early Norman poetry, whose fusion with the pure north Saxon ballad school produced Chaucer and the poets previous to the Reformation. We shall proceed to Chaucer himself; then to the rise of the drama; then to the poets of the Elizabethan age. I shall analyse a few of Shakespeare's masterpieces; then speak of Milton and Spenser; thence pass to the prose of Sidney, Hooker, Bacon, Taylor, and our later great authors. Thus our Composition lectures will follow an historical method, parallel with, and I hope illustrative of, the lectures on English History.

But it will not be enough, I am afraid, to study the style of others without attempting something yourselves. No criticism teaches so much as the criticism of our own works. And I hope therefore that you will not think that I ask too much of you when I propose that weekly prose and verse compositions, on set subjects, be sent in by the class. To the examination of these the latter half of each lecture may be devoted, and the first half-hour to the study of various authors: and in order that I may be able to speak my mind freely on them I should propose that they be anonymous. I hope that you will all trust me when I tell you that those who have themselves experienced what labour attends the task of composition, are generally most tender and charitable in judging of the work of others, and that whatever remarks I may make will be such only as a man has a right to make on a woman's composition.

And if I may seem to be asking anything new or troublesome, I beg you to remember, that it is the primary idea of this College to vindicate women's right to an education in all points equal to that of men; the difference between them being determined not by any fancied inferiority of mind, but simply by the distinct offices and character of the sexes. And surely when you recollect the long drudgery at Greek and Latin verses which is required of every highly-educated man, and the high importance which has attached to them for centuries in the opinion of Englishmen, you cannot think that I am too *exigeant* in asking you for a few sets of English verses. Believe me, that you ought to find their beneficial effect in producing, as I said before, a measured deliberate style of expression, a habit of calling up clear and distinct images on all subjects, a power of condensing and arranging your thoughts, such as no practice in prose themes can ever give. If you are disappointed of these results it will not be the fault of this long-proved method of teaching, but of my own inability to carry it out. Indeed I cannot too strongly confess my own ignorance or fear my own inability. I stand aghast when I compare my means and my idea, but I believe that "by teaching thou shalt learn," is a rule of which I too shall take the benefit, and having begun these lectures in the name of Him who is The Word, and with the firm intention of asserting throughout His claims as the inspirer of all language and of all art, I may perhaps hope for the fulfilment of His own promise: "Be not anxious what you shall speak, for it shall be given you in that day and in that hour what you shall speak."

ON ENGLISH LITERATURE.

ON ENGLISH LITERATURE.

Introductory Lecture given at Queen's College, London, 1848.

An introductory lecture must, I suppose, be considered as a sort of art-exhibition, or advertisement of the wares hereafter to be furnished by the lecturer. If these, on actual use, should prove to fall far short of the promise conveyed in the programme, hearers must remember that the lecturer is bound, even to his own shame, to set forth in all commencements the most perfect method of teaching which he can devise, in order that human frailty may have something at which to aim; at the same time begging all to consider that in this piecemeal world, it is sufficient not so much to have realised one's ideal, as earnestly to have tried to realise it, according to the measure of each man's gifts. Besides, what may not be fulfilled in a first course, or in a first generation of teachers, may still be effected by those who follow them. It is but fair to expect that if this Institution shall prove, as I pray God it may, a centre of female education worthy of the wants of the coming age, the method and the practice of the College will be developing, as years bring experience and wider eye-range, till we become truly able to teach the English woman of the nineteenth century to bear her part in an era, which, as I believe, more and more bids fair to eclipse, in faith and in art, in science and in polity, any and every period of glory which Christendom has yet beheld.

The first requisite, I think, for a modern course of English Literature is, that it be a whole course or none. The literary education of woman has too often fallen into the fault of our "Elegant Extracts," and "Beauties of British Poetry." It has neither begun at the beginning nor ended at the end. The young have been taught to admire the laurels of Parnassus, but only after they have been clipped and pollarded like a Dutch shrubbery. The roots which connect them with mythic antiquity, and the fresh leaves and flowers of the growing present, have been generally cut off with care, and the middle part only has been allowed to be used—too often, of course, a sufficiently tough and dry stem. This method is no doubt easy, because it saves teachers the trouble of investigating antiquity, and saves them too the still more delicate task of judging contemporaneous authors—but like all half measures, it has bred less good than evil. If we could silence a free press, and the very free tongues of modern society; if we could clip the busy, imaginative, craving mind of youth on the Procrustean bed of use and wont, the method might succeed; but we can do neither—the young *will* read and *will* hear; and the consequence is, a general complaint that the minds of young women are outgrowing their mothers' guidance, that they are reading books which their mothers never dreamt of reading, of many of which they never heard, many at least whose good and evil they have had no means of investigating; that the authors which really interest and influence the minds of the young are just the ones which have formed no part of their education, and therefore those for judging of which they have received no adequate rules; that, in short, in literature as in many things, education in England is far behind the wants of the age.

Now this is all wrong and ruinous. The mother's mind should be the lodestar of the daughter's. Any thing which loosens the bond of filial reverence, of filial resignation, is even more destructive, if possible, to womanhood than to manhood—the certain bane of both. And the evil fruits are evident enough—self-will and self-conceit in the less gentle, restlessness and dissatisfaction in many of the meekest and gentlest; talents seem with most a curse instead of a blessing; clever and earnest young women, like young men, are beginning to wander up and down in all sorts of eclecticisms and dilettanteisms—one year they find out that the dark ages were not altogether barbarous, and by a revulsion of feeling natural to youth, they begin to adore them as a very galaxy of light, beauty, and holiness. Then they begin to crave naturally enough for some real understanding of this strange ever-developing nineteenth century, some real sympathy with its new wonders, some real sphere of labour in it; and this drives them to devour the very newest authors—any book whatever which seems to open for them the riddle of the mighty and mysterious present, which is forcing itself on their attention through every sense. And so up and down, amid confusions and oscillations from pole to pole, and equally eclectic at either pole, from St. Augustin and Mr. Pugin to Goethe and George Sand, and all intensified and coloured by that tender enthusiasm, that craving for something to worship, which is a woman's highest grace, or her bitterest curse — wander these poor Noah's doves, without either ark of shelter or rest for the sole of their foot, sometimes, alas! over strange ocean-wastes, into gulfs of error—too sad to speak of here—and *will* wander more and more till teachers begin boldly to face reality, and interpret to them both the old and the new, lest they misinterpret them for themselves. The educators of the present generation must meet the cravings of the young spirit with the bread of life, or they will gorge themselves with poison. Telling them that they ought not to be hungry, will not stop their hunger; shutting our eyes to facts, will only make us stumble over them the sooner; hiding our eyes in the sand, like the hunted ostrich, will not hide us from the iron necessity of circumstances, or from the Almighty will of Him, who is saying in these days to society, in language unmistakable: "Educate, or fall to pieces! Speak the *whole* truth to the young, or take the consequences of your cowardice!"

On these grounds I should wish to see established in this College a really entire course of English Literature, such as shall give correct, reverent, and loving views of every period, from the earliest legends and poetry of the Middle Age, up to the latest of our modern authors, and in the case of the higher classes, if it should hereafter be found practicable, lectures devoted to the criticism of such authors as may be exercising any real influence upon the minds of English women. This, I think, should be our ideal. It must be attempted cautiously and step by step. It will not be attained at the first trial, certainly not by the first lecturer. Sufficient, if each succeeding teacher shall leave something more taught, some fresh extension of the range of knowledge which is thought fit for his scholars.

I said that the ages of history were analogous to the ages of man, and that each age of literature was the truest picture of the history of its day; and for this very reason English literature is the best perhaps, the only teacher of English history, to women especially. For it seems to me that it is principally by the help of such an extended literary course, that we can cultivate a just and enlarged taste, which will connect education with the deepest feelings of the heart. It seems hardly fair, or reasonable either, to confine the reading of the young to any certain fancied Augustan age of authors, I mean those of the seventeenth and eighteenth centuries; especially when that age requires, in order to appreciate it, a far more developed mind, a far greater experience of mankind and of the world, than falls to the lot of one young woman out of a thousand. Strong meat for men, and milk for babes. But why are we to force on any age spiritual food unfitted for it? If we do we shall be likely only to engender a lasting disgust for that by which our pupils might have fully profited, had they only been introduced to it when they were ready for it. And this actually happens with English literature: by having the so-called standard works thrust upon them too early, and then only in a fragmentary form, not fresh and whole, but cut up into the very driest hay, the young too often neglect in after-life the very books which then might become the guides of their taste. Hence proceed in the minds of the young sudden and irregular revulsions of affection for different schools of writing: and all revolutions in the individual as well as in the nation are sure to be accompanied by some dead loss of what has been already gained, some disruption of feelings, some renunciation of principles, which ought to have been preserved; something which might have borne fruit is sure to be crushed in the earthquake. Many before me must surely have felt this. Do none here remember how, when they first escaped from the dry class-drudgery of Pope and Johnson, they snatched greedily at the forbidden fruit of Byron, perhaps of Shelley, and sentimental novel-writers innumerable? How when the luscious melancholy of their morbid self-consciousness began to pall on the appetite, they fled for refuge as suddenly to mere poetry of description and action, to Southey, Scott, the ballad-literature of all ages? How when the craving returned (perhaps unconsciously to themselves) to understand the wondrous heart of man, they tried to satisfy it with deep draughts of Wordsworth's celestial and pure simplicity? How again, they tired of that too gentle and unworldly strain, and sought in Shakespeare something more exciting, more genial, more rich in the facts and passions of daily life? How even his all-embracing genius failed to satisfy them, because he did not palpably connect for them their fancy and their passions with their religious faith—and so they wandered out again over the sea of literature, heaven only knows whither, in search of a school of authors yet, alas! unborn. For the true literature of the nineteenth century, the literature which shall set forth in worthy strains the relation of the two greatest facts, namely, of the universe and of Christ, which shall transfigure all our enlarged knowledge of science and of society, of nature, of art, and man, with the eternal truths of the gospel, that poetry of the future is not yet here: but it is coming, ay even at the doors, when this great era shall become conscious of its high vocation, and the author too shall claim his priestly calling, and the poets of the world, like the kingdoms of the world, shall become the poets of God and of His Christ.

But to return. Should we not rather in education follow that method which Providence has already mapped out for us? If we are bound, as of course we are, to teach our pupils to breathe freely on the highest mountain-peaks of Shakespeare's art, how can we more certainly train them to do so, than by leading them along the same upward path by which Shakespeare himself rose—through the various changes of taste, the gradual developments of literature, through which the English mind had been passing before Shakespeare's time? For there was a literature before Shakespeare. Had there not been, neither would there have been a Shakespeare. Critics are now beginning to see that the old fancy which made Shakespeare spring up at once, a self-perfected poet, like Minerva full-armed from the head of Jove, was a superstition of pedants, who neither knew the ages before the great poet, nor the man himself, except that little of him which seemed to square with their shallow mechanical taste. The old fairy superstition, the old legends and ballads, the old chronicles of feudal war and chivalry, the earlier moralities and mysteries, and tragi-comic attempts—these were the roots of his poetic tree—they must be the roots of any literary education which can teach us to appreciate him. These fed Shakespeare's youth; why should they not feed our children's? Why indeed? That inborn delight of the young in all that is marvellous and fantastic—has that a merely evil root? No surely! It is a most pure part of their spiritual nature; a part of "the heaven which lies about us in our infancy;" angel-wings with which the free child leaps the prison-walls of sense and custom, and the drudgery of earthly life—like the wild dreams of childhood, it is a God-appointed means for keeping alive what noble Wordsworth calls

> those obstinate questionings
> Of sense and outward things,
> Fallings from us, vanishings;
> Blank misgivings of a creature
> Moving about in worlds not realised;
> * * * * *

by which

> Though inland far we be,
> Our souls have sight of that immortal sea
> Which brought us hither:
> Can in a moment travel thither,
> And see the children sporting on the shore,
> And hear the mighty waters rolling evermore.

And those old dreams of our ancestors in the childhood of England, they are fantastic enough, no doubt, and unreal, but yet they are most true and most practical, if we but use them as parables and symbols of human feeling and everlasting truth. What, after all, is any event of earth, palpable as it may seem, but, like them, a shadow and a ghostly dream, till it has touched our *hearts*, till we have found out and obeyed its spiritual lesson? Be sure that one really pure legend or ballad may bring God's truth and heaven's beauty more directly home to the young spirit than whole volumes of dry abstract didactic morality. Outward things, beauty, action, nature, are the great problems for the young. God has put them in a visible world, that by what they *see* they may learn to know the *unseen*; and we must begin to feed their minds with that literature which deals most with visible things, with passion manifested in action, which we shall find in the early writing of our Middle Ages; for then the collective mind of our nation was passing through its natural stages of childhood and budding youth, as every nation and every single individual must at some time or other do; a true "young England," always significant and precious to the young. I said there was a literary art before Shakespeare—an art more simple, more childlike, more girlish as it were, and therefore all the more adapted for young minds. But also an art most vigorous and pure in point of style: thoroughly fitted to give its readers the first elements of taste, which must lie at the root of even the most complex æsthetics. I know no higher specimens of poetic style, considering the subject, and the belief of the time about them, than may be found in many of our old ballads. How many poets are there in England now, who could have written "The Twa Bairns," or "Sir Patrick Spens?" How many such histories as old William of Malmesbury, in spite of all his foolish monk miracles? As few now as there were then; and as for lying legends—they had their superstitions, and we have ours; and the next generation will stare at our strange doings as much as we stare at our forefathers. For our forefathers they were; we owe them filial reverence, thoughtful attention, and more—we must know them ere we can know ourselves. The only key to the present is the *past*.

But I must go farther still, and after premising that the English classics, so called, of the sixteenth and eighteenth centuries will of course form the bulk of the lectures, I must plead for some instruction in the works of recent and living authors. I cannot see why we are to teach the young about the past and not about the present. After all, they have to live now, and at no other time; in this same nineteenth century lies their work: it may be unfortunate, but we cannot help it. I do not see why we should wish to help it. I know no century which the world has yet seen so well worth living in. Let us thank God that we are here now, and joyfully try to understand *where* we are, and what our work is *here*. As for all superstitions about "the good old times," and fancies that *they* belonged to God, while this age belongs only to man, blind chance, and the Evil One, let us cast them from us as the suggestions of an evil lying spirit, as the natural parents of laziness, pedantry, popery, and unbelief.

And therefore let us not fear to tell our children the meaning of this present day, and of all its different voices. Let us not be content to say to them, as we have been doing: "We will see you well instructed in the past, but you must make out the present for yourselves." Why, if the past is worth explaining, far more is the present—the pressing, noisy, complex present, where our work-field lies, the most intricate of all states of society, and of all schools of literature yet known, and therefore the very one requiring most explanation.

How rich in strange and touching utterances have been the last fifty years of English literature. Do you think that God has been teaching us nothing in them? Will He not *make* our children listen to that teaching, whether we like or not? And suppose our most modern writers *had* added nothing to the stock of national knowledge, which I most fervently deny, yet are they not actually influencing the minds of the young? and can we prevent their doing so either directly or indirectly? If we do not find them right teaching about their own day, will they not be sure to find self-chosen teachers about it themselves, who will be almost certainly the first who may come to hand, and therefore as likely as not to be *bad* teachers? And do we not see every day that it is just the most tender, the most enthusiastic, the most precious spirits, who are most likely to be misled, because their honest disgust at the follies of the day has most utterly outgrown their critical training? And that lazy wholesale disapprobation of living writers, so common and convenient, what does it do but injure all reverence for parents and teachers, when the young find out that the poet, who, as they were told, was a bungler and a charlatan, somehow continues to touch the purest and noblest nerves of their souls, and that the author who was said to be dangerous and unchristian, somehow makes them more dutiful, more earnest, more industrious, more loving to the poor? I speak of actual cases. Would to God they were not daily ones!

Is it not then the wiser, because the more simple and trustful method, both to God and our children, to say: "You shall read living authors, and we will teach you how to read them; you, like every child that is born into the world, must eat the fruit of the tree of knowledge of good and evil; we will see that you have your senses exercised to discern between that good and that evil. You shall have the writers for whom you long, as far as consists with common prudence and morality, and more, you shall be taught them: all we ask of you is to be patient and humble; believe us, you will never really appreciate these writers, you will not even rationally enjoy their beauties, unless you submit to a course of intellectual training like that through which most of them have passed, and through which certainly this nation which produced them has passed, in the successive stages of its growth."

The best method, I think, of working out these principles would be to devote a few lectures in the last term of every complete course, to the examination of some select works of recent writers, chosen under the sanction of the Educational Committee. But I must plead for *whole* works. "Extracts" and "Select Beauties" are about as practical as the worthy in the old story, who, wishing to sell his house, brought one of the bricks to market as a specimen. It is equally unfair on the author and on the pupil; for it is impossible to show the merits or demerits of a work of art, even to explain the truth or falsehood of any particular passage, except by viewing the book as an organic whole. And as for the fear of raising a desire to read more of an author than may be proper—when a work has once been pointed out as really hurtful, the rest must be left to the best safeguard which I have yet discovered, in man or woman—the pupil's own honour.

Such a knowledge of English literature would tend no less, I think, to the spread of healthy historic views among us. The literature of every nation is its autobiography. Even in its most complex and artistic forms, it is still a wonderfully artless and unconscious record of its doubts and its faith, its sorrows and its triumphs, at each era of its existence. Wonderfully artless and correct—because all utterances which were not faithful to their time, which did not touch some sympathetic chord in their heart's souls, are pretty sure to have been swept out into wholesome oblivion, and only the most genuine and earnest left behind for posterity. The history of England indeed is the literature of England—but one very different from any school history or other now in vogue. You will find it neither a mere list of acts of parliament and record-office, like some; nor yet an antiquarian gallery of costumes and armour, like others; nor a mere war-gazette and report of killed and wounded from time to time; least of all not a "Debrett's Peerage," and catalogue of kings and queens (whose names are given, while their souls are ignored), but a true spiritual history of England—a picture of the spirits of our old forefathers, who worked, and fought, and sorrowed, and died for us; on whose accumulated labours we now here stand. *That* I call a history—not of one class of offices or events, but of the living human souls of English men and English women. And therefore one most adapted to the mind of woman; one which will call into fullest exercise her blessed faculty of sympathy, that pure and tender heart of flesh, which teaches her always to find her highest interest in mankind, simply as mankind; to see the Divine most completely in the human; to prefer the incarnate to the disembodied, the personal to the abstract, the pathetic to the intellectual; to see, and truly, in the most common tale of village love or sorrow, a mystery deeper and more divine than lies in all the theories of politicians or the fixed ideas of the sage.

Such a course of history would quicken women's inborn *personal interest* in the actors of this life-drama, and be quickened by it in return, as indeed it ought: for it is thus that God intended woman to look instinctively at the world. Would to God that she would teach us men to look at it thus likewise! Would to God that she would in these days claim and fulfil to the uttermost her vocation as the priestess of charity!—that woman's heart would help to deliver man from bondage to his own tyrannous and all-too-exclusive brain—from our idolatry of mere dead laws and printed books—from our daily sin of looking at men, not as our struggling and suffering brothers, but as mere symbols of certain formulæ, incarnations of sets of opinions, wheels in some iron liberty-grinding or Christianity-spinning machine, which we miscall society, or civilisation, or, worst misnomer of all, the Church!

This I take to be one of the highest aims of woman—to preach charity, love, and brotherhood: but in this nineteenth century, hunting everywhere for law and organisation, refusing loyalty to anything which cannot range itself under its theories, she will never get a hearing, till her knowledge of the past becomes more organised and methodic. As it is now, for want of large many-sided views of the past, her admiration is too apt to attach itself to some two or three characters only in the hero-list of all the ages. Then comes the temptation to thrust aside all which interferes with her favourite idols, and so the very heart given her for universal sympathy becomes the organ of an exclusive bigotry, and she who should have taught man to love, too often only embitters his hate.

I claim, therefore, as necessary for the education of the future, that woman should be initiated into the thoughts and feelings of her countrymen in every age, from the wildest legends of the past to the most palpable naturalism of the present; and that not merely in a chronological order, sometimes not in chronological order at all; but in a true spiritual sequence; that knowing the hearts of many, she may in after life be able to comfort the hearts of all.

But there is yet another advantage in an extended study of English literature—I mean the more national tone which it ought to give the thoughts of the rising generation. Of course to repress the reading of foreign books, to strive after any national exclusiveness, or mere John-Bullism of mind, in an age of railroads and free press, would be simply absurd—and more, it would be fighting against the will of God revealed in events. He has put the literary treasures of the Continent into our hands; we must joyfully accept them, and earnestly exhaust them. This age is craving for what it calls catholicity; for more complete interchange and brotherhood of thought between all the nations of the earth. This spirit is stirring in the young especially, and I believe that God Himself has inspired it, because I see that He has first revealed the means of gratifying the desire, at that very time in which it has arisen.

But every observant person must be aware that this tendency has produced its evils as well as its good. There is a general complaint that the minds of young women are becoming un-English; that their foreign reading does not merely supply the deficiencies of their English studies, but too often completely supersedes them; that the whole tone of their thoughts is too often taken from French or German writings; that by some means or other, the standard works of English literature are becoming very much undervalued and neglected by the young people of this day; and that selfwill and irregular eclecticism are the natural results.

I must say that I consider the greater part of these evils as the natural consequence of past miseducation; as the just punishment of the old system, which attached the most disproportionate importance to mere acquirements, and those mostly of foreign languages, foreign music, and so forth, while the "well of English undefiled," and not only that, but English literature, history, patriotism, too often English religion, have been made quite minor considerations. Therefore so few of the young have any healthy and firm English standard whereby to try and judge foreign thought. Therefore they fancy, when they meet with anything deep and attractive in foreign works, that because they have no such thoughts put before them in English authors, no such thoughts exist in them.

But happily we may do much towards mending this state of things, by making our pupils thoroughly conversant with the æsthetic treasures of English literature. From them I firmly believe they may derive sufficient rules whereby to separate in foreign books the true from the false, the necessary from the accidental, the eternal truth from its peculiar national vesture. Above all, we shall give them a better chance of seeing things from that side from which God intended English women to see them: for as surely as there is an English view of everything, so surely God intends us to take that view; and He who gave us our English character intends us to develop its peculiarities, as He intends the French woman to develop hers, that so each nation by learning to understand itself, may learn to understand, and therefore to profit, by its neighbour. He who has not cultivated his own plot of ground will hardly know much about the tillage of his neighbour's land. And she who does not appreciate the mind of her own countrymen will never form any true judgment of the mind of foreigners. Let English women be sure that the best way to understand the heroines of the Continent is not by mimicking them, however noble they may be, not by trying to become a sham Rahel, or a sham De Sévigné, but a real Elizabeth Fry, Felicia Hemans, or Hannah More. What indeed entitles either Madame de Sévigné or Rahel to fame, but their very nationality—that intensely local style of language and feeling which clothes their genius with a living body instead of leaving it in the abstractions of a dreary cosmopolitism? The one I suppose would be called the very beau-ideal, not of woman, but of the French woman—the other the ideal, not even of the Jewess, but of the German Jewess. We may admire wherever we find worth; but if we try to imitate, we only caricature. Excellence grows in all climes, transplants to none: the palm luxuriates only in the tropics, the Alp-rose only beside eternal snows. Only by standing on our own native earth can we enjoy or even see aright the distant stars: if we try to reach them, we shall at once lose sight of them, and drop helpless in a new element, unfitted for our limbs.

Teach, then, the young, by an extended knowledge of English literature, thoroughly to comprehend the English spirit, thoroughly to see that the English mind has its peculiar calling on God's earth, which alone, and no other, it can fulfil. Teach them thoroughly to appreciate the artistic and intellectual excellences of their own country; but by no means in a spirit of narrow bigotry: tell them fairly our national faults—teach them to unravel those faults from our national virtues; and then there will be no danger of the prejudiced English woman becoming by a sudden revulsion an equally prejudiced cosmopolite and eclectic, as soon as she discovers that her own nation does not monopolise all human perfections; and so trying to become German, Italian, French woman, all at once—a heterogeneous chaos of imitations, very probably with the faults of all three characters, and the graces of none. God has given us our own prophets, our own heroines. To recognise those prophets, to imitate those heroines, is the duty which lies nearest to the English woman, and therefore the duty which God intends her to fulfil.

I should wish therefore in the first few lectures on English literature to glance at the character of our old Saxon ancestors, and the legends connected with their first invasion of the country; and above all at the magnificent fables of King Arthur and his times which exercised so great an influence on the English mind, and were in fact, although originally Celtic, so thoroughly adopted and naturalised by the Saxon, as to reappear under different forms in every age, and form the keynote of most of our fictions, from Geoffrey of Monmouth and the medieval ballads, up to Chaucer, Spenser, Shakespeare, and at last Milton and Blackmore. This series of legends will, I think, as we trace its development, bring us in contact one by one with the corresponding developments of the English character; and, unless I am much mistaken, enable us to explain many of its peculiarities.

Of course nothing more than sketches can be given; but I think nothing more is required for any one but the professed historian. For young people especially, it is sufficient to understand the tone of human feeling expressed by legends, rather than to enter into any critical dissertations on their historic truth. They need, after all, principles rather than facts. To educate them truly we must give them inductive habits of thought, and teach them to deduce from a few facts a law which makes plain all similar ones, and so acquire the habit of extracting from every story somewhat of its kernel of spiritual meaning. But again, to educate them truly we must ourselves have faith; we must believe that in every one there is a spiritual eye which can perceive those great principles when they are once fairly presented to it, that in all there are some noble instincts, some pure yearnings after wisdom, and taste, and usefulness, which, if we only appeal to them trustfully through the examples of the past, and the excitements of the present, will wake into conscious life. Above all, both pupils and teachers must never forget that all these things were written for their examples; that though circumstances and creeds, schools and tastes, may alter, yet the heart of man, and the duty of man, remain unchanged, and that while

> The old order changes, giving place to the new,
> And God fulfils himself in many ways—

yet again

> Through the ages one unaltered purpose runs—

and the principles of truth and beauty are the same as when the everlasting Spirit from whom they come "brooded upon the face" of the primeval seas.

But once more, we must and will by God's help try

to realise the purpose of this College, by boldly facing the facts of the age and of our own office. And therefore we shall not shrink from the task, however delicate and difficult, of speaking to our hearers as to women. Our teaching must be no sexless, heartless abstraction. We must try to make all which we tell them bear on the great purpose of unfolding to woman her own calling in all ages—her especial calling in this one. We must incite them to realise the chivalrous belief of our old forefathers among their Saxon forests, that something Divine dwelt in the counsels of woman; but, on the other hand, we must continually remind them that they will attain that divine instinct, not by renouncing their sex, but by fulfilling it; by becoming true women, and not bad imitations of men; by educating their heads for the sake of their hearts, not their hearts for the sake of their heads; by claiming woman's divine vocation, as the priestess of purity, of beauty, and of love; by educating themselves to become, with God's blessing, worthy wives and mothers of a mighty nation of workers, in an age when the voice of the ever-working God is proclaiming through the thunder of falling dynasties, and crumbling idols: "He that will not work, neither shall he eat."

GROTS AND GROVES.

GROTS AND GROVES.*

This lecture is intended to be suggestive rather than didactic; to set you thinking and inquiring for yourselves, rather than learning at second-hand from me. Some among my audience, I doubt not, will neither need to be taught by me, nor to be stirred up to inquiry for themselves. They are already, probably, antiquarians; already better acquainted with the subject than I am. But they will, I hope, remember that I am only trying to excite a general interest in that very architecture in which they delight, and so to make the public do justice to their labours. They will therefore, I trust—

> Be to my faults a little blind,
> Be to my virtues very kind—

and if my architectural theories do not seem to them correct in all details—well-founded I believe them myself to be—remember that if it be a light matter to me, or to the audience, whether any special and pet

* This Lecture was given at Chester in 1871.

fancy of mine should be exactly true or not; yet it is not a light matter that my hearers should be awakened—and too many just now need an actual awakening—to a right, pure, and wholesome judgment on questions of art, especially when the soundness of that judgment depends, as in this case, on sound judgments about human history, as well as about natural objects.

Now, it befell me that, fresh from the tropic forests, and with their forms hanging always as it were in the background of my eye, I was impressed more and more vividly the longer I looked, with the likeness of those forest forms to the forms of our own Cathedral of Chester. The grand and graceful Chapter-house transformed itself into one of those green bowers, which, once seen, and never to be seen again, make one at once richer and poorer for the rest of life. The fans of groining sprang from the short columns, just as do the feathered boughs of the far more beautiful Maximiliana palm, and just of the same size and shape; and met overhead, as I have seen them meet, in aisles longer by far than our cathedral nave. The free upright shafts, which give such strength, and yet such lightness, to the mullions of each window, pierced upward through those curving lines, as do the stems of young trees through the fronds of palm; and, like them, carried the eye and the fancy up into the infinite, and took off a sense of oppression and captivity which the weight of the roof might have produced. In the nave, in the choir, the same vision of the tropic forest haunted me. The fluted columns not only resembled, but seemed copied from the fluted stems beneath which I had ridden in the primeval woods; their bases, their capitals, seemed copied from the bulgings at the collar of the root, and at the spring of the boughs, produced by a check of the redundant sap; and were garlanded often enough, like the capitals of the columns, with delicate tracery of parasite leaves and flowers; the mouldings of the arches seemed copied from the parallel bundles of the curving bamboo shoots; and even the flatter roof of the nave and transepts had its antitype in that highest level of the forest aisles where the trees, having climbed at last to the light-food which they seek, care no longer to grow upward, but spread out in huge limbs, almost horizontal, reminding the eye of the four-centred arch which marks the period of perpendicular Gothic.

Nay, to this day there is one point in our cathedral which, to me, keeps up the illusion still. As I enter the choir, and look upward toward the left, I cannot help seeing, in the tabernacle work of the stalls, the slender and aspiring forms of the "rastrajo;" the delicate second growth which, as it were, rushes upward from the earth wherever the forest is cleared; and above it, in the tall lines of the north-west pier of the tower—even though defaced, along the inner face of the western arch, by ugly and needless perpendicular panelling—I seem to see the stems of huge cedars, or balatas, or ceibas, curving over, as they would do, into the great beams of the transept roof, some seventy feet above the ground.

Nay, so far will the fancy lead, that I have seemed to see, in the stained glass between the tracery of the windows, such gorgeous sheets of colour as sometimes flash on the eye, when, far aloft, between high stems and boughs, you catch sight of some great tree ablaze with flowers, either its own or those of a parasite; yellow or crimson, white or purple; and over them again the cloudless blue.

Now, I know well that all these dreams are dreams; that the men who built our northern cathedrals never saw these forest forms; and that the likeness of their work to those of tropic nature is at most only a corroboration of Mr. Ruskin's dictum, that "the Gothic did not arise out of, but developed itself into, a resemblance to vegetation. . . . . It was no chance suggestion of the form of an arch from the bending of a bough, but the gradual and continual discovery of a beauty in natural forms which could be more and more transferred into those of stone, which influenced at once the hearts of the people and the form of the edifice." So true is this, that by a pure and noble copying of the vegetable beauty which they had seen in their own clime, the medieval craftsmen went so far—as I have shown you—as to anticipate forms of vegetable beauty peculiar to tropic climes, which they had not seen; a fresh proof, if proof were needed, that beauty is something absolute and independent of man; and not, as some think, only relative, and what happens to be pleasant to the eye of this man or that.

But thinking over this matter, and reading over, too, that which Mr. Ruskin has written thereon in his "Stones of Venice," vol. ii. cap. vi., on the nature of Gothic, I came to certain further conclusions—or at least surmises—which I put before you to-night, in hopes that if they have no other effect on you, they will at least stir some of you up to read Mr. Ruskin's works.

Now Mr. Ruskin says: "That the original conception of Gothic architecture has been derived from vegetation, from the symmetry of avenues and the interlacing of branches, is a strange and vain supposition. It is a theory which never could have existed for a moment in the mind of any person acquainted with early Gothic; but, however idle as a theory, it is most valuable as a testimony to the character of the perfected style."

Doubtless so. But you must remember always that the subject of my lecture is Grots and Groves; that I am speaking not of Gothic architecture in general, but of Gothic ecclesiastical architecture; and more, almost exclusively of the ecclesiastical architecture of the Teutonic or northern nations; because in them, as I think, the resemblance between the temple and the forest reached the fullest exactness.

Now the original idea of a Christian church was that of a grot—a cave. That is a historic fact. The Christianity which was passed on to us began to worship, hidden and persecuted, in the catacombs of Rome, it may be often around the martyrs' tombs, by the dim light of candle or of torch. The candles on the Roman altars, whatever they have been made to symbolise since then, are the hereditary memorials of that fact. Throughout the North, in these isles as much as in any land, the idea of the grot was, in like wise, the idea of a church. The saint or hermit built himself a cell; dark, massive, intended to exclude light as well as weather; or took refuge in a cave. There he prayed and worshipped, and gathered others to pray and worship round him, during his life. There he, often enough, became an object of worship in his turn, after his death. In after ages his cave was ornamented, like that of the hermit of Montmajour by Arles; or his cell-chapel enlarged, as those of the Scotch and Irish saints have been, again and again; till at last a stately minster rose above it. Still, the idea that the church was to be a grot haunted the minds of builders.

But side by side with the Christian grot there was throughout the North another form of temple, dedicated to very different gods, namely, the trees from whose mighty stems hung the heads of the victims of Odin or of Thor—the horse, the goat, and, in time of calamity or pestilence, of men. Trees and not grots were the temples of our forefathers.

Scholars know well—but they must excuse my quoting it for the sake of those who are not scholars—the famous passage of Tacitus which tells how our forefathers "held it beneath the dignity of the gods to coop them within walls, or liken them to any human countenance; but consecrated groves and woods, and called by the name of gods that mystery which they held by faith alone;" and the equally famous passage of Claudian, about "the vast silence of the Black Forest, and groves awful with ancient superstition; and oaks, barbarian deities;" and Lucan's "groves inviolate from all antiquity, and altars stained with human blood."

To worship in such spots was an abomination to

the early Christian. It was as much a test of heathendom as the eating of horse-flesh, sacred to Odin, and therefore unclean to Christian men. The Lombard laws and others forbid expressly the lingering remnants of grove worship. St. Boniface and other early missionaries hewed down in defiance the sacred oaks, and paid sometimes for their valour with their lives.

It is no wonder, then, if long centuries elapsed ere the likeness of vegetable forms began to reappear in the Christian churches of the North. And yet both grot and grove were equally the natural temples which the religious instinct of all deep-hearted peoples, conscious of sin, and conscious, too, of yearnings after a perfection not to be found on earth, chooses from the earliest stage of awakening civilisation. In them, alone, before he had strength and skill to build nobly for himself, could man find darkness, the mother of mystery and awe, in which he is reminded perforce of his own ignorance and weakness; in which he learns first to remember unseen powers, sometimes to his comfort and elevation, sometimes only to his terror and debasement; darkness; and with it silence and solitude, in which he can collect himself, and shut out the noise and glare, the meanness and the coarseness of the world; and be alone awhile with his own thoughts, his own fancy, his own conscience, his own soul.

But for awhile, as I have said, that darkness, solitude, and silence were to be sought in the grot, not in the grove.

Then Christianity conquered the Empire. It adapted,

not merely its architecture, but its very buildings, to its worship. The Roman Basilica became the Christian church; a noble form of building enough, though one in which was neither darkness, solitude, nor silence, but crowded congregations, clapping—or otherwise—the popular preacher; or fighting about the election of a bishop or a pope, till the holy place ran with Christian blood. The deep-hearted Northern turned away, in weariness and disgust, from those vast halls, fitted only for the feverish superstition of a profligate and worn-out civilisation; and took himself, amid his own rocks and forests, moors and shores, to a simpler and sterner architecture, which should express a creed, sterner, and at heart far simpler, though dogmatically the same.

And this is, to my mind, the difference, and the noble difference, between the so-called Norman architecture, which came hither about the time of the Conquest; and that of Romanised Italy.

But the Normans were a conquering race; and one which conquered, be it always remembered, in England at least, in the name and by the authority of Rome. Their ecclesiastics, like the ecclesiastics on the Continent, were the representatives of Roman civilisation, of Rome's right, intellectual and spiritual, to rule the world.

Therefore their architecture, like their creed, was Roman. They took the massive towering Roman forms, which expressed domination; and piled them one on the other, to express the domination of Christian Rome over the souls, as they had represented the domination of heathen Rome over the bodies of men. And so side by side with the towers of the Norman keep rose the towers of the Norman cathedral—the two signs of a double servitude.

But with the thirteenth century there dawned an age in Northern Europe which I may boldly call an heroic age—heroic in its virtues and in its crimes; an age of rich passionate youth, or rather of early manhood; full of aspirations of chivalry, of self-sacrifice as strange and terrible as it was beautiful and noble, even when most misguided. The Teutonic nations of Europe—our own forefathers most of all—having absorbed all that heathen Rome could teach them, at least for the time being, began to think for themselves; to have poets, philosophers, historians, architects, of their own. The thirteenth century was especially an age of aspiration; and its architects expressed, in building, quite unlike those of the preceding centuries, the aspirations of the time.

The Pointed Arch had been introduced half a century before. It may be that the Crusaders saw it in the East and brought it home. It may be that it originated from the quadripartite vaulting of the Normans, the segmental groins of which, crossing diagonally, produced to appearance the pointed arch. It may be that it was derived from that mystical figure of a pointed oval form, the vesica piscis. It may be, lastly, that it was suggested simply by the intersection of semicircular arches, so frequently found in ornamental arcades. The last cause may perhaps be the true one; but it matters little whence the pointed arch came. It matters much what it meant to those who introduced it. And at the beginning of the Transition or semi-Norman period, it seems to have meant nothing. It was not till the thirteenth century that it had gradually received, as it were, a soul, and had become the exponent of a great idea. As the Norman architecture and its forms had signified domination, so the Early English, as we call it, signified aspiration—an idea which was perfected, as far as it could be, in what we call the Decorated style.

There is an evident gap, I had almost said a gulf, between the architectural mind of the eleventh and that of the thirteenth century. A vertical tendency, a longing after lightness and freedom appears; and with them a longing to reproduce the graces of nature and art. And here I ask you to look for yourselves at the buildings of this new era—there is a beautiful specimen in yonder arcade*—and judge for yourselves whether they, and even more than they the Decorated style into which they developed, do not remind you of the forest shapes?

And if they remind you, must they not have reminded those who shaped them? Can it have been otherwise? We know that the men who built were earnest. The carefulness, the reverence, of their work have given a subject for some of Mr. Ruskin's noblest chapters, a text for some of his noblest sermons. We know that they were students of vegetable form. That is proved by the flowers, the leaves, even the birds, with which they enwreathed their capitals and enriched their mouldings. Look up there, and see.

You cannot look at any good church-work from the thirteenth to the middle of the fifteenth century, with-

* An arcade in the King's School, Chester.

out seeing that leaves and flowers were perpetually in the workman's mind. Do you fancy that stems and boughs were never in his mind? He kept, doubtless, in remembrance the fundamental idea, that the Christian church should symbolise a grot or cave. He could do no less; while he again and again saw hermits around him dwelling and worshipping in caves, as they had done ages before in Egypt and Syria; while he fixed, again and again, the site of his convent and his minster in some secluded valley guarded by cliffs and rocks, like Vale Crucis in North Wales. But his minster stood often not among rocks only, but amid trees; in some clearing in the primeval forest, as Vale Crucis was then. At least he could not pass from minster to minster, from town to town, without journeying through long miles of forest. Do you think that the awful shapes and shadows of that forest never haunted his imagination as he built? He would have cut down ruthlessly, as his predecessors the early missionaries did, the sacred trees amid which Thor and Odin had been worshipped by the heathen Saxons; amid which still darker deities were still worshipped by the heathen tribes of Eastern Europe. But he was the descendant of men who had worshipped in those groves, and the glamour of them was upon him still. He peopled the wild forest with demons and fairies; but that did not surely prevent his feeling its ennobling grandeur, its chastening loneliness. His ancestors had held the oaks for trees of God, even as the Jews held the cedar, and the Hindoos likewise; for the Deodara pine is not only, botanists tell us, the same as the cedar of Lebanon, but its very name—

the Deodara—signifies naught else but "the tree of God."

His ancestors, I say, had held the oaks for trees of God. It may be that as the monk sat beneath their shade with his bible on his knee, like good St. Boniface in the Fulda forest, he found that his ancestors were right.

To understand what sort of trees they were from which he got his inspiration, you must look, not at an average English wood, perpetually thinned out as the trees arrive at middle age. Still less must you look at the pines, oaks, beeches, of an English park, where each tree has had space to develop itself freely into a more or less rounded form. You must not even look at the tropic forests. For there, from the immense diversity of forms, twenty varieties of tree will grow beneath each other, forming a close-packed heap of boughs and leaves, from the ground to a hundred feet and more aloft.

You should look at the North American forests of social trees—especially of pines and firs, where trees of one species, crowded together, and competing with equal advantages for the air and light, form themselves into one wilderness of straight smooth shafts, surmounted by a flat sheet of foliage, held up by boughs like the ribs of a groined roof, while underneath the ground is bare as a cathedral floor.

You all know, surely, the Hemlock spruce of America; which, while growing by itself in open ground, is the most wilful and fantastic, as well as the most graceful, of all the firs; imitating the shape, not of its kindred, but of an enormous tuft of fern.

Yet if you look at the same tree, when it has struggled long for life from its youth amid other trees of its own kind and its own age, you find that the lower boughs have died off from want of light, leaving not a scar behind. The upper boughs have reached at once the light and their natural term of years. They are content to live, and little more. The central trunk no longer sends up each year a fresh perpendicular shoot to aspire above the rest, but, as weary of struggling ambition as they are, is content to become more and more their equal as the years pass by. And this is a law of social forest trees, which you must bear in mind whenever I speak of the influence of tree-forms on Gothic architecture.

Such forms as these are rare enough in Europe now.

I never understood how possible, how common they must have been in medieval Europe, till I saw in the forest of Fontainebleau a few oaks, like the oak of Charlemagne and the Bouquet du Roi, at whose age I dare not guess, but whose size and shape showed them to have once formed part of a continuous wood, the like whereof remains not in these isles—perhaps not east of the Carpathian mountains. In them a clear shaft of at least sixty, it may be eighty feet, carries a flat head of boughs, each in itself a tree. In such a grove, I thought, the heathen Gaul, even the heathen Frank, worshipped beneath "trees of God." Such trees, I thought, centuries after, inspired the genius of every builder of Gothic aisles and roofs.

Thus, at least, we can explain that rigidity, which Mr. Ruskin tells us, "is a special element of Gothic architecture. Greek and Egyptian buildings," he says —and I should have added, Roman building also, in proportion to their age, *i.e.* to the amount of the Roman elements in them—"stand for the most part by their own weight and mass, one stone passively incumbent on another: but in the Gothic vaults and traceries there is a stiffness analogous to that of the bones of a limb, or fibres of a tree; an elastic tension and communication of force from part to part; and also a studious expression of this throughout every part of the building." In a word, Gothic vaulting and tracery have been studiously made like to boughs of trees. Were those boughs present to the mind of the architect? Or is the coincidence merely fortuitous? You know already how I should answer. The cusped arch, too, was it actually not intended to imitate vegetation? Mr. Ruskin seems to think so. He says that it is merely the special application to the arch of the great ornamental system of foliation, which, "whether simple as in the cusped arch, or complicated as in tracery, arose out of the love of leafage. Not that the form of the arch is intended to imitate a leaf," but to be invested with the same characters of beauty which the designer had discovered in the leaf." Now I differ from Mr. Ruskin with extreme hesitation. I agree that the cusped arch is not meant to imitate a leaf. I think with Mr. Ruskin, that it was probably first adopted on account of its superior strength; and that it afterwards took the form of a bough. But I cannot as yet believe that it was not at last intended to imitate a bough; a bough of a very common form, and one in which "active rigidity" is peculiarly shown. I mean a bough which has forked. If the lower fork has died off, for want of light, we obtain something like the simply cusped arch. If it be still living—but short and stunted in comparison with the higher fork—we obtain, it seems to me, something like the foliated cusp; both likenesses being near enough to those of common objects to make it possible that those objects may have suggested them. And thus, more and more boldly, the medieval architect learnt to copy boughs, stems, and at last, the whole effect, as far always as stone would allow, of a combination of rock and tree, of grot and grove.

So he formed his minsters, as I believe, upon the model of those leafy minsters in which he walked to meditate, amid the aisles which God, not man, has built. He sent their columns aloft like the boles of ancient trees. He wreathed their capitals, sometimes their very shafts, with flowers and creeping shoots. He threw their arches out, and interwove the groinings of their vaults, like the bough-roofage overhead. He decked with foliage and fruit the bosses above and the corbels below. He sent up out of those corbels upright shafts along the walls, in the likeness of the trees which sprang out of the rocks above his head. He raised those walls into great cliffs. He pierced them with the arches of the triforium, as with hermits' cells. He represented in the horizontal sills of his windows, and in his horizontal string-courses, the horizontal strata of the rocks. He opened the windows into high and lofty glades, broken, as in the forest, by the tracery of stems and boughs, through which was seen, not merely the outer, but the upper world. For he craved, as all true artists crave, for light and colour; and had the sky above been one perpetual blue, he might have been content with it, and left his glass transparent. But in that dark, dank, northern clime, rain and snow-storm, black cloud and gray mist, were all that he was like to see outside for nine months in the year. So he took such light and colour as nature gave in her few gayer moods; and set aloft his stained-glass windows, the hues of the noonday and the rainbow, and the sun-rise and the sunset, and the purple of the heather, and the gold of the gorse, and the azure of the bugloss, and the crimson of the poppy; and among them, in gorgeous robes, the angels and the saints of heaven, and the memories of heroic virtues and heroic sufferings, that he might lift up his own eyes and heart for ever out of the dark, dank, sad world of the cold north, with all its coarsenesses and its crimes, toward a realm of perpetual holiness, amid a perpetual summer of beauty and of light; as one who—for he was true to nature, even in that—from between the black jaws of a narrow glen, or from beneath the black shade of gnarled trees, catches a glimpse of far lands gay with gardens and cottages, and purple mountain ranges, and the far-off sea, and the hazy horizon melting into the hazy sky; and finds his heart carried out into an infinite at once of freedom and of repose.

And so out of the cliffs and the forests he shaped the inside of his church. And how did he shape the outside? Look for yourselves, and judge. But look, not at Chester, but at Salisbury. Look at those churches which carry not mere towers, but spires, or at least pinnacled towers approaching the pyramidal form. The outside form of every Gothic cathedral must be considered imperfect if it does not culminate in something pyramidal.

The especial want of all Greek and Roman buildings with which we are acquainted is the absence—save in a few and unimportant cases—of the pyramidal form. The Egyptians knew at least the worth of the obelisk; but the Greeks and Romans hardly knew even that: their buildings are flat-topped. Their builders were contented with the earth as it was. There was a great truth involved in that; which I am the last to deny.

But religions which, like the Buddhist or the Christian, nurse a noble self-discontent, are sure to adopt sooner or later an upward and aspiring form of building. It is not merely that, fancying heaven to be above earth, they point towards heaven. There is a deeper natural language in the pyramidal form of a growing tree. It symbolises growth, or the desire of growth. The Norman tower does nothing of the kind. It does not aspire to grow. Look—I mention an instance with which I am most familiar—at the Norman tower of Bury St. Edmund's. It is graceful—awful, if you will—but there is no aspiration in it. It is stately, but self-content. Its horizontal courses, circular arches, above all, its flat sky-line, seem to have risen enough, and wish to rise no higher. For it has no touch of that unrest of soul which is expressed by the spire, and still more by the compound spire, with its pinnacles, crockets, finials—which are finials only in name; for they do not finish, and are really terminal buds, as it were, longing to open and grow upward, even as the crockets are bracts and leaves thrown off as the shoot has grown.

You feel, surely, the truth of these last words. You cannot look at the canopy work or the pinnacle work of this cathedral without seeing that they do not merely suggest buds and leaves, but that the buds and leaves are there carven before your eyes. I myself cannot look at the tabernacle work of our stalls without being reminded of the young pine forests which clothe the Hampshire moors. But if the details are copied from vegetable forms, why not the whole? Is not a spire like a growing tree, a tabernacle like a fir-tree, a compound spire like a group of firs? And if we can see that, do you fancy that the man who planned the spire did not see it as clearly as we do; and perhaps more clearly still?

I am aware, of course, that Norman architecture had sometimes its pinnacle, a mere conical or polygonal capping. I am aware that this form, only more and more slender, lasted on in England during the thirteenth and the early part of the fourteenth century; and on the Continent under many modifications, one English kind whereof is usually called a "broach," of which you have a beautiful specimen in the new church at Hoole.

Now, no one will deny that that broach is beautiful. But it would be difficult to prove that its form was taken from a North European tree. The cypress was unknown, probably, to our northern architects. The Lombardy poplar—which has wandered hither, I know not when, all the way from Cashmere—had not wandered then, I believe, farther than North Italy. The form is rather that of mere stone; of the obelisk or of the mountain-peak; and they, in fact, may have at first suggested the spire. The grandeur of an isolated mountain, even of a dolmen or single upright stone, is evident to all.

But it is the grandeur not of aspiration, but of defiance; not of the Christian, not even of the Stoic, but rather of the Epicurean. It says—I cannot rise. I do not care to rise. I will be contentedly and valiantly that which I am; and face circumstances, though I cannot conquer them. But it is defiance under defeat. The mountain-peak does not grow, but only decays. Fretted by rains, peeled by frost, splintered by lightning, it must down at last; and crumble into earth, were it as old, as hard, as lofty as the Matterhorn itself. And while it stands, it wants not only aspiration, it wants tenderness; it wants humility; it wants the unrest which tenderness and humility must breed, and which Mr. Ruskin so clearly recognises in the best Gothic art. And, meanwhile, it wants naturalness. The mere smooth spire or broach—I had almost said, even the spire of Salisbury—is like no tall or commanding object in nature. It is merely the caricature of one—it may be of the mountain-peak. The outline must be broken, must be softened, before it can express the soul of a creed which in the thirteenth and fourteenth centuries, far more than now, was one of penitence as well as of aspiration, of passionate emotion as well as of lofty faith. But a shape which will express that soul must be sought, not among mineral, but among vegetable, forms. And remember always, if we feel thus even now, how much more must those medieval men of genius have felt thus, whose work we now dare only copy line by line?

So—as it seems to me—they sought among vegetable forms for what they needed: and they found it at once in the pine, or rather the fir—the spruce and silver firs of their own forests. They are not, of course, indigenous to England. But they are so common through all the rest of Europe, that not only would the form suggest itself to a continental architect, but to any English clerk who travelled, as all did who could, across the Alps to Rome. The fir-tree, not growing on level ground, like the oaks of Fontainebleau, into one flat roof of foliage, but clinging to the hillside and the crag, old above young, spire above spire, whorl above whorl—for the young shoots of each whorl of boughs point upward in the spring; and now and then a whole bough breaking away, as it were, into free space, turns upward altogether, and forms a secondary spire on the same tree—this surely was the form which the medieval architect seized, to clothe with it the sides and roof of the stone mountain which he had built; piling up pinnacles and spires, each crocketed at the angles; that, like a group of firs upon an isolated rock, every point of the building might seem in act to grow toward heaven, till his idea culminated in that glorious Minster of Cologne, which, if it ever be completed, will be the likeness of one forest-clothed group of cliffs, surrounded by three enormous pines.

One feature of the Norman temple he could keep; for it was copied from the same Nature which he was trying to copy—namely, the high-pitched roof and gables. Mr. Ruskin lays it down as a law, that the acute angle in roofs, gables, spires, is the distinguishing mark of northern Gothic. It was adopted, most probably, at first from domestic buildings. A northern house or barn must have a high-pitched roof, or the snow will not slip off it. But that fact was not discovered by man; it was copied by him from the rocks around. He saw the mountain-peak jut black and bare above the snows of winter; he saw those snows slip down in sheets, rush down in torrents under the sun, from the steep slabs of rock which coped the hillside; and he copied, in his roofs, the rocks above his town. But as the love for decorations arose, he would deck his roofs as nature had decked hers, till the gray sheets of the cathedral slates should stand out amid pinnacles and turrets rich with foliage, as the gray mountain-sides stood out amid knolls of feathery birch and towering pine.

He failed, though he failed nobly. He never succeeded in attaining a perfectly natural style.

The medieval architects were crippled to the last by the tradition of artificial Roman forms. They began improving them into naturalness, without any clear notion of what they wanted; and when that notion became clear, it was too late. Take, as an instance, the tracery of their windows. It is true, as Mr. Ruskin says, that they began by piercing holes in a wall of the form of a leaf, which developed, in the rose window, into the form of a star inside, and of a flower outside. Look at such aloft there. Then, by introducing mullions and traceries into the lower part of the window, they added stem and bough forms to those flower forms. But the two did not fit. Look at the west window of our choir, and you will see what I mean. The upright mullions break off into bough curves graceful enough:

but these are cut short—as I hold, spoiled—by circular and triangular forms of rose and trefoil resting on them as such forms never rest in nature; and the whole, though beautiful, is only half beautiful. It is fragmentary, unmeaning—barbaric, because unnatural.

They failed too, it may be, from the very paucity of the vegetable forms they could find to copy among the flora of this colder clime; and so, stopped short in drawing from nature, ran off into mere purposeless luxuriance. Had they been able to add to their stock of memories a hundred forms which they would have seen in the tropics, they might have gone on for centuries copying nature without exhausting her.

And yet, did they exhaust even the few forms of beauty which they saw around them? It must be confessed that they did not. I believe that they could not, because they dared not. The unnaturalness of the creed which they expressed always hampered them. It forbade them to look Nature freely and lovingly in the face. It forbade them—as one glaring example—to know anything truly of the most beautiful of all natural objects—the human form. They were tempted perpetually to take Nature as ornament, not as basis; and they yielded at last to the temptation; till, in the age of Perpendicular architecture, their very ornament became unnatural again; because conventional, untrue, meaningless.

But the creed for which they worked was dying by that time, and therefore the art which expressed it must needs die too. And even that death, or rather the approach of it, was symbolised truly in the flatter roof, the four-centred arch, the flat-topped tower of the fifteenth-century church. The creed had ceased to aspire: so did the architecture. It had ceased to grow: so did the temple. And the arch sank lower; and the rafters grew more horizontal; and the likeness to the old tree, content to grow no more, took the place of the likeness to the young tree struggling toward the sky.

And now—unless you are tired of listening to me—a few practical words.

We are restoring our old cathedral stone by stone after its ancient model. We are also trying to build a new church. We are building it—as most new churches in England are now built—in a pure Gothic style.

Are we doing right? I do not mean morally right. It is always morally right to build a new church, if needed, whatever be its architecture. It is always morally right to restore an old church, if it be beautiful and noble, as an heirloom handed down to us by our ancestors, which we have no right—I say no right—for the sake of our children, and of our children's children, to leave to ruin.

But are we artistically, æsthetically right? Is the best Gothic fit for our worship? Does it express our belief? Or shall we choose some other style?

I say that it is; and that it is so because it is a style which, if not founded on Nature, has taken into itself more of nature, of nature beautiful and healthy, than any other style.

With greater knowledge of nature, both geographical and scientific, fresh styles of architecture may and will arise, as much more beautiful, and as much more natural, than the Gothic, as Gothic is more beautiful and natural than the Norman. Till then we must take the best models which we have; use them; and, as it were, use them up and exhaust them. By that time we may have learnt to improve on them; and to build churches more Gothic than Gothic itself, more like grot and grove than even a northern cathedral.

That is the direction in which we must work. And if any shall say to us, as it has been said ere now—"After all, your new Gothic churches are but imitations, shams, borrowed symbols, which to you symbolise nothing. They are Romish churches, meant to express Romish doctrine, built for a Protestant creed which they do not express, and for a Protestant worship which they will not fit." Then we shall answer—Not so. The objection might be true if we built Norman or Romanesque churches; for we should then be returning to that very foreign and unnatural style which Rome taught our forefathers, and from which they escaped gradually into the comparative freedom, the comparative naturalness, of that true Gothic of which Mr. Ruskin says so well:

> It is gladdening to remember that, in its utmost nobleness, the very temper which has been thought most adverse to it, the Protestant temper of self-dependence and inquiry, were expressed in every case. Faith and aspiration there were in every Christian ecclesiastical building from the first century to the fifteenth: but the moral habits to which England in this age owes the kind of greatness which she has—the habits of philosophical investigation, of accurate thought, of domestic seclusion and independence, of stern self-reliance, and sincere upright searching into religious truth—were only traceable in the features which were the distinctive creations of the Gothic schools, in the varied foliage and thorny fretwork, and shadowy niche, and buttressed pier, and fearless height of subtle pinnacle and crested tower, sent "like an unperplexed question up to heaven."

So says Mr. Ruskin. I, for one, endorse his gallant words. And I think that a strong proof of their truth is to be found in two facts, which seem at first paradoxical. First, that the new Roman Catholic churches on the Continent—I speak especially of France, which is the most highly-cultivated Romanist country—are like those which the Jesuits built in the seventeenth and eighteenth centuries, less and less Gothic. The former were sham-classic; the latter are rather of a new fantastic Romanesque, or rather Byzantinesque style, which is a real retrogression from Gothic towards earlier and less natural schools. Next, that the Puritan communions, the Kirk of Scotland and the English Nonconformists, as they are becoming more cultivated—and there are now many highly-cultivated men among them—are introducing Gothic architecture more and more into their churches. There are elements in it, it seems, which do not contradict their Puritanism; elements which they can adapt to their own worship; namely, the very elements which Mr. Ruskin has discerned.

But if they can do so, how much more can we of the Church of England? As long as we go on where our medieval forefathers left off; as long as we keep to the most perfect types of their work, in waiting for the day when we shall be able to surpass them, by making our work even more naturalistic than theirs, more truly expressive of the highest aspirations of humanity; so long we are reverencing them, and that latent Protestantism in them, which produced at last the Reformation.

And if any should say: "Nevertheless your Protestant Gothic Church, though you made it ten times more beautiful, and more symbolic than Cologne Minster itself, would still be a sham. For where would be your images? And still more, where would be your Host? Do you not know that in the medieval church the vistas of its arcades, the alternation of its lights and shadows, the gradations of its colouring, and all its carefully subordinated wealth of art, pointed to, were concentrated round, one sacred spot, as a curve, however vast its sweep through space, tends at every moment toward a single focus? And that spot, that focus was, and is still in every Romish church, the body of God, present upon the altar in the form of bread? Without Him, what is all your building? Your church is empty; your altar bare; a throne without a king; an eye-socket without an eye."

My friends, if we be true children of those old worthies, whom Tacitus saw worshipping beneath the German oaks, we shall have but one answer to that scoff:

"We know it; and we glory in the fact. We glory in it, as the old Jews gloried in it, when the Roman soldiers, bursting through the Temple and into the Holy of Holies itself, paused in wonder and in awe when they beheld neither God, nor image of God, but —blank yet all-suggestive—the empty mercy-seat.

Like theirs, our altar is an empty throne; for it symbolises our worship of Him who dwelleth not in temples made with hands; whom the heaven and the heaven of heavens cannot contain. Our eye-socket holds no eye. For it symbolises our worship of that Eye which is over all the earth; which is about our path, and about our bed, and spies out all our ways.

We need no artificial and material presence of Deity. For we believe in That One Eternal and Universal Real Presence—of which it is written 'He is not far from anyone of us; for in God we live and move and have our being;' and again: 'Lo, I am with you even to the end of the world;' and again: 'Wheresoever two or three are gathered together in My Name there am I in the midst of them.'

He is the God of nature, as well as the God of grace. Forever He looks down on all things which He has made, and behold, they are very good. And, therefore, we dare offer to Him, in our churches, the most perfect works of naturalistic art, and shape them into copies of whatever beauty He has shown us, in man or woman, in cove or mountain-peak, in tree or flower, even in bird or butterfly

But Himself?—Who can see Him? Except the humble and the contrite heart, to whom He reveals Himself as a Spirit to be worshipped in spirit and in truth, and not in bread, nor wood, nor stone, nor gold, nor quintessential diamond."

So we shall obey the sound instinct of our Christian forefathers, when they shaped their churches into forest aisles, and decked them with the boughs of the woodland and the flowers of the field: but we shall obey too, that sounder instinct of theirs, which made them at last cast out of their own temples, as misplaced and unnatural things, the idols which they had inherited from Rome.

So we shall obey the sound instinct of our heathen forefathers when they worshipped the unknown God beneath the oaks of the primeval forests: but we shall obey, too, that sounder instinct of theirs, which taught them this, at least, concerning God—That it was beneath His dignity to coop Him within walls; and that the grandest forms of nature, as well as the deepest consciousness of their own souls, revealed to them a mysterious Being, who was to be beheld by faith alone.

HOURS WITH THE MYSTICS.

HOURS WITH THE MYSTICS.*

Few readers of this magazine probably know anything about "Mystics;" know even what the term means: but as it is plainly connected with the adjective "mystical," they probably suppose it to denote some sort of vague, dreamy, sentimental, and therefore useless and undesirable personage. Nor can we blame them if they do so; for mysticism is a form of thought and feeling now all but extinct in England. There are probably not ten thorough mystics among all our millions; the mystic philosophers are very little read by our scholars, and read not for, but in spite of, their mysticism; and our popular theology has so completely rid itself of any mystic elements, that our divines look with utter disfavour upon it, use the word always as a term of opprobrium, and interpret the mystic expressions in our liturgy—which mostly occur in the Collects—according to the philosophy of Locke, really ignorant,

* Fraser's Magazine, September, 1856.— "Hours with the Mystics." By Robert Alfred Vaughan, B.A. Two Volumes. London: John W. Parker and Son. 1856.

it would seem, that they were written by Platonist mystics.

We do not blame them either, save in as far as teachers of men are blameworthy for being ignorant of any form of thought which has ever had a living hold upon good and earnest men, and may therefore take hold of them again. But the English are not now a mystic people, any more than the old Romans were; their habit of mind, their destiny in the world, are like those of the Romans, altogether practical; and who can be surprised if they do not think about what they are not called upon to think about?

Nevertheless, it is quite a mistake to suppose that mysticism is by its own nature unpractical. The greatest and most prosperous races of antiquity—the Egyptians, Babylonians, Hindoos, Greeks—had the mystic element as strong and living in them as the Germans have now; and certainly we cannot call them unpractical peoples. They fell and came to ruin—as the Germans may do—when their mysticism became unpractical: but their thought remained, to be translated into practice by sounder-hearted races than themselves. Rome learnt from Greece, and did in some confused imperfect way that which Greece only dreamed; just as future nations may act hereafter, nobly and usefully, on the truths which Germans discover, only to put in a book and smoke over. For they are terribly practical people, these mystics, quiet students and devotees as they may seem. They go, or seem to go, down to the roots of things, after a way of their own; and lay foundations on which—be they sound or unsound—those who come after them cannot choose but build; as we are building now. For our forefathers were mystics for generations; they were mystics in the forests of Germany and in the dales of Norway; they were mystics in the convents and the universities of the Middle Ages; they were mystics, all the deepest and noblest minds of them, during the Elizabethan era.

Even now the few mystic writers of this island are exercising more influence on thought than any other men, for good or for evil. Coleridge and Alexander Knox have changed the minds, and with them the acts, of thousands; and when they are accused of having originated, unknowingly, the whole "Tractarian" movement, those who have watched English thought carefully can only answer, that on the confession of the elder Tractarians themselves, the allegation is true: but that they originated a dozen other "movements" beside in the most opposite directions, and that free-thinking Emersonians will be as ready as Romish perverts and good plain English churchmen to confess that the critical point of their life was determined by the writings of the fakeer of Highgate. At this very time too, the only real mystic of any genius who is writing and teaching is exercising more practical influence, infusing more vigorous life into the minds of thousands of men and women, than all the other teachers of England put together; and has set rolling a ball which may in the next half century gather into an avalanche, perhaps utterly different in form, material, and direction, from all which he expects.

So much for mystics being unpractical. If we look faithfully into the meaning of their name, we shall see why, for good or for evil, they cannot be unpractical;

why they, let them be the most self-absorbed of recluses, are the very men who sow the seeds of great schools, great national and political movements, even great religions.

A mystic—according to the Greek etymology—should signify one who is initiated into mysteries, one whose eyes are opened to see things which other people cannot see. And the true mystic in all ages and countries, has believed that this was the case with him. He believes that there is an invisible world as well as a visible one—so do most men: but the mystic believes also that this same invisible world is not merely a supernumerary one world more, over and above the earth on which he lives, and the stars over his head, but that it is the cause of them and the ground of them; that it was the cause of them at first, and is the cause of them now, even to the budding of every flower, and the falling of every pebble to the ground; and therefore, that having been before this visible world, it will be after it, and endure just as real, living, and eternal, though matter were annihilated to-morrow.

"But, on this showing, every Christian, nay, every religious man, is a mystic; for he believes in an invisible world?" The answer is found in the plain fact, that good Christians here in England do not think so themselves; that they dislike and dread mysticism; would not understand it if it were preached to them; are more puzzled by those utterances of St. John, which mystics have always claimed as justifying their theories, than by any part of their bibles. There is a positive and conscious difference between popular metaphysics and mysticism; and it seems to lie in this: the invisible world in which Englishmen in general believe, is one which happens to be invisible now, but which will not be so hereafter. When they speak of the other world they mean a place which their bodily eyes will see some day, and could see now if they were allowed; when they speak of spirits they mean ghosts who could, and perhaps do, make themselves visible to men's bodily eyes. We are not inquiring here whether they be right or wrong; we are only specifying a common form of human thought.

The mystic, on the other hand, believes that the invisible world is so by its very nature, and must be so for ever. He lives therein now, he holds, and will live in it through eternity: but he will see it never with any bodily eyes, not even with the eyes of any future "glorified" body. It is ipso facto not to be seen, only to be believed in; never for him will "faith be changed for sight," as the popular theologians say that it will; for this invisible world is only to be "spiritually discerned."

This is the mystic idea, pure and simple; of course there are various grades of it, as there are of the popular one; for no man holds his own creed and nothing more; and it is good for him, in this piecemeal and shortsighted world, that he should not. Were he over-true to his own idea, he would become a fanatic, perhaps a madman. And so the modern evangelical of the Venn and Newton school, to whom mysticism is neology and nehushtan, when he speaks of "spiritual experiences," uses the adjective in its purely mystic sense; while Bernard of Cluny, in his once famous hymn, "Hic breve vivitur," mingles the two conceptions of the unseen world in inextricable confusion. Between these two extreme poles, in fact, we have every variety of thought; and it is good for us that we should have them; for no one man or school of men can grasp the whole truth, and every intermediate modification supplies some link in the great cycle of facts which its neighbours have overlooked.

In the minds who have held this belief, that the unseen world is the only real and eternal one, there has generally existed a belief, more or less confused, that the visible world is in some mysterious way a pattern or symbol of the invisible one; that its physical laws are the analogues of the spiritual laws of the eternal world: a belief of which Mr. Vaughan seems to think lightly; though if it be untrue we can hardly see how that metaphoric illustration in which he indulges so freely, and which he often uses in a masterly and graceful way, can be anything but useless trifling. For what is a metaphor or a simile but a mere paralogism—having nothing to do with the matter in hand, and not to be allowed for a moment to influence the reader's judgment, unless there be some real and objective analogy—homology we should call it—between the physical phenomenon from which the symbol is taken, and the spiritual truth which it is meant to illustrate? What divineness, what logical weight, in our Lord's parables, unless He was by them trying to show his hearers that the laws which they saw at work in the lilies of the field, in the most common occupations of men, were but lower manifestations of the laws by which are governed the inmost workings of the human spirit? What triflers, on any other ground, were Socrates and

Plato. What triflers, too, Shakespeare and Spenser. Indeed, we should say that it is the belief, conscious or unconscious, of the eternal correlation of the physical and spiritual worlds, which alone constitutes the essence of a poet.

Of course this idea led, and would necessarily lead, to follies and fancies enough, as long as the phenomena of nature were not carefully studied, and her laws scientifically investigated; and all the dreams of Paracelsus or Van Helmont, Cardan or Crollius, Baptista Porta or Behmen, are but the natural and pardonable errors of minds which, while they felt deeply the sanctity and mystery of Nature, had no Baconian philosophy to tell them what Nature actually was, and what she actually said. But their idea lives still, and will live as long as the belief in a one God lives. The physical and spiritual worlds cannot be separated by an impassable gulf. They must, in some way or other, reflect each other, even in their minutest phenomena, for so only can they both reflect that absolute primeval unity, in whom they both live and move and have their being. Mr. Vaughan's object, however, has not been to work out in his book such problems as these. Had he done so, he would have made his readers understand better what Mysticism is; he would have avoided several hasty epithets, by the use of which he has, we think, deceived himself into the notion that he has settled a matter by calling it a hard name; he would have explained, perhaps, to himself and to us, many strange and seemingly contradictory facts in the annals of Mysticism. But he would also not have written so readable a book. On the whole he has taken the right course, though one wishes that he had carried it out more methodically.

A few friends, literate and comfortable men, and right-hearted Christians withal, meet together to talk over these same mystics, and to read papers and extracts which will give a general notion of the subject from the earliest historic times. The gentlemen talk about and about a little too much; they are a little toc fond of illustrations of the popular pulpit style; they are often apt to say each his say, with very little care of what the previous speaker has uttered; in fact these conversations are, as conversations, not good, but as centres of thought they are excellent. There is not a page nor a paragraph in which there is not something well worth recollecting, and often reflections very wise and weighty indeed, which show that whether or not Mr. Vaughan has thoroughly grasped the subject of Mysticism, he has grasped and made part of his own mind and heart many things far more practically important than Mysticism, or any other form of thought; and no one ought to rise up from the perusal of his book without finding himself if not a better, at least a more thoughtful man, and perhaps a humble one also, as he learns how many more struggles and doubts, discoveries, sorrows and joys, the human race has passed through, than are contained in his own private experience.

The true value of the book is, that though not exhaustive of the subject, it is suggestive. It affords the best, indeed the only general, sketch of the subject which we have in England, and gives therein boundless food for future thought and reading; and the country parson, or the thoughtful professional man, who has no time to follow out the question for himself, much less to hunt out and examine original documents, may learn from these pages a thousand curious and interesting hints about men of like passions with himself, and about old times, the history of which—as of all times—was not the history of their kings and queens, but of the creeds and deeds of the "masses" who worked, and failed, and sorrowed, and rejoiced again, unknown to fame. Whatsoever, meanwhile, their own conclusions may be on the subject-matter of the book, they will hardly fail to admire the extraordinary variety and fulness of Mr. Vaughan's reading, and wonder when they hear—unless we are wrongly informed—that he is quite a young man—

> How one small head could compass all he knew.

He begins with the mysticism of the Hindoo Yogis. And to this, as we shall hereafter show, he hardly does justice; but we wish now to point out in detail the extended range of subjects, of each of which the book gives some general notion. From the Hindoos he passes to Philo and the neo-Platonists; from them to the pseudo-Dionysius, and the Mysticism of the early Eastern Church. He then traces, shrewdly enough, the influence of the pseudo-Areopagite and the Easterns on the bolder and more practical minds of the Western Latins, and gives a sketch of Bernard and his Abbey of Clairvaux, which brings pleasantly enough before us the ways and works of a long-dead world, which was all but inconceivable to us till Mr. Carlyle disinterred it in his picture of Abbot Sampson, the hero of "Past and Present."

We are next introduced to the mystic schoolmen—Hugo and Richard of St. Victor; and then to a far more interesting class of men, and one with which Mr. Vaughan has more sympathy than with any of his characters, perhaps because he knows more about them. His chapters on the German Mysticism of the fourteenth century; his imaginary, yet fruitful chronicle of Adolf of Arnstein, with its glimpses of Meister Eckart, Suso, the "Nameless Wild," Ruysbroek, and Tauler himself, are admirable, if merely as historic studies, and should be, and we doubt not will be, read by many as practical commentaries on the "Theologia Germanica," and on the selection from Tauler's "Sermons," now in course of publication. Had all the book been written as these chapters are, we should not have had a word of complaint to make, save when we find the author passing over without a word of comment, utterances which, right or wrong, contain the very keynote and central idea of the men whom he is holding up to admiration, and as we think, of Mysticism itself. There is, for instance, a paragraph attributed to Ruysbroek, in p. 275, vol. i., which, whether true or false—and we believe it to be essentially true—is so inexpressibly important, both in the subject which it treats, and in the way in which it treats it, that twenty pages of comment on it would not have been misdevoted. Yet it is passed by without a word.

Going forward to the age of the Reformation, the book then gives us a spirited glimpse of John Bokelson and the Munster Anabaptists, of Carlstadt and the

Zurichian prophets, and then dwells at some length on the attempt of that day to combine physical and spiritual science in occult philosophy. We have enough to make us wish to hear more of Cornelius Agrippa, Paracelsus, and Behmen, with their alchemy, "true magic," doctrines of sympathies,* signatures of things, Cabbala, and Gamahea, and the rest of that (now fallen) inverted pyramid of pseudo-science. His estimate of Behmen and his writings, we may observe in passing, is both sound and charitable, and speaks as much for Mr. Vaughan's heart as for his head. Then we have a little about the Rosicrucians and the Comte de Gabalis, and the theory of the Rabbis, from whom the Rosicrucians borrowed so much, all told in the same lively manner, all utterly new to ninety-nine readers out of a hundred, all indicating, we are bound to say, a much more extensive reading than appears on the page itself.

From these he passes to the Mysticism of the counter-Reformation, especially to the two great Spanish mystics, St. Theresa and St. John of the Cross. Here again he is new and interesting; but we must regret that he has not been as merciful to Theresa as he has to poor little John.

He then devotes some eighty pages—and very well employed they are—in detailing the strange and sad story of Madame Guyon and the "Quietist" movement

* Why has Mr. Vaughan omitted to give us a few racy lines on Sir Matthew Hale's "Divine Contemplations of the Magnet," Sir Kenelm Digby's "Weapon-Salve," and Valentine Greatrake's "Magnetic Cures"? He should have told the world a little, too, about the strange phenomenon of the Jesuit Kircher, in whom Popery attempted to recover the very ground which Behmen and the Protestant Nature-mystics were conquering from them.

at Louis Quatorze's Court. Much of this he has taken, with all due acknowledgment, from Upham; but he has told the story most pleasantly, in his own way, and these pages will give a better notion of Fénelon, and of the "Eagle" (for eagle read vulture) "of Meaux," old Bossuet, than they are likely to find elsewhere in the same compass.

Following chronological order as nearly as he can, he next passes to George Fox and the early Quakers, introducing a curious—and in our own case quite novel —little episode concerning "The History of Hai Ebn Yokhdan," a medieval Arabian romance, which old Barclay seems to have got hold of and pressed into the service of his sect, taking it for literal truth.

The twelfth book is devoted to Swedenborg, and a very valuable little sketch it is, and one which goes far to clear up the moral character, and the reputation for sanity also, of that much-calumniated philosopher, whom the world knows only as a dreaming false prophet, forgetting that even if he was that, he was also a sound and severe scientific labourer, to whom our modern physical science is most deeply indebted.

This is a short sketch of the contents of a book which is a really valuable addition to English literature, and which is as interesting as it is instructive. But Mr. Vaughan must forgive us if we tell him frankly that he has not exhausted the subject; that he has hardly defined Mysticism at all—at least, has defined it by its outward results, and that without classifying them; and that he has not grasped the central idea of the subject. There were more things in these same mystics than are dreamt of in his philosophy; and he has missed seeing them, because he has put himself rather in the attitude of a judge than of an inquirer.

He has not had respect and trust enough for the men and women of whom he writes; and is too much inclined to laugh at them, and treat them *de haut en bas*. He has trusted too much to his own great power of logical analysis, and his equally great power of illustration, and is therefore apt to mistake the being able to put a man's thoughts into words for him, for the being really able to understand him. To understand any man we must have sympathy for him, even affection. No intellectual acuteness, no amount even of mere pity for his errors, will enable us to see the man from within, and put our own souls into the place of his soul. To do that, one must feel and confess within oneself the seed of the same errors which one reproves in him; one must have passed more or less through his temptations, doubts, hunger of heart and brain; and one cannot help questioning, as one reads Mr. Vaughan's book, whether he has really done this in the case of those of whom he writes. He should have remembered too how little any young man can have experienced of the terrible sorrows which branded into the hearts of these old devotees the truths to which they clung more than to life, while they too often warped their hearts into morbidity, and caused alike their folly and their wisdom. Gently indeed should we speak even of the dreams of some self-imagined "Bride of Christ," when we picture to ourselves the bitter agonies which must have been endured ere a human soul could develop so fantastically diseased a growth. "She was only a hysterical nun." Well, and what more tragical object, to those who will look patiently and lovingly at human nature, than a hysterical nun? She may have been driven into a convent by some disappointment in love. And has not disappointed affection been confessed, in all climes and ages, to enshroud its victim ever after in a sanctuary of reverent pity? If sorrow "broke her brains," as well as broke her heart, shall we do aught but love her the more for her capacity of love? Or she may have entered the convent, as thousands did, in girlish simplicity, to escape from a world she had not tried, before she had discovered that the world could give her something which the convent could not. What more tragical than her discovery in herself of a capacity for love which could never be satisfied within that prison? And when that capacity began to vindicate itself in strange forms of disease, seemingly to her supernatural, often agonising, often degrading, and at the same time (strange contradiction) mixed itself up with her noblest thoughts, to ennoble them still more, and inspire her not only with a desire of physical self-torture, which would seem holy both in her own eyes and her priest's, but with a love for all that is fair and lofty, for self-devotion and self-sacrifice—shall we blame her—shall we even smile at her if, after the dreadful question: "Is this the possession of a demon?" had alternated with, "Is this the inspiration of a god?" she settled down, as the only escape from madness and suicide, into the latter thought and believed that she found in the idea l and perfect man hood of One whom she was told to revere and love as a God, and who had sacrificed His own life for her, a substitute for that merely human affection from which she was for ever debarred? Why blame her for not numbering that which was wanting, or making straight that which was crooked? Let God judge her, not we: and the fit critics of her conduct are not the easy gentleman-like scholars, like Mr. Vaughan's Athertons and Gowers, discussing the "aberrations of fanaticism" over wine and walnuts; or the gay girl, Kate; hardly even the happy mother, Mrs. Atherton; but those whose hairs are gray with sorrow; who have been softened at once and hardened in the fire of God; who have cried out of the bottomless deep like David, while lover and friend were hid away from them, and laid amid the corpses of their dead hopes, dead health, dead joy, as on a ghastly battle-field, "stript among the dead, like those who are wounded, and cut away from God's hands;" who have struggled drowning in the horrible mire of doubt, and have felt all God's billows and waves sweep over them, till they were weary of crying, and their sight failed for waiting so long upon God; and all the faith and prayer which was left was "Thou wilt not leave my soul in hell, nor suffer thy Holy One to see corruption." Be it understood, however, for fear of any mistake, that we hold Mr. Vaughan to be simply and altogether right in his main idea. His one test for all these people, and all which they said or did, is—Were they made practically better men and women thereby? He sees clearly that the "spiritual" is none other than the "moral"—that which has to do with right and wrong; and he has a righteous contempt for everything and anything, however graceful and reverent, and artistic and devout, and celestial and super-celestial, except in as far as he finds it making better men and women do better work at every-day life.

But even on this ground we must protest against such a sketch as this; even of one of the least honourable of the Middle-age saints:

> ATHERTON. Angela de Foligni, who made herself miserable—I must say something the converse of flourished—about the beginning of the fourteenth century, was a fine model pupil of this sort, a genuine daughter of St. Francis. Her mother, her husband, her children dead, she is alone and sorrowful. She betakes herself to violent devotion—falls ill—suffers incessant anguish from a complication of disorders—has rapturous consolations and terrific temptations—is dashed in a moment from a seat of glory above the empyrean . . .

Very amusing, is it not? To have one's mother, husband, children die—the most commonplace sort of things—what (over one's wine and walnuts) one describes as being "alone and sorrowful." Men who having tasted the blessings conveyed in those few words, have also found the horror conveyed in them, have no epithets for the state of mind in which such a fate would leave them. They simply pray that if that hour came, they might just have faith enough left not to curse God and die. Amusing, too, her falling ill, and suffering under a complication of disorders, especially if those disorders were the fruit of combined grief and widowhood. Amusing also her betaking herself to violent devotion! In the first place, if devotion be a good thing, could she have too much of it? If it be the way to make people good (as is commonly held by all Christian sects), could she become too good? The more important question which springs out of the fact we will ask presently. "She has rapturous consolations and terrific temptations." Did the consolations come first, and were the temptations a revulsion from "spiritual" exaltation into "spiritual" collapse and melancholy? or did the temptations come first, and the consolations come after, to save her from madness and despair? Either may be the case; perhaps both were: but somewhat more of care should have been taken in expressing so important a spiritual sequence as either case exhibits.

It is twelve years and more since we studied the history of the "B. Angela de Foligni," and many another kindred saint; and we cannot recollect what were the terrific temptations, what was the floor of hell which the poor thing saw yawning beneath her feet. But we must ask Mr. Vaughan, has he ever read Boccaccio, or any of the Italian novelists up to the seventeenth century? And if so, can he not understand how Angela de Foligni, the lovely Italian widow of the fourteenth century, had her terrific temptations, to which, if she had yielded, she might have fallen to the lowest pit of hell, let that word mean what it may; and temptations all the more terrific because she saw every widow round her considering them no temptations at all, but yielding to them, going out to invite them in the most business-like, nay, duty-like, way? What if she had "rapturous consolations"? What if she did pour out to One who was worthy not of less but of more affection than she offered in her passionate southern heart, in language which in our colder northerns would be mere hypocrisy, yet which she had been taught to believe lawful by that interpretation of the Canticles which (be it always remembered) is common to Evangelicals and to Romanists? What if even, in reward for her righteous belief, that what she saw all widows round her doing was abominable and to be avoided at all risks, she were permitted to enjoy a passionate affection, which after all was not misplaced? There are mysteries in religion as in all things, where it is better not to intrude behind the veil. Wisdom is justified of all her children: and folly may be justified of some of her children also.

Equally unfair it seems to us is the notice of St. Brigitta—in our eyes a beautiful and noble figure. A widow she, too—and what worlds of sorrow are there in that word, especially when applied to the pure deep-hearted Northern woman, as she was—she leaves her Scandinavian pine-forests to worship and to give wherever she can, till she arrives at Rome, the centre of the universe, the seat of Christ's vicegerent, the city of God, the gate of Paradise. Thousands of weary miles she travels, through danger and sorrow—and when she finds it, behold it is a lie and a sham! not the gate of Paradise, but the gate of Sodom and of hell. Was not that enough to madden her, if mad she became? What matter after that her "angel dictated discourses on the Blessed Virgin," "bombastic invocations to the Saviour's eyes, ears, hair?"—they were at least the best objects of worship which the age gave her. In one thing she was right, and kept her first love. "What was not quite so bad, she gives to the world a series of revelations, in which the vices of popes and prelates are lashed unsparingly and threatened with speedy judgment." Not quite so bad? To us the whole phenomenon wears an utterly different aspect. At the risk of her life, at the risk of being burned alive—did anyone ever consider what that means?—the noble Norsewoman, like an Alruna maid of old, hurls out her divine hereditary hatred of sin and filth and lies. At last she falls back on Christ Himself, as the only home for a homeless soul in such an evil time. And she is not burnt alive. The hand of One mightier than she is over her, and she is safe under the shadow of His wings till her weary work is done and she goes home, her righteousness accepted for His sake: her folly, hysterics, dreams—call them by what base name we will—forgiven and forgotten for the sake of her many sorrows and her faithfulness to the end.

But whatever fault we can find with these sketches, we can find none with Mr. Vaughan's reflections on them:

What a condemning comment on the pretended tender mercies of the Church are those narratives which Rome delights to parade of the sufferings, mental and bodily, which her devotees were instructed to inflict upon themselves! I am reminded of the thirsting mule, which has, in some countries, to strike with his hoof among the spines of the cactus, and drink, with lamed foot and bleeding lips, the few drops of milk which ooze from the broken thorns. Affectionate, suffering natures came to Rome for comfort; but her scanty kindness is only to be drawn with anguish from the cruel sharpness of asceticism. The worldly, the audacious, escape easily; but these pliant excitable temperaments, so anxiously in earnest, may be made useful. The more dangerous, frightful, or unnatural their performances, the more profit for their keepers. Men and women are trained by torturing processes to deny their nature, and then they are exhibited to bring grist to the mill—like birds and beasts forced to postures and services against the laws of their being—like those who must perform perilous feats on ropes or with lions, nightly hazarding their lives to fill the pockets of a manager. The self-devotedness of which Rome boasts so much is a self-devotion she has always thus made the most of for herself. Calculating men who have thought only of the interest of the priesthood, have known well how best to stimulate and to display the spasmodic movements of a brainsick disinterestedness. I have not the shadow of a doubt that, once and again, some priest might have been seen, with cold gray eye, endeavouring to do a stroke of diplomacy by means of the enthusiastic Catherine, making the fancied ambassadress of Heaven in reality the tool of a schemer. Such unquestionable virtues as these visionaries may some of them have possessed cannot be fairly set down to the credit of the Church, which has used them all for mercenary or ambitious purposes, and infected them everywhere with a morbid character. Some of these mystics, floating down the great ecclesiastical current of the Middle Age, appear to me like the trees carried away by the inundation of some mighty tropical river. They drift along the stream, passive, lifeless, broken; yet they are covered with gay verdure, the aquatic plants hang and twine about the sodden timber and the draggled leaves, the trunk is a sailing garden of flowers. But the adornment is that of Nature—it is the decoration of another and a strange element: the roots are in the air: the boughs which should be full of birds, are in the flood, covered by its alien products, swimming side by side with the alligator. So has this priestcraft swept its victims from their natural place and independent growth, to clothe them in their helplessness with a false spiritual adornment, neither scriptural nor human, but ecclesiastical—the native product of that overwhelming superstition which has subverted and enslaved their nature. The Church of Rome takes care that while simple souls think they are cultivating Christian graces they shall be forging their own chains; that their attempts to honour God shall always dishonour, because they disenfranchise themselves. To be humble, to be obedient, to be charitable, under such direction, is to be contentedly ignorant, pitiably abject, and notoriously swindled.

Mr. Vaughan cannot be too severe upon the Romish priesthood. But it is one thing to dismiss with summary contempt men, who, as they do, keep the keys of knowledge, and neither enter in themselves nor suffer others to enter, and quite another thing to apply the same summary jurisdiction to men who, under whatsoever confusions, are feeling earnestly and honestly after truth. And therefore we regret exceedingly the mock trial which he has introduced into his Introduction. We regret it for his own sake; for it will drive away from the book—indeed it has driven—thoughtful and reverent people who, having a strong though vague inclination toward the Mystics, might be very profitably taught by the after pages to separate the evil from the good in the Bernards and Guyons whom they admire, they scarce know why; and will shock, too, scholars, to whom Hindoo and Persian thoughts on these subjects are matters not of ridicule but of solemn and earnest investigation.

Besides, the question is not so easily settled. Putting aside the flippancy of the passage, it involves something very like a petitio principii to ask offhand: "Does the man mean a living union of heart to Christ, a spiritual fellowship or converse with the Father, when he talks of the union of the believer with God—participation in the Divine nature?" For first, what we want to know is, the meaning of the words—what means "living"? what "union"? what "heart"? They are terms common to the Mystic and to the popular religionist, only differently interpreted; and in the meanings attributed to them lies nothing less than the whole world-old dispute between Nominalist and Realist not yet to be settled in two lines by two gentlemen over their wine, much less ignored as a thing settled beyond all dispute already. If by "living union of heart with"—Mr. Vaughan meant "identity of morals with"—he should have said so: but he should have borne in mind that all the great evangelicals have meant much more than this by those words; that on the whole, instead of considering—as he seems to do, and we do—the moral and the spiritual as identical, they have put them in antithesis to each other, and looked down upon "mere morality" just because it did not seem to them to involve that supernatural, transcendental, "mystic" element which they considered that they found in Scripture. From Luther to Owen and Baxter, from them to Wesley, Cecil, and Venn, Newton, Bridges, the great evangelical authorities would (not very clearly or consistently, for they were but poor metaphysicians, but honestly and earnestly) have accepted some modified form of the Mystic's theory, even to the "discerning in particular thoughts, frames, impulses, and inward witnessings, immediate communications from heaven." Surely Mr. Vaughan must be aware that the majority of "vital Christians" on this ground are among his mystic offenders; and that those who deny such possibilities are but too liable to be stigmatised as "Pelagians," and "Rationalists." His friend Atherton is bound to show cause why those names are not to be applied to him, as he is bound to show what he means by "living union with Christ," and why he complains of the Mystic for desiring "participation in the Divine nature." If he does so, he only desires what the New Testament formally, and word for word, promises him; whatsoever be the meaning of the term, he is not to be blamed for using it. Mr. Vaughan cannot have forgotten the many expressions, both of St. Paul and St. John, which do at first sight go far to justify the Mystic, though they are but seldom heard, and more seldom boldly commented on, in modern pulpits—of Christ being formed in men, dwelling in men; of God dwelling in man and man in God; of Christ being the life of men; of men living, and moving, and having their being in God; and many another passage. If these be mere metaphors let the fact be stated, with due reason for it. But there is no sin or shame in interpreting them in that literal and realist sense in which they seem at first sight to have been written. The first duty of a scholar who sets before himself to investigate the phenomena of "Mysticism," so called, should be to answer these questions: Can there be a direct communication, above and beyond sense or consciousness, between the human spirit and God the Spirit? And if so, what are its conditions, where its limits, to transcend which is to fall into "mysticism"?

And it is just this which Mr. Vaughan fails in doing. In his sketch, for instance, of the Mysticism of India, he gives us a very clear and (save in two points) sound summary of that "round of notions, occurring to minds of similar make under similar circumstances," which is "common to Mystics in ancient India and in modern Christendom."

Summarily, I would say this Hindoo mysticism—

(1) Lays claim to disinterested love as opposed to a mercenary religion;

(2) Reacts against the ceremonial prescription and pedantic literalism of the Vedas;

(3) Identifies, in its pantheism, subject and object, worshipper and worshipped ;

(4) Aims at ultimate absorption in the Infinite;

(5) Inculcates, as the way to this dissolution, absolute passivity, withdrawal into the inmost self, cessation of all the powers: giving recipes for procuring this beatific torpor or trance;

(6) Believes that eternity may thus be realised in time;

(7) Has its mythical miraculous pretensions, *i.e.* its theurgic department;

(8) And, finally, advises the learner in this kind of religion to submit himself implicitly to a spiritual guide—his Guru.

Against the two latter articles we except. The theurgic department of Mysticism—unfortunately but too common—seems to us always to have been (as it certainly was in neo-Platonism) the despairing return to that ceremonialism which it had begun by shaking off, when it was disappointed in reaching its high aim by its proper method. The use of the Guru, or Father Confessor (which Mr. Vaughan confesses to be inconsistent with Mysticism), is to be explained in the same way—he is a last refuge after disappointment.

But as for the first six counts. Is the Hindoo mystic a worse or a better man for holding them? Are they on the whole right or wrong? Is not disinterested love nobler than a mercenary religion? Is it not right to protest against ceremonial prescriptions, and to say, with the later prophets and psalmists of the Jews: "Thinkest thou that He will eat bull's flesh, and drink the blood of goats. Sacrifice and burnt-offering Thou wouldst not. . . . I come to do thy will, O God!" What is, even, if he will look calmly into it, the "pantheistic identification of subject and object, worshipper and worshipped," but the clumsy yet honest effort of the human mind to say to itself: "Doing God's will is the real end and aim of man?" The Yogi looks round upon his fellow-men, and sees that all their misery and shame come from self-will; he looks within, and finds that all which makes him miserable, angry, lustful, greedy after this and that, comes from the same self-will. And he asks himself: How shall I escape from this torment of self?—how shall I tame my wayward will, till it shall become one with the harmonious, beautiful, and absolute Will which made all things? At least I will try to do it, whatever it shall cost me. I will give up all for which men live—wife and child, the sights, scents, sounds of this fair earth, all things, whatever they be, which men call enjoyment; I will make this life one long torture, if need be; but this rebel will of mine I will conquer. I ask for no reward. That may come in some future life. But what care I? I am now miserable by reason of the lusts which war in my members; the peace which I shall gain in being freed from them will be its own reward. After all I give up little. All these things round me—the primeval forest, and the sacred stream of Ganga, the mighty Himalaya, mount of God, ay, the illimitable vault of heaven above me, sun and stars—what are they but "such stuff as dreams are made of"? Brahm thought, and they became something and somewhere. He may think again, and they will become nothing and nowhere. Are these eternal, greater than I, worth troubling my mind about? Nothing is eternal, but the Thought which made them, and will unmake them. They are only venerable in my eyes, because each of them is a thought of Brahm's. And I too have thought; I alone of all the kinds of living things. Am I not, then, akin to God? what better for me than to sit down and think, as Brahm thinks, and so enjoy my eternal heritage, leaving for those who cannot think the passions and pleasures which they share in common with the beasts of the field? So I shall become more and more like Brahm—will his will, think his thoughts, till I lose utterly this house-fiend of self, and become one with God.

Is this a man to be despised? Is he a sickly dreamer, or a too valiant hero? and if any one be shocked at this last utterance, let him consider carefully the words which he may hear on Sunday: "Then we dwell in Christ, and Christ in us; we are one with Christ, and Christ with us." That belief is surely not a false one. Shall we abhor the Yogi because he has seen, sitting alone there amid idolatry and licentiousness, despotism and priestcraft, that the ideal goal of man is what we confess it to be in the communion service? Shall we not rather wonder and rejoice over the magnificent utterance in that Bhagavat-Gita which Mr. Vaughan takes for the text-book of Hindoo Mysticism, where Krishna, the teacher human, and yet God himself, speaks thus:

> There is nothing greater than I; all things hang on me, as precious gems upon a string. . . . I am life in all things, and zeal in the zealous. I am the eternal seed of nature: I am the understanding of the wise, the glory of the proud, the strength of the strong, free from lust and anger. . . . Those who trust in me know Brahm, the supreme and incorruptible. . . . In this body I am the teacher of worship. He who thinks of me will find me. He who finds me returns not again to mortal birth. . . . I am the sacrifice, I am the worship,

I am the incense, I am the fire, I am the victim, I am the father and mother of the world; I am the road of the good, the comforter, the creator, the witness, the asylum, and the friend. They who serve other Gods with a firm belief, involuntarily worship me. I am the same to all mankind. They who serve me in adoration are in me. If one whose ways are ever so evil serve me alone, he becometh of a virtuous spirit and obtaineth eternal happiness. Even women, and the tribes of Visya and Soodra, shall go the supreme journey if they take sanctuary with me; how much more my holy servants the Brahmins and the Ragarshees! Consider this world as a finite and joyless place, and serve me.

There may be confused words scattered up and down here; there are still more confused words—not immoral ones—round them, which we have omitted; but we ask, once and for all, is this true, or is it not? Is there a being who answers to this description, or is there not? And if there be, was it not a light price to pay for the discovery of Him "to sit upon the sacred grass called koos, with his mind fixed on one object alone; keeping his head, neck, and body steady, without motion; his eyes fixed upon the point of his nose, looking at no other place around"—or any other simple, even childish, practical means of getting rid of the disturbing bustle and noise of the outward time-world, that he might see the eternal world which underlies it? What if the discovery be imperfect, the figure in many features erroneous? Is not the wonder to us, the honour to him, that the figure should be there at all? Inexplicable to us on any ground, save that one common to the Bhagavat-Gita, to the gospel. "He who seeks me shall find me." What if he knew but in part, and saw through a glass darkly? Was there not an inspired apostle, who could but say the very same thing of himself, and look forward to a future life in which he would "know even as he was known"?

It is well worth observing too, that so far from the moral of this Bhagavat-Gita issuing in mere contemplative Quietism, its purpose is essentially practical. It arises out of Arjoun's doubt whether he shall join in the battle which he sees raging below him; it results in his being commanded to join in it, and fight like a man. We cannot see, as Mr. Vaughan does, an "unholy indifference" in the moral. Arjoun shrinks from fighting because friends and relatives are engaged on both sides, and he dreads hell if he kills one of them. The answer to his doubt is, after all, the only one which makes war permissible to a Christian, who looks on all men as his brothers:

"You are a Ksahtree, a soldier; your duty is to fight. Do your duty, and leave the consequences of it to him who commanded the duty. You cannot kill these men's souls any more than they can yours. You can only kill their mortal bodies; the fate of their souls and yours depends on their moral state. Kill their bodies, then, if it be your duty, instead of tormenting yourself with scruples, which are not really scruples of conscience, only selfish fears of harm to yourself, and leave their souls to the care of Him who made them, and knows them, and cares more for them than you do."

This seems to be the plain outcome of the teaching. What is it, mutatis mutandis, but the sermon "cold-blooded" or not, which every righteous soldier has to preach to himself, day by day, as long as his duty commands him to kill his human brothers?

Yet the fact is undeniable that Hindoo Mysticism has failed of practical result—that it has died down into brutal fakeerism. We look in vain, however, in Mr. Vaughan's chapter for an explanation of this fact, save his assertion, which we deny, that Hindoo Mysticism was in essence and at its root wrong and rotten. Mr. Maurice ("Moral and Metaphysical Philosophy," p. 46) seems to point to a more charitable solution. "The Hindoo," he says, "whatsoever vast discovery he may have made at an early period of a mysterious Teacher near him, working on his spirit, who is at the same time Lord over nature, began the search from himself—he had no other point from whence to begin—and therefore it ended in himself. The purification of his individual soul became practically his highest conceivable end; to carry out that he must separate from society. Yet the more he tries to escape self the more he finds self; for what are his thoughts about Brahm, his thoughts about Krishna, save his own thoughts? Is Brahm a projection of his own soul? To sink in him, does it mean to be nothing? Am I, after all, my own law? And hence the downward career into stupid indifferentism, even into Antinomian profligacy."

The Hebrew, on the other hand, begins from the belief of an objective external God, but One who cares for more than his individual soul; as One who is the ever-present guide, and teacher, and ruler of his whole nation; who regards that nation as a whole, a one person, and that not merely one present generation, but all, past or future, as a one "Israel"—lawgivers, prophets, priests, warriors. All classes are His ministers.

He is essentially a political deity, who cares infinitely for the polity of a nation, and therefore bestows one upon them—"a law of Jehovah." Gradually, under this teaching, the Hebrew rises to the very idea of an inward teacher, which the Yogi had, and to a far purer and clearer form of that idea; but he is not tempted by it to selfish individualism, or contemplative isolation, as long as he is true to the old Mosaic belief, that this being is the Political Deity. "the King of Kings." The Pharisee becomes a selfish individualist just because he has forgotten this; the Essene, a selfish "mystic" for the same reason; Philo and the Jewish mystics of Alexandria lose in like manner all notion that Jehovah is the lawgiver, and ruler, and archetype of family and of national life. Christianity retained the idea; it brought out the meaning of the old Jewish polity in its highest form; for that very reason it was able to bring out the meaning of the "mystic" idea in its highest form also, without injury to men's work as members of families, as citizens, as practical men of the world; and so to conquer at last that Manichæan hatred of marriage and parentage, which from the first to the sixteenth century shed its Upas shade over the Church.

And here let us say boldly to Mr. Vaughan and to our readers: As long as "the salvation of a man's own soul" is set forth in all pulpits as the first and last end and aim of mortal existence; as long as Christianity is dwelt on merely as influencing individuals each apart —as "brands plucked, one here and another there, from the general burning"—so long will Mysticism, in its highest form be the refuge of the strongest spirits, and in its more base and diseased forms the refuge of the weak and sentimental spirits. They will say, each in his own way: "You confess that there can be a direct relation, communion, inspiration, from God to my soul, as I sit alone in my chamber. You do not think that there is such between God and what you call the world; between Him and nations as wholes—families, churches, schools of thought, as wholes; that He does not take a special interest, or exercise a special influence, over the ways and works of men—over science, commerce, civilisation, colonisation, all which affects the earthly destinies of the race. All these you call secular; to admit His influence over them for their own sake (though of course He overrules them for the sake of His elect) savours of Pantheism. Is it so? Then we will give up the world. We will cling to the one fact which you confess to be certain about us—that we can take refuge in God, each in the loneliness of his chamber, from all the vain turmoil of a race which is hastening heedless into endless misery. You may call us Mystics, or what you will. We will possess our souls in patience, and turn away our eyes from vanity. We will commune with our own hearts in solitude, and be still. We will not even mingle in your religious world, the world which you have invented for yourselves, after denying that God's human world is sacred; for it seems to us as full of intrigue, ambition, party-spirit, falsehood, bitterness, and ignorance, as the political world, or the fashionable world, or the scientific world; and we will have none of it. Leave us alone with God."

This has been the true reason of mystical isolation

in every age and country. So thought Macarius and the Christian fakeers of the Thebaid. So thought the medieval monks and nuns. So thought the German Quietists when they revolted from the fierce degradation of decaying Lutheranism. So are hundreds thinking now; so may thousands think ere long. If the individualising phase of Christianity which is now dominant shall long retain its ascendancy, and the creed of Dr. Cumming and Mr. Spurgeon become that of the British people, our purest and noblest spirits will act here, with regard to religion, as the purest and noblest in America have acted with regard to politics. They will withdraw each into the sanctuary of his own heart, and leave the battle-field to rival demagogues. They will do wrong, it may be. Isolation involves laziness, pride, cowardice; but if sober England, during the next half-century, should be astonished by an outburst of Mysticism, as grand in some respects, as fantastic in others, as that of the thirteenth or the seventeenth centuries, the blame, if blame there be, will lie with those leaders of the public conscience who, after having debased alike the Church of England and the dissenting sects with a selfish individualism which was as foreign to the old Cromwellite Ironside as to the High Church divine, have tried to debar their disciples from that peaceful and graceful Mysticism which is the only excusable or tolerable form of religion beginning and ending in self.

Let it be always borne in mind, that Quakerism was not a protest against, or a revulsion from, the Church of England, but from Calvinism. The steeple-houses, against which George Fox testified, were not served by

Henry Mores, Cudworths, or Norrises: not even by dogmatist High-Churchmen, but by Calvinist ministers, who had ejected them. George Fox developed his own scheme, such as it was, because the popular Protestantism of his day failed to meet the deepest wants of his heart; because, as he used to say, it gave him "a dead Christ," and he required "a living Christ." Doctrines about who Christ is, he held, are not Christ Himself. Doctrines about what He has done for man, are not He himself. Fox held, that if Christ be a living person, He must act (when He acted) directly on the most inward and central personality of him, George Fox; and his desire was satisfied by the discovery of the indwelling Logos, or rather by its re-discovery, after it had fallen into oblivion for centuries. Whether he were right or wrong, he is a fresh instance of a man's arriving, alone and unassisted, at the same idea at which Mystics of all ages and countries have arrived: a fresh corroboration of our belief, that there must be some reality corresponding to a notion which has manifested itself so variously, and among so many thousands of every creed, and has yet arrived, by whatsoever different paths, at one and the same result.

That he was more or less right—that there is nothing in the essence of Mysticism contrary to practical morality, Mr. Vaughan himself fully confesses. In his fair and liberal chapters on Fox and the Early Quakers, he does full justice to their intense practical benevolence; to the important fact that Fox only lived to do good, of any and every kind, as often as a sorrow to be soothed, or an evil to be remedied, crossed his path. We only wish that he had also brought in the curious and affecting account of Fox's interview with Cromwell, in which he tells us (and we will take Fox's word against any man) that the Protector gave him to understand, almost with tears, that there was that in Fox's faith which he was seeking in vain from the "ministers" around him.

All we ask of Mr. Vaughan is, not to be afraid of his own evident liking for Fox; of his own evident liking for Tauler and his school; not to put aside the question which their doctrines involve, with such half-utterances as—

> The Quakers are wrong, I think, in separating particular movements and monitions as Divine. But, at the same time, the "witness of the Spirit," as regards our state before God, is something more, I believe, than the mere attestation to the written word.

As for the former of these two sentences, he may be quite right, for aught we know. But it must be said on the other hand, that not merely Quakers, but decent men of every creed and age, have—we may dare to say, in proportion to their devoutness—believed in such monitions; and that it is hard to see how any man could have arrived at the belief that a living person was working on him, and not a mere unpersonal principle, law, or afflatus—(spirit of the universe, or other metaphor for hiding materialism)—unless by believing, rightly or wrongly, in such monitions. For our only inductive conception of a living person demands that that person shall make himself felt by separate acts.

But against the second sentence we must protest. The question in hand is not whether this "witness of the Spirit" "is something more" than anything else, but whether it exists at all, and what it is. Why was the book written, save to help toward the solution of this very matter? The question all through has been: Can an immediate influence be exercised by the Spirit of God on the spirit of man? Mr. Vaughan assents, and says (we cannot see why) that there is no mysticism in such a belief. Be that as it may, what that influence is, and how exercised, is all through the de quo agitur of Mysticism. Mr. Vaughan, however, seems here for awhile to be talking realism through an admirable page, well worth perusal (pp. 264, 265). Yet his grasp is not sure. We soon find him saying what More and Fox would alike deny, that "The story of Christ's life and death is our soul's food." No; Christ Himself is—would the Catholic Church and the Mystic alike answer. And here again the whole matter in dispute is (unconsciously to Mr. Vaughan) opened up in one word. And if this sentence does not bear directly on that problem, on what does it bear? It was therefore with extreme disappointment that on reading this, and saying to ourselves: "Now we shall hear at last what Mr. Vaughan himself thinks on the matter," we found that he literally turned the subject off, as if not worth investigation, by making the next speaker answer, apropos of nothing, that "the traditional ascetism of the Friends is their fatal defect as a body."

Why, too, has Mr. Vaughan devoted a few lines only to the great English Platonists, More, Norris, Smith of Jesus, Gale, and Cudworth? He says, indeed, that they are scarcely Mystics, except in as far as Platonism is always in a measure mystical. In our sense of the word they were all of them Mystics, and of a very lofty type; but surely Henry More is a Mystic in Mr. Vaughan's sense also. If the author of "Conjectura Cabbalistica" be not a mystical writer (he himself uses the term without shame), who is?

We hope to see much in this book condensed, much modified, much worked out, instead of being left fragmentary and embryotic; but whether our hope be fulfilled or not, a useful and honourable future is before the man who could write such a book as this is, in spite of all defects.

* * * * *

Since the above was written, Mr. Vaughan's premature death has robbed us of a man who might have done brave work, by lessening, through his own learning, the intellectual gulf which now exists between English Churchmen and Dissenters. Dîs aliter visum. But Mr. Vaughan's death does not, I think, render it necessary for me to alter any of the opinions expressed here; and least of all that in the last sentence, fulfilled now more perfectly than I could have foreseen.

FREDERICK DENISON MAURICE.

IN MEMORIAM.

FREDERICK DENISON MAURICE.*

IN MEMORIAM.

On Friday, the fifth of April, a noteworthy assemblage gathered round an open vault in a corner of Highgate Cemetery. Some hundreds of persons, closely packed up the steep banks among the trees and shrubs, had found in that grave a common bond of brotherhood. I say, in that grave. They were no sect, clique, or school of disciples, held together by community of opinions. They were simply men and women, held together, for the moment at least, by love of a man, and that man, as they had believed, a man of God. All shades of opinion, almost of creed, were represented there; though the majority were members of the Church of England—many probably reconciled to that Church by him who lay below. All sorts and conditions of men, and indeed of women, were there; for he had had a word for all sorts and conditions of men. Most of them had never seen each other before—would never see each other again. But each felt that the man, however unknown to him who stood next

* Macmillan's Magazine, May 1872.

him, was indeed a brother in loyalty to that beautiful soul, beautiful face, beautiful smile, beautiful voice, from which, in public or in secret, each had received noble impulses, tender consolation, loving correction, and clearer and juster conceptions of God, of duty, of the meaning of themselves and of the universe. And when they turned and left his body there, the world—as one said who served him gallantly and long—seemed darker now he had left it; but he had stayed here long enough to do the work for which he was fitted. He had wasted no time, but died, like a valiant man, at his work, and of his work.

He might have been buried in Westminster Abbey. There was no lack of men of mark who held that such a public recognition of his worth was due, not only to the man himself, but to the honour of the Church of England. His life had been one of rare sanctity; he was a philosopher of learning and acuteness, unsurpassed by any man of his generation; he had done more than any man of that generation to defend the Church's doctrines; to recommend her to highly-cultivated men and women; to bring within her pale those who had been born outside it, or had wandered from it; to reconcile the revolutionary party among the workmen of the great cities with Christianity, order, law; to make all ranks understand that if Christianity meant anything, it meant that a man should not merely strive to save his own soul after death, but that he should live here the life of a true citizen, virtuous, earnest, helpful to his human brethren. He had been the originator of, or at least the chief mover in, working-men's colleges, schemes for the higher education of women, for the protection of the weak and the oppressed. He had been the champion, the organiser, the helper with his own money and time, of that co-operative movement—the very germ of the economy of the future—which seems now destined to spread, and with right good results, to far other classes, and in far other forms, than those of which Mr. Maurice was thinking five-and-twenty years ago. His whole life had been one of unceasing labour for that which he believed to be truth and right, and for the practical amelioration of his fellow-creatures. He had not an enemy, unless it were here and there a bigot or a dishonest man—two classes who could not abide him, because they knew well that he could not abide them. But for the rest, those from whom he had differed most, with whom he had engaged, ere now, in the sharpest controversy, had learned to admire his sanctity, charity, courtesy—for he was the most perfect of gentlemen—as well as to respect his genius and learning. He had been welcomed to Cambridge, by all the finer spirits of the University, as Professor of Moral Philosophy; and as such, and as the parish priest of St. Edward's, he had done his work—as far as failing health allowed—as none but he could do it. Nothing save his own too-scrupulous sense of honour had prevented him from accepting some higher ecclesiastical preferment—which he would have used, alas! not for literary leisure, nor for the physical rest which he absolutely required, but merely as an excuse for greater and more arduous toil. If such a man was not the man whom the Church of England would delight to honour, who was the man? But he was gone; and a grave among England's worthies was all that could be offered him now; and it was offered. But those whose will on such a point was law, judged it to be more in keeping with the exquisite modesty and humility of Frederick Denison Maurice, that he should be laid out of sight, though not out of mind, by the side of his father and his mother. Well: be it so. At least that green nook at Highgate will be a sacred spot to hundreds—it may be to thousands—who owe him more than they will care to tell to any created being.

It was, after all, in this—in his personal influence—that Mr. Maurice was greatest. True, he was a great and rare thinker. Those who wish to satisfy themselves of this should measure the capaciousness of his intellect by studying—not by merely reading—his Boyle Lectures on the Religions of the world; and that Kingdom of Christ, the ablest "Apology" for the Catholic Faith which England has seen for more than two hundred years. The ablest, and perhaps practically the most successful; for it has made the Catholic Faith look living, rational, practical, and practicable, to hundreds who could rest neither in modified Puritanism nor modified Romanism, and still less in scepticism, however earnest. The fact that it is written from a Realist point of view, as all Mr. Maurice's books are, will make it obscure to many readers. Nominalism is just now so utterly in the ascendant, that most persons seem to have lost the power of thinking, as well as of talking, by any other method. But when the tide of thought shall turn, this, and the rest of Mr. Maurice's works, will become not only precious but luminous, to a generation which will have recollected that substance does not mean matter, that a person is not the net result of his circumstances, and that the real is not the visible Actual, but the invisible Ideal.

If anyone, again, would test Mr. Maurice's faculty as an interpreter of Scripture, let him study the two volumes on the Gospel and the Epistles of St. John; and study, too, the two volumes on the Old Testament, which have been (as a fact) the means of delivering more than one or two from both the Rationalist and the Mythicist theories of interpretation. I mention these only as peculiar examples of Mr. Maurice's power. To those who have read nothing of his, I would say: "Take up what book you will, you will be sure to find in it something new to you, something noble, something which, if you can act on it, will make you a better man." And if anyone, on making the trial, should say: "But I do not understand the book. It is to me a new world;" then it must be answered: "If you wish to read only books which you can understand at first sight confine yourself to periodical literature. As for finding yourself in a new world, is it not good sometimes to do that?—to discover how vast the universe of mind, as well as of matter, is; that it contains many worlds; and that wise and beautiful souls may and do live in more worlds than your own?" Much has been said of the obscurity of Mr. Maurice's style. It is a question whether any great thinker will be anything but obscure at times; simply because he is possessed by conceptions beyond his powers of expression. But the conceptions may be clear enough; and it may be worth the wise man's while to search for them under the imperfect words. Only thus—to take an illustrious instance—has St. Paul, often the most obscure of writers, become luminous to students; and there are those who will hold that St. Paul is by no means understood yet; and that the Calvinistic system which has been built upon his Epistles, has been built up upon a total ignoring of the greater part of them, and a total misunderstanding of the remainder: yet, for all that, no Christian man will lightly shut up St. Paul as too obscure for use. Really, when one considers what worthless verbiage which men have ere now, and do still, take infinite pains to make themselves fancy that they understand, one is tempted to impatience when men confess that they will not take the trouble of trying to understand Mr. Maurice.

Yet after all, I know no work which gives a fairer measure of Mr. Maurice's intellect, both political and exegetic, and a fairer measure likewise, of the plain downright common sense which he brought to bear on each of so many subjects, than his Commentary on the very book which is supposed to have least connection with common sense, and on which common sense has as yet been seldom employed—namely, the Apocalypse of St. John. That his method of interpretation is the right one can hardly be doubted by those who perceive that it is the one and only method on which any fair exegesis is possible—namely, to ask: What must these words have meant to those to whom they were actually spoken? That Mr. Maurice is more reverent, by being more accurate, more spiritual, by being more practical, in his interpretation than commentators on this book have usually been, will be seen the more the book is studied, and found to be what any and every commentary on the Revelation ought to be—a mine of political wisdom. Sayings will be found which will escape the grasp of most readers, as indeed they do mine, so pregnant are they, and swift revealing, like the lightning-flash at night, a whole vision: but only for a moment's space. The reader may find also details of interpretation which are open to doubt; if so, he will remember that no man would have shrunk with more horror than Mr. Maurice from the assumption of infallibility. Meanwhile, that the author's manly confidence in the reasonableness of his method will be justified hereafter, I must hope, if the Book of Revelation is to remain, as God grant it may, the political text-book of the Christian Church.

On one matter, however, Mr. Maurice is never obscure—on questions of right and wrong. As with St. Paul, his theology, however seemingly abstruse, always results in some lesson of plain practical morality. To do the right and eschew the wrong, and that not from hope of reward or fear of punishment—in which case the right ceases to be right—but because a man loves the right and hates the wrong; about this there is no hesitation or evasion in Mr. Maurice's writings. If any man is in search of a mere philosophy, like the neo-Platonists of old, or of a mere system of dogmas, by assenting to which he will gain a right to look down on the unorthodox, while he is absolved from the duty of becoming a better man than he is and as good a man as he can be—then let him beware of Mr. Maurice's books, lest, while searching merely for "thoughts that breathe," he should stumble upon "words that burn," and were meant to burn. His books, like himself, are full of that θυμός, that capacity of indignation, which Plato says is the root of all virtues. "There was something," it has been well said, "so awful, and yet so Christ-like in its awful sternness, in the expression which came over that beautiful face when he heard of anything base or cruel or wicked, that it brought home to the bystander our Lord's judgment of sin."

And here, perhaps, lay the secret of the extraordinary personal influence which he exercised; namely, in that truly formidable element which underlaid a character which (as one said of him) "combined all that was noblest in man and woman; all the tenderness and all the strength, all the sensitiveness and all the fire, of both; and with that a humility which made men feel the utter baseness, meanness, of all pretension." For can there be true love without wholesome fear? And does not the old Elizabethan "My dear dread" express the noblest voluntary relation in which two human souls can stand to each other? Perfect love casteth out fear. Yes: but where is love perfect among imperfect beings, save a mother's for her child? For all the rest, it is through fear that love is made perfect; fear which bridles and guides the lover with awe—even though misplaced—of the beloved one's perfections; with dread—never misplaced—of the beloved one's contempt. And therefore it is that souls who have the germ of nobleness within, are drawn to souls more noble than themselves, just because, needing guidance, they cling to one before whom they dare not say or do, or even think, an ignoble thing. And if these higher souls are—as they usually are—not merely formidable, but tender likewise, and true, then the influence which they may gain is unbounded, for good—or, alas! for evil—both to themselves and to those that worship them. Woe to the man who, finding that God has given him influence over human beings for their good, begins to use it after awhile, first only to carry out through them his own little system of the Universe, and found a school or sect; and at last by steady and necessary degradation, mainly to feed his own vanity and his own animal sense of power.

But Mr. Maurice, above all men whom I have ever met, conquered both these temptations. For, first, he had no system of the Universe. To have founded a sect, or even a school, would be, he once said, a sure sign that he was wrong and was leading others wrong. He was a Catholic and a Theologian, and he wished all men to be such likewise. To be so, he held, they must know God in Christ. If they knew God, then with them, as with himself, they would have the key which would unlock all knowledge, ecclesiastical, eschatological (religious, as it is commonly called), historic, political, social. Nay even, so he hoped, that knowledge of God would prove at last to be the key to the right understanding of that physical science of which he, unfortunately for the world, knew but too little, but which he accepted with a loyal trust in God, and in fact as the voice of God, which won him respect and love from men of science to whom his theology was a foreign world. If he could make men know God, and therefore if he could make men know that God was teaching them; that no man could see a thing unless God first showed it to him—then all would go well, and they might follow the Logos, with old Socrates, whithersoever he led. Therefore he tried not so much to alter men's convictions, as, like Socrates, to make them respect their own convictions, to be true to their own deepest instincts, true to the very words which they used so carelessly, ignorant alike of their meaning and their wealth. He wished all men, all churches, all nations, to be true to the light which they had already, to whatsoever was godlike, and therefore God-given, in their own thoughts; and so to rise from their partial apprehensions, their scattered gleams of light, toward that full knowledge and light which was contained—so he said, even with his dying lips—in the orthodox Catholic faith. This was the ideal of the man and his work; and it left him neither courage nor time to found a school or promulgate a system. God had His own system: a system vaster than Augustine's, vaster than Dante's, vaster than all the thoughts of all thinkers, orthodox and heterodox, put together; for God was His own system, and by Him all things consisted, and in Him they lived and moved and had their being; and He was here, living and working, and we were living and working in Him, and had, instead of building systems of our own, to find out His eternal laws for men, for nations, for churches; for only in obedience to them is Life. Yes, a man who held this could found no system. "Other foundation," he used to say, "can no man lay, save that which is laid, even

Jesus Christ." And as he said it, his voice and eye told those who heard him that it was to him the most potent, the most inevitable, the most terrible, and yet the most hopeful, of all facts.

As for temptations to vanity, and love of power—he may have had to fight with them in the heyday of youth, and genius, and perhaps ambition. But the stories of his childhood are stories of the same generosity, courtesy, unselfishness, which graced his later years. At least, if he had been tempted, he had conquered. In more than five-and-twenty years, I have known no being so utterly unselfish, so utterly humble, so utterly careless of power or influence, for the mere enjoyment—and a terrible enjoyment it is—of using them. Staunch to his own opinion only when it seemed to involve some moral principle, he was almost too ready to yield it, in all practical matters, to anyone whom he supposed to possess more practical knowledge than he. To distrust himself, to accuse himself, to confess his proneness to hard judgments, while, to the eye of those who knew him and the facts, he was exercising a splendid charity and magnanimity; to hold himself up as a warning of "wasted time," while he was, but too literally, working himself to death—this was the childlike temper which made some lower spirits now and then glad to escape from their consciousness of his superiority by patronising and pitying him; causing in him—for he was, as all such great men are like to be, instinct with genial humour—a certain quiet good-natured amusement, but nothing more.

But it was that very humility, that very self-distrust, combined so strangely with manful strength and sternness, which drew to him humble souls, self-distrustful souls, who, like him, were full of the "Divine discontent;" who lived—as perhaps all men should live—angry with themselves, ashamed of themselves, and more and more angry and ashamed as their own ideal grew, and with it their consciousness of defection from that ideal. To him, as to David in the wilderness, gathered those who were spiritually discontented and spiritually in debt; and he was a captain over them, because, like David, he talked to them, not of his own genius or his own doctrines, but of the Living God, who had helped their forefathers, and would help them likewise. How great his influence was; what an amount of teaching, consolation, reproof, instruction in righteousness, that man found time to pour into heart after heart, with a fit word for man and for woman; how wide his sympathies, how deep his understanding of the human heart; how many sorrows he has lightened; how many wandering feet set right, will never be known till the day when the secrets of all hearts are disclosed. His forthcoming biography, if, as is hoped, it contains a selection from his vast correspondence, will tell something of all this: but how little! The most valuable of his letters will be those which were meant for no eye but the recipient's, and which no recipient would give to the world—hardly to an ideal Church; and what he has done will have to be estimated by wise men hereafter, when (as in the case of most great geniuses) a hundred indirect influences, subtle, various, often seemingly contradictory, will be found to have had their origin in Frederick Maurice.

And thus I end what little I have dared to say. There is much behind, even more worth saying, which must not be said. Perhaps some far wiser men than I will think that I have said too much already, and be inclined to answer me as Elisha of old answered the over-meddling sons of the prophets:

"Knowest thou that the Lord will take away thy master from thy head to-day?"

"Yea, I know it: hold ye your peace."

PHAETHON;

OR,

LOOSE THOUGHTS FOR LOOSE THINKERS.

PHAETHON;

OR,

LOOSE THOUGHTS FOR LOOSE THINKERS.

1852.

TEMPLETON and I were lounging by the clear limestone stream which crossed his park and wound away round wooded hills toward the distant Severn. A lovelier fishing morning sportsman never saw. A soft gray under-roof of cloud slid on before a soft west wind, and here and there a stray gleam of sunlight shot into the vale across the purple mountain-tops, and awoke into busy life the denizens of the water, already quickened by the mysterious electric influences of the last night's thunder-shower. The long-winged cinnamon-flies spun and fluttered over the pools; the sand-bees hummed merrily round their burrows in the marly bank; and delicate iridescent ephemeræ rose by hundreds from the depths, and, dropping their shells, floated away, each a tiny Venus Anadyomene, down the glassy ripples of the reaches. Every moment a heavy splash beneath some overhanging tuft of milfoil or water hemlock proclaimed the death-doom of a hapless beetle who had dropped into the stream beneath; yet still we fished and fished, and caught nothing, and seemed utterly careless about catching anything; till the old keeper who followed us, sighing and shrugging his shoulders, broke forth into open remonstrance:

"Excuse my liberty, gentlemen, but what ever is the matter with you and master, sir? I never did see you miss so many honest rises before."

"It is too true," said Templeton to me with a laugh. "I must confess I have been dreaming instead of fishing the whole morning. But what has happened to you, who are not as apt as I am to do nothing by trying to do two things at once?"

"My hand may well be somewhat unsteady; for to tell the truth, I sat up all last night writing."

"A hopeful preparation for a day's fishing in limestone water! But what can have set you on writing all night after so busy and talkative an evening as the last, ending too, as it did, somewhere about half-past twelve?"

"Perhaps the said talkative evening itself; and I suspect, if you will confess the truth, you will say that your morning's meditations are running very much in the same channel."

"Lewis," said he, after a pause, "go up to the hall, and bring some luncheon for us down to the lower waterfall."

"And a wheelbarrow to carry home the fish, sir?"

"If you wish to warm yourself, certainly. And now, my good fellow," said he, as the old keeper toddled away up the park, "I will open my heart—a process for which I have but few opportunities here—to an old college friend. I am disturbed and saddened by last night's talk and by last night's guest."

"By the American professor? How, in the name of English exclusiveness, did such a rampantly heterodox spiritual guerilla invade the respectabilities and conservatisms of Herefordshire?"

"He was returning from a tour through Wales, and had introductions to me from some Manchester friends of mine, to avail himself of which I found he had gone some thirty miles out of his way."

"Complimentary to you, at least."

"To Lady Jane, I suspect, rather than to me; for he told me broadly enough that all the flattering attentions which he had received in Manchester—where, you know, all such prophets are received with open arms, their only credentials being that, whatsoever they believe, they shall not believe the Bible—had not given him the pleasure which he had received from that one introduction to what he called 'the inner hearth-life of the English landed aristocracy.' But what did you think of him?"

"Do you really wish to know?"

"I do."

"Then, honestly, I never heard so much magniloquent unwisdom talked in the same space of time. It was the sense of shame for my race which kept me silent all the evening. I could not trust myself to argue with a gray-haired Saxon man, whose fifty years of life seemed to have left him a child in all but the childlike heart which alone can enter into the kingdom of heaven."

"You are severe," said Templeton, smilingly though, as if his estimate were not very different from mine.

"Can one help being severe when one hears irreverence poured forth from reverend lips? I do not mean merely irreverence for the Catholic Creeds; that to my mind—God forgive me if I misjudge him—seemed to me only one fruit of a deep root of irreverence for all things as they are, even for all things as they seem. Did you not remark the audacious contempt for all ages but 'our glorious nineteenth century,' and the still deeper contempt for all in the said glorious time who dared to believe that there was any ascertained truth independent of the private fancy and opinion of—for I am afraid it came to that—him, Professor Windrush, and his circle of elect souls? 'You may believe nothing if you like, and welcome; but if you do take to that unnecessary act, you are a fool if you believe anything but what I believe—though I do not choose to state what that is.' Is not that, now, a pretty fair formulisation of his doctrine?"

"But, my dear raver," said Templeton, laughing, "the man believed at least in physical science. I am sure we heard enough about its triumphs."

"It may be so. But to me his very 'spiritualism' seemed more materialistic than his physics. His notion seemed to be, though heaven forbid that I should say that he ever put it formally before himself——"

"Or anything else," said Templeton, sotto voce.

"—that it is the spiritual world which is governed by physical laws, and the physical by spiritual ones; that while men and women are merely the puppets of cerebrations and mentations, and attractions and repulsions, it is the trees, and stones, and gases, who have the wills and the energies, and the faiths and the virtues and the personalities."

"You are caricaturing."

"How so? How can I judge otherwise, when I hear a man talking, as he did, of God in terms which, every one of them involved what we call the essential properties of matter—space, time, passibility, motion; setting forth phrenology and mesmerism as the great organs of education, even of the regeneration of mankind; apologising for the earlier ravings of the Poughkeepsie seer, and considering his later eclectico-pantheist farragos as great utterances: while, whenever he talked of Nature, he showed the most credulous craving after everything which we, the countrymen of Bacon, have been taught to consider unscientific—Homœopathy, Electro-biology, Loves of the Plants à la Darwin, Vestiges of Creation, Vegetarianisms, Teetotalisms—never mind what, provided it was unaccredited or condemned by regularly educated men of science?"

"But you don't mean to assert that there is nothing in any of these theories?"

"Of course not. I can no more prove a universal negative about them than I can about the existence of life on the moon. But I do say that this contempt for that which has been already discovered—this carelessness about induction from the normal phenomena, coupled with this hankering after theories built upon exceptional ones—this craving for 'signs and wonders,' which is the sure accompaniment of a dying faith in

God, and in nature as God's work—are symptoms which make me tremble for the fate of physical as well as of spiritual science, both in America and in the Americanists here at home. As the Professor talked on, I could not help thinking of the neo-Platonists of Alexandria, and their exactly similar course—downward from a spiritualism of notions and emotions, which in every term confessed its own materialism, to the fearful discovery that consciousness does not reveal God, not even matter, but only its own existence; and then onward, in desperate search after something external wherein to trust, towards theurgic fetish worship, and the secret virtues of gems and flowers and stars; and, last of all, to the lowest depth of bowing statues and winking pictures. The sixth century saw that career, Templeton; the nineteenth may see it re-enacted, with only these differences, that the Nature-worship which seems coming will be all the more crushing and slavish, because we know so much better how vast and glorious Nature is; and that the superstitions will be more clumsy and foolish in proportion as our Saxon brain is less acute and discursive, and our education less severely scientific, than those of the old Greeks."

"Silence, raver!" cried Templeton, throwing himself on the grass in fits of laughter. "So the Professor's grandchildren will have either turned Papists, or be bowing down before rusty locomotives and broken electric telegraphs? But, my good friend, you surely do not take Professor Windrush for a fair sample of the great American people?"

"God forbid that so unpractical a talker should be

a sample of the most practical people upon earth. The Americans have their engineers, their geographers, their astronomers, their scientific chemists; few indeed, but such as bid fair to rival those of any nation upon earth. But these, like other true workers, hold their tongues and do their business."

"And they have a few indigenous authors too: you must have read the 'Biglow Papers,' and the 'Fable for Critics,' and last but not least, 'Uncle Tom's Cabin'?"

"Yes; and I have had far less fear for Americans since I read that book; for it showed me that there was right healthy power, artistic as well as intellectual, among them even now—ready, when their present borrowed peacocks' feathers have fallen off, to come forth and prove that the Yankee Eagle is a right gallant bird, if he will but trust to his own natural plumage."

"And they have a few statesmen also."

"But they are curt, plain-spoken, practical—in everything antipodal to the knot of hapless men, who, unable from some defect or morbidity to help on the real movement of their nation, are fain to get their bread with tongue and pen, by retailing to 'silly women,' 'ever learning and never coming to the knowledge of the truth,' second-hand German eclecticisms, now exploded even in the country where they arose, and the very froth and scum of the Medea's caldron, in which the disjecta membra of old Calvinism are pitiably seething."

"Ah! It has been always the plan, you know, in England, as well as in America, courteously to avoid taking up a German theory till the Germans had quite done with it, and thrown it away for something new. But what are we to say of those who are trying to introduce into England these very Americanised Germanisms, as the only teaching which can suit the needs of the old world?"

"We will, if we are in a vulgar humour, apply to them a certain old proverb about teaching one's grandmother a certain simple operation on the egg of the domestic fowl; but we will no less take shame to ourselves, as sons of Alma Mater, that such nonsense can get even a day's hearing, either among the daughters of Manchester manufacturers, or among London working men. Had we taught them what we were taught in the schools, Templeton——"

"Alas, my friend, we must ourselves have learnt it first. I have no right to throw stones at the poor Professor, for I could not answer him."

"Do not suppose that I can either. All I say is—mankind has not lived in vain. Least of all has it lived in vain during the last eighteen hundred years. It has gained something of eternal truth in every age, and that which it has gained is as fresh and young now as ever; and I will not throw away the bird in the hand for any number of birds in the bush."

"Especially when you suspect most of them to be only wooden pheasants, set up to delude poachers. Well, you are far more of a Philister and a Conservative than I thought you."

"The New is coming, I doubt not; but it must grow organically out of the Old—not root the old up, and stick itself full-grown into the place thereof, like a French tree of liberty—sure of much the same fate. Other foundation can no man lay than that which is laid already, in spiritual things or in physical; as the Professor and his school will surely find."

"You recollect to whom the Bible applies that text?"

"I do."

"And yet you say you cannot answer the Professor?"

"I do not care to do so. There are certain root-truths which I know, because they have been discovered and settled for ages; and instead of accepting the challenge of every I-know-not-whom to re-examine them, and begin the world's work all over again, I will test his theories by them; and if they fail to coincide, I will hear no more speech about the details of the branches and flowers, for I shall know the root is rotten."

"But he, too, acknowledged certain of those root-truths," said Templeton, who seemed to have a lingering sympathy with my victim; "he insisted most strongly, and spoke, you will not deny, eloquently and nobly on the Unity of the Deity."

"On the non-Trinity of *it*, rather; for I will not degrade the word 'Him,' by applying it here. But, tell me honestly—*c'est le timbre qui fait la musique*—did his 'Unity of the Deity' sound in your English Bible-bred heart at all like that ancient, human, personal 'Hear, O Israel! the Lord thy God is one Lord'?"

"Much more like 'The Something our Nothing is one Something.'"

"May we not suspect, then, that his notion of the 'Unity of the Deity' does not quite coincide with the foundation already laid, whosesoever else may?"

"You are assuming rather hastily."

"Perhaps I may prove also, some day or other. Do you think, moreover, that the theory which he so boldly started, when his nerves and his manners were relieved from the unwonted pressure by Lady Jane and the ladies going upstairs, was part of the same old foundation?"

"Which, then?"

"That, if a man does but believe a thing, he has a right to speak it and act on it, right or wrong. Have you forgotten his vindication of your friend, the radical voter, and his 'spirit of truth'?"

"What, the worthy who, when I canvassed him as the Liberal candidate for ——, and promised to support complete freedom of religious opinion, tested me by breaking out into such blasphemous ribaldry as made me run out of the house, and then went and voted against me as a bigot?"

"I mean him, of course. The Professor really seemed to admire the man, as a more brave and conscientious hero than himself. I am not squeamish, as you know; but I am afraid that I was quite rude to him when he went as far as that."

"What—when you told him that you thought that, after all, the old theory of the Divine Right of Kings was as plausible as the new theory of the Divine Right of Blasphemy? My dear fellow, do not fret yourself on that point. He seemed to take it rather as a compliment to his own audacity, and whispered to me that

'The Divine Right of Blasphemy' was an expression of which Theodore Parker himself need not have been ashamed."

"He was pleased to be complimentary. But, tell me, what was it in his oratory which has so vexed the soul of the country squire?"

"That very argument of his, among many things. I saw, or rather felt, that he was wrong; and yet, as I have said already, I could not answer him; and, had he not been my guest, should have got thoroughly cross with him, as a pis-aller."

"I saw it. But, my friend, used we not to read Plato together, and enjoy him together, in old Cambridge days? Do you not think that Socrates might at all events have driven the Professor into a corner?"

"He might: but I cannot. Is that, then, what you were writing about all last night?"

"It was. I could not help, when I went out on the terrace to smoke my last cigar, fancying to myself how Socrates might have seemed to set you, and the Professor, and that warm-hearted, right-headed, wrong-tongued High-Church Curate, all together by the ears, and made confusion worse confounded for the time being, and yet have left for each of you some hint whereby you might see the darling truth for which you were barking, all the more clearly in the light of the one which you were howling down."

"And so you sat up, and—I thought the corridor smelt somewhat of smoke."

"Forgive, and I will confess. I wrote a dialogue; —and here it is, if you choose to hear it. If there are a few passages, or even many, which Plato would not have written, you will consider my age and inexperience, and forgive."

"My dear fellow, you forget that I, like you, have been ten years away from dear old Alma-Mater, Plato, the boats, and Potton Wood. My authorities now are 'Morton on Soils,' and 'Miles on the Horse's Foot.' Read on, fearless of my criticisms. Here is the waterfall; we will settle ourselves on Jane's favourite seat. You shall discourse, and I, till Lewis brings the luncheon, will smoke my cigar; and if I seem to be looking at the mountain, don't fancy that I am only counting how many young grouse those heath-burning worthies will have left me by the twelfth."

So we sat down, and I began:

PHAETHON.

ALCIBIADES and I walked into the Pnyx early the other morning, before the people assembled. There we saw Socrates standing, having his face turned toward the rising sun. Approaching him, we perceived that he was praying; and that so ardently, that we touched him on the shoulder before he became aware of our presence.

"You seem like a man filled with the God, Socrates," said Alcibiades.

"Would that were true," answered he, "both of me and of all who will counsel here this day. In fact, I was praying for that very thing; namely, that they might have light to see the truth, in whatsoever matter might be discussed here."

"And for me also?" said Alcibiades; "but I have prepared my speech already."

"And for you also, if you desire it—even though some of your periods should be spoiled thereby. But why are you both here so early, before any business is stirring?"

"We were discussing," said I, "that very thing for which we found you praying—namely, truth, and what it might be."

"Perhaps you went a worse way toward discovering it than I did. But let us hear. Whence did the discussion arise?"

"From something," said Alcibiades, "which Protagoras said in his lecture yesterday—How truth was what each man troweth, or believeth, to be true. 'So that,' he said, 'one thing is true to me, if I believe it true, and another opposite thing to you, if you believe that opposite. For,' continued he, 'there is an objective and a subjective truth; the former, doubtless, one and absolute, and contained in the nature of each thing; but the other manifold and relative, varying with the faculties of each perceiver thereof.' But as each man's faculties, he said, were different from his neighbour's, and all more or less imperfect, it was impossible that the absolute objective truth of anything could be seen by any mortal, but only some partial approximation, and, as it were, sketch of it, according as the object was represented with more or less refraction on the mirror of his subjectivity. And therefore, as the true inquirer deals only with the possible, and lets the impossible go, it was the business of the wise man, shunning the search after absolute truth as an impious attempt of the Titans to scale Olympus, to busy himself humbly and practically with subjective truth, and with those methods—rhetoric, for instance—by which he can make the subjective opinions of others either similar to his own, or, leaving them as they are—for it may be very often unnecessary to change them—useful to his own ends."

Then Socrates, laughing:

"My fine fellow, you will have made more than one oration in the Pnyx to-day. And indeed, I myself felt quite exalted, and rapt aloft, like Bellerophon on Pegasus, upon the eloquence of Protagoras and you. But yet forgive me this one thing; for my mother bare me, as you know, a man-midwife, after her own trade, and not a sage."

ALCIBIADES. "What then?"

SOCRATES. "This, my astonishing friend—for really I am altogether astonished and struck dumb, as I always am whensoever I hear a brilliant talker like you discourse concerning objectivities and subjectivities, and such mysterious words; at such moments I am like an old war-horse, who, though he will rush on levelled lances, shudders and sweats with terror at a boy rattling pebbles in a bladder; and I feel altogether dizzy, and dread lest I should suffer some such transformation as Scylla, when I hear awful words, like incantations, pronounced over me, of which I, being no sage, understand nothing. But tell me now, Alcibiades, did the opinion of Protagoras altogether please you?"

A. "Why not? Is it not certain that two equally honest men may differ in their opinions on the same matter?"

S. "Undeniable."

A. "But if each is equally sincere in speaking what he believes, is not each equally moved by the spirit of truth?"

S. "You seem to have been lately initiated, and that not at Eleusis merely, nor in the Cabiria, but rather in some Persian or Babylonian mysteries, when you discourse thus of spirits. But you, Phaethon" (turning to me), "how did you like the periods of Protagoras?"

"Do not ask me, Socrates," said I, "for indeed we have fought a weary battle together ever since sundown last night, and all that I had to say I learnt from you."

S. "From me, good fellow?"

PHAETHON. "Yes, indeed. I seemed to have heard from you that truth is simply 'facts as they are.' But when I urged this on Alcibiades, his arguments seemed superior to mine."

A. "But I have been telling him, drunk and sober, that it is my opinion also as to what truth is. Only I, with Protagoras, distinguish between objective fact and subjective opinion."

S. "Doing rightly, too, fair youth. But how comes it then that you and Phaethon cannot agree?"

"That," said I, "you know better than either of us."

"You seem both of you," said Socrates, "to be, as usual, in the family way. Shall I exercise my profession on you?"

"No, by Zeus!" answered Alcibiades, laughing; "I fear thee, thou juggler, lest I suffer once again the same fate with the woman in the myth, and after I have conceived a fair man-child, and, as I fancy, brought it forth, thou hold up to the people some dead puppy, or log, or what not, and cry: 'Look what Alcibiades has produced!'"

S. "But, beautiful youth, before I can do that, you will have spoken your oration on the bema, and all the people will be ready and able to say 'Absurd! Nothing but what is fair can come from so fair a body.' Come, let us consider the question together."

I assented willingly; and Alcibiades, mincing and pouting, after his fashion, still was loath to refuse.

S. "Let us see, then. Alcibiades distinguishes, he says, between objective fact and subjective opinion?"

A. "Of course I do."

S. "But not, I presume, between objective truth and subjective truth, whereof Protagoras spoke?"

A. "What trap are you laying now? I distinguish between them also, of course."

S. "Tell me, then, dear youth, of your indulgence, what they are; for I am shamefully ignorant on the matter."

A. "Why, do they not call a thing objectively true, when it is true absolutely in itself; but subjectively true, when it is true in the belief of a particular person?"

S. "—Though not necessarily true objectively, that is, absolutely and in itself?"

A. "No."

S. "But possibly true so?"

A. "Of course."

S. "Now, tell me—a thing is objectively true, is it not, when it is a fact as it is?"

A. "Yes."

S. "And when it is a fact as it is not, it is objectively false; for such a fact would not be true absolutely, and in itself, would it?"

A. "Of course not."

S. "Such a fact would be, therefore, no fact, and nothing."

A. "Why so?"

S. "Because, if a thing exists, it can only exist as it is, not as it is not; at least my opinion inclines that way."

"Certainly not," said I; "why do you haggle so, Alcibiades?"

S. "Fair and softly, Phaethon! How do you know that he is not fighting for wife and child, and the altars of his gods? But if he will agree with you and me, he will confess that a thing which is objectively false does not exist at all, and is nothing."

A. "I suppose it is necessary to do so. But I know whither you are struggling."

S. "To this, dear youth, that, therefore, if a thing subjectively true be also objectively false, it does not exist, and is nothing."

"It is so," said I.

S. "Let us, then, let nothing go its own way, while we go on ours with that which is only objectively true, lest coming to a river over which it is subjectively true to us that there is a bridge, and trying to walk over that work of our own mind, but no one's hands, the bridge prove to be objectively false, and we, walking over the bank into the water, be set free from that which is subjectively on the farther bank of Styx."

Then I, laughing: "This hardly coincides, Alcibiades, with Protagoras's opinion, that subjective truth was alone useful."

"But rather proves," said Socrates, "that undiluted draughts of it are of a hurtful and poisonous nature, and require to be tempered with somewhat of objective truth, before it is safe to use them—at least in the case of bridges."

"Did I not tell you," interrupted Alcibiades, "how the old deceiver would try to put me to bed of some dead puppy or log? Or do you not see how, in order, after his custom, to raise a laugh about the whole question by vulgar examples, he is blinking what he knows as well as I?"

S. "What then, fair youth?"

A. "That Protagoras was not speaking about bridges, or any other merely physical things, on which no difference of opinion need occur, because every one can satisfy himself by simply using his senses; but concerning moral and intellectual matters, which are not cognisable by the senses, and therefore permit, without blame, a greater diversity of opinion. Error on such points, he told us—on the subject of religion, for example—was both pardonable and harmless; for no blame could be imputed to the man who acted faithfully up to his own belief, whatsoever that might be."

S. "Bravely spoken of him, and worthily of a free

state. But tell me, Alcibiades, with what matters does religion deal?"

A. "With the Gods."

S. "Then it is not hurtful to speak false things of the Gods?"

A. "Not unless you know them to be false."

S. "But answer me this, Alcibiades. If you made a mistake concerning numbers, as that twice two made five, might it not be hurtful to you?"

A. "Certainly; for I might pay away five obols instead of four."

S. "And so be punished, not by any anger of two and two against you, but by those very necessary laws of number, which you had mistaken?"

A. "Yes."

S. "Or if you made a mistake concerning music, as that two consecutive notes could produce harmony, that opinion also, if you acted upon it, would be hurtful to you?"

A. "Certainly; for I should make a discord, and pain my own ears, and my hearers'."

S. "And in this case also, be punished, not by any anger of the lyre against you, but by those very necessary laws of music which you had mistaken?"

A. "Yes."

S. "Or if you mistook concerning a brave man, believing him to be a coward, might not this also be hurtful to you? If, for instance, you attacked him carelessly, expecting him to run away, and he defended himself valiantly, and conquered you; or if you neglected to call for his help in need, expecting him falsely, as in the former case, to run away; would not such a mistake be hurtful to you, and punish you, not by any anger of the man against you, but by your mistake itself?"

A. "It is evident."

S. "We may assume, then, that such mistakes at least are hurtful, and that they are liable to be punished by the very laws of that concerning which we mistake?"

A. "We may so assume."

S. "Suppose, then, we were to say: 'What argument is this of yours, Protagoras?—that concerning lesser things, both intellectual and moral, such as concerning number, music, or the character of a man, mistakes are hurtful, and liable to bring punishment, in proportion to our need of using those things: but concerning the Gods, the very authors and lawgivers of number, music, human character, and all other things whatsoever, mistakes are of no consequence, nor in any way hurtful to man, who stands in need of their help, not only in stress of battle, once or twice in his life, as he might of the brave man, but always and in all things both outward and inward? Does it not seem strange to you, for it does to me, that to make mistakes concerning such beings should not bring an altogether infinite and daily punishment, not by any resentment of theirs, but, as in the case of music or numbers, by the very fact of our having mistaken the laws of their being, on which the whole universe depends?'—What do you suppose Protagoras would be able to answer, if he faced the question boldly?"

A. "I cannot tell."

S. "Nor I either. Yet one thing more it may be worth our while to examine. If one should mistake concerning God, will his error be one of excess, or defect?"

A. "How can I tell?"

S. "Let us see. Is not Zeus more perfect than all other beings?"

A. "Certainly, if it be true that, as they say, the perfection of each kind of being is derived from him; he must therefore be himself more perfect than any one of those perfections."

S. "Well argued. Therefore, if he conceived of himself, his conception of himself would be more perfect than that of any man concerning him?"

A. "Assuredly; if he have that faculty, he must needs have it in perfection."

S. "Suppose, then, that he conceived of one of his own properties, such as his justice; how large would that perfect conception of his be?"

A. "But how can I tell, Socrates?"

S. "My good friend, would it not be exactly commensurate with that justice of his?"

A. "How then?"

S. "Wherein consists the perfection of any conception, save in this, that it be the exact copy of that whereof it is conceived, and neither greater nor less?"

A. "I see now."

S. "Without the Pythia's help, I should say. But, tell me—We agree that Zeus's conception of his own justice will be exactly commensurate with his justice?"

A. "We do."

S. "But man's conception thereof, it has been agreed, would be certainly less perfect than Zeus's?"

A. "It would."

S. "Man, then, it seems, would always conceive God to be less just than God conceives himself to be?"

A. "He would."

S. "And therefore to be less just, according to the argument, than he really is?"

A. "True."

S. "And therefore his error concerning Zeus, would be in this case an error of defect?"

A. "It would."

S. "And so on of each of his other properties?"

A. "The same argument would likewise, as far as I can see, apply to them."

S. "So that, on the whole, man, by the unassisted power of his own faculty, will always conceive Zeus to be less just, wise, good, and beautiful than he is?"

A. "It seems probable."

S. "But does not that seem to you hurtful?"

A. "Why so?"

S. "As if, for instance, a man believing that Zeus loves him less than he really does, should become superstitious and self-tormenting. Or, believing that Zeus will guide him less than he really will, he should go his own way through life without looking for that guidance: or if, believing that Zeus cares about his conquering his passions less than he really does, he should become careless and despairing in the struggle: or if, believing that Zeus is less interested in the welfare of mankind than he really is, he should himself neglect to assist them, and so lose the glory of being called a benefactor of his country: would not all these mistakes be hurtful ones?"

"Certainly," said I: but Alcibiades was silent.

S. "And would not these mistakes, by the hypothesis, themselves punish him who made them, without any resentment whatsoever, or Nemesis of the Gods being required for his chastisement?"

"It seems so," said I.

S. "But can we say of such mistakes, and of the harm which may accrue from them, anything but that they must both be infinite; seeing that they are mistakes concerning an infinite Being, and his infinite properties, on every one of which, and on all together, our daily existence depends?"

P. "It seems so."

S. "So that, until such a man's error concerning Zeus, the source of all things, is cleared up, either in this life or in some future one, we cannot but fear for him infinite confusion, misery, and harm, in all matters which he may take in hand?"

Then Alcibiades, angrily: "What ugly mask is this you have put on, Socrates? You speak rather like a priest trying to frighten rustics into paying their first-fruits, than a philosopher inquiring after that which is beautiful. But you shall never terrify me into believing that it is not a noble thing to speak out whatsoever a man believes, and to go forward boldly in the spirit of truth."

S. "Feeling first, I hope, with your staff, as would be but reasonable in the case of the bridge, whether your belief was objectively or only subjectively true, lest you should fall through your subjective bridge into objective water. Nevertheless, leaving the bridge and the water, let us examine a little what this said spirit of truth may be. How do you define it?"

A. "I assert that whosoever says honestly what he believes, does so by the spirit of truth."

S. "Then if Lyce, patting those soft cheeks of yours, were to say: 'Alcibiades, thou art the fairest youth in Athens,' she would speak by the spirit of truth?"

A. "They say so."

S. "And they say rightly. But if Lyce, as is her custom, wished, by so saying, to cheat you into believing that she loved you, and thereby to wheedle you out of a new shawl, she would still speak by the spirit of truth?"

A. "I suppose so."

S. "But if, again, she said the same thing to Phaethon, she would still speak by the spirit of truth?"

"By no means, Socrates," said I, laughing.

S. "Be silent, fair boy; you are out of court as an interested party. Alcibiades shall answer. If Lyce, being really mad with love, like Sappho, were to believe Phaethon to be fairer than you, and say so, she would still speak by the spirit of truth?"

A. "I suppose so."

S. "Do not frown; your beauty is in no question. Only she would then be saying what is not true?"

"I must answer for him after all," said I.

S. "Then it seems, from what has been agreed, that it is indifferent to the spirit of truth, whether it speak truth or not. The spirit seems to be of an enviable serenity. But suppose again, that I believed that Alcibiades had an ulcer on his leg, and were to proclaim the same now to the people, when they come into the Pnyx, should I not be speaking by the spirit of truth?"

A. "But that would be a shameful and blackguardly action."

S. "Be it so. It seems, therefore, that it is indifferent to the spirit of truth whether that which it affirms be honourable or blackguardly. Is it not so?"

A. "It seems so, most certainly, in that case at least."

S. "And in others, as I think. But tell me—Is not the man who does what he believes, as much moved by this your spirit of truth as he who says what he believes?"

A. "Certainly he is."

S. "Then if I believed it right to lie or steal, I, in lying or stealing, should lie or steal by the spirit of truth?"

A. "Certainly: but that is impossible."

S. "My fine fellow, and wherefore? I have heard of a nation among the Indians who hold it a sacred duty to murder every one not of their own tribe, whom they can waylay: and when they are taken and punished by the rulers of that country, die joyfully under the greatest torments, believing themselves certain of an entrance into the Elysian fields, in proportion to the number of murders which they have committed."

A. "They must be impious wretches."

S. "Be it so. But believing themselves to be right, they commit murder by the spirit of truth."

A. "It seems to follow from the argument."

S. "Then it is indifferent to the spirit of truth whether the action which it prompts be right or wrong?"

A. "It must be confessed."

S. "It is therefore not a moral faculty, this spirit of truth. Let us see now whether it be an intellectual one. How are intellectual things defined, Phaethon? Tell me, for you are cunning in such matters."

P. "Those things which have to do with processes of the mind."

S. "With right processes, or with wrong?"

P. "With right, of course."

S. "And processes for what purpose?"

P. "For the discovery of facts."

S. "Of facts as they are, or as they are not?"

P. "As they are."

S. "And he who discovers facts as they are, discovers truth; while he who discovers facts as they are not, discovers falsehood?"

P. "He discovers nothing, Socrates."

S. "True; but it has been agreed already that the spirit of truth is indifferent to the question whether facts be true or false, but only concerns itself with the sincere affirmation of them, whatsoever they may be. Much more then must it be indifferent to those processes by which they are discovered."

P. "How so?"

S. "Because it only concerns itself with affirmation concerning facts; but these processes are anterior to that affirmation."

P. "I comprehend."

S. "And much more is it indifferent to whether those are right processes or not."

P. "Much more so."

S. "It is therefore not intellectual. It remains, therefore, that it must be some merely physical faculty, like that of fearing, hungering, or enjoying the sexual appetite."

A. "Absurd, Socrates!"

S. "That is the argument's concern, not ours: let us follow manfully whithersoever it may lead us."

A. "Lead on, thou sophist!"

S. "It was agreed, then, that he who does what he thinks right, does so by the spirit of truth—was it not?"

A. "It was."

S. "Then he who eats when he thinks that he ought to eat, does so by the spirit of truth?"

A. "What next?"

S. "This next, that he who blows his nose when he thinks that it wants blowing, blows his nose by the spirit of truth."

A. "What next?"

S. "Do not frown, friend. Believe me, in such days as these, I honour even the man who is honest enough to blow his nose because he finds that he ought to do so. But tell me—a horse, when he shies at a beggar, does not he also do so by the spirit of truth? For he believes sincerely the beggar to be something formidable, and honestly acts upon his conviction."

"Not a doubt of it," said I, laughing, in spite of myself, at Alcibiades's countenance.

S. "It is in danger, then, of proving to be something quite brutish and doggish, this spirit of truth. I should not wonder, therefore, if we found it proper to be restrained."

A. "How so, thou hair-splitter?"

S. "Have we not proved it to be common to man and animals; but are not those passions which we have in common with animals to be restrained?"

P. "Restrain the spirit of truth, Socrates?"

S. "If it be doggishly inclined. As, for instance, if a man knew that his father had committed a shameful act, and were to publish it, he would do so by the spirit of truth. Yet such an act would be blackguardly, and to be restrained."

P. "Of course."

S. "But much more, if he accused his father only on his own private suspicion, not having seen him commit the act; while many others, who had watched his father's character more than he did, assured him that he was mistaken."

P. "Such an act would be to be restrained, not merely as blackguardly, but as impious."

S. "Or if a man believed things derogatory to the character of the Gods, not having seen them do wrong himself, while all those who had given themselves to the study of divine things assured him that he was mistaken, would he not be bound to restrain an inclination to speak such things, even if he believed them?"

P. "Surely, Socrates; and that even if he believed that the Gods did not exist at all. For there would be far more chance that he alone was wrong, and the many right, than that the many were wrong, and he alone right. He would therefore commit an insolent and conceited action, and, moreover, a cruel and shameless one; for he would certainly make miserable, if he were believed, the hearts of many virtuous persons who had never harmed him, for no immediate or demonstrable purpose except that of pleasing his own self-will; and that much more, were he wrong in his assertion."

S. "Here, then, is another case in which it seems proper to restrain the spirit of truth, whatsoever it may be?"

P. "What, then, are we to say of those who speak fearlessly and openly their own opinions on every subject? for, in spite of all this, one cannot but admire them, whether rationally or irrationally."

S. "We will allow them at least the honour which we do to the wild boar, who rushes fiercely through thorns and brambles upon the dogs, not to be turned aside by spears or tree-trunks, and indeed charges forward the more valiantly the more tightly he shuts his eyes. That praise we can bestow on him, but, I fear, no higher one. It is expedient, nevertheless, to have such a temperament as it is to have a good memory, or a loud voice, or a straight nose unlike mine; only, like other animal passions, it must be restrained and regulated by reason and the law of right, so as to employ itself only on such matters and to such a degree as they prescribe."

"It may seem so in the argument," said I. "Yet no argument, even of yours, Socrates, with your pardon, shall convince me that the spirit of truth is not fair and good, ay, the noblest possession of all; throwing away which, a man throws away his shield, and becomes unworthy of the company of gods or men."

S. "Or of beasts either, as it seems to me and the argument. Nevertheless, to this point has the argument, in its cunning and malice, brought us by crooked paths. Can we find no escape?"

P. "I know none."

S. "But may it not be possible that we, not having been initiated, like Alcibiades, into the Babylonian mysteries, have somewhat mistaken the meaning of that expression, 'spirit of truth'? For truth we defined to be 'facts as they are.' The spirit of truth then should mean, should it not, the spirit of facts as they are?"

P. "It should."

S. "But what shall we say that this expression, in its turn, means? The spirit which makes facts as they are?"

A. "Surely not. That would be the supreme Demiurgus himself."

S. "Of whom you were not speaking, when you spoke of the spirit of truth?"

A. "Certainly not. I was speaking of a spirit in man."

S. "And belonging to him?"

A. "Yes."

S. "And doing—what, with regard to facts as

they are? for this is just the thing which puzzles me."

A. "Telling facts as they are."

S. "Without seeing them as they are?"

A. "How you bore one! of course not. It sees facts as they are, and therefore tells them."

S. "But perhaps it might see them as they are, and find it expedient, being of the same temperament as I, to hold its tongue about them? Would it then be still the spirit of truth?"

A. "It would, of course."

S. "The man then who possesses the spirit of truth will see facts as they are?"

A. "He will."

S. "And conversely?"

A. "Yes."

S. "But if he sees anything only as it seems to him, and is not in fact, he will not, with regard to that thing, see it by the spirit of truth?"

A. "I suppose not."

S. "Neither then will he be able to speak of it by the spirit of truth."

A. "Why?"

S. "Because, by what we agreed before, it will not be there to speak of, my wondrous friend. For it appeared to us, if I recollect right, that facts can only exist as they are, and not as they are not, and that therefore the spirit of truth had nothing to do with any facts but those which are."

"But," I interrupted, "O dear Socrates, I fear much that if the spirit of truth be such as this, it must be beyond the reach of man."

S. "Why then?"

P. "Because the immortal gods only can see things as they really are, having alone made all things, and ruling them all according to the laws of each. They therefore, I much fear, will be alone able to behold them, how they are really in their inner nature and properties, and not merely from the outside, and by guess, as we do. How then can we obtain such a spirit ourselves?"

S. "Dear boy, you seem to wish that I should, as usual, put you off with a myth, when you begin to ask me about those who know far more about me than I do about them. Nevertheless, shall I tell you a myth?"

P. "If you have nothing better."

S. "They say, then, that Prometheus, when he grew to man's estate, found mankind, though they were like him in form, utterly brutish and ignorant, so that, as Æschylus says:

> Seeing they saw in vain,
> Hearing they heard not; but were like the shapes
> Of dreams, and long time did confuse all things
> At random:

being, as I suppose, led, like the animals, only by their private judgments of things as they seemed to each man, and enslaved to that subjective truth, which we found to be utterly careless and ignorant of facts as they are. But Prometheus, taking pity on them, determined in his mind to free them from that slavery and to teach them to rise above the beasts, by seeing things as they are. He therefore made them acquainted with the secrets of nature, and taught them to build houses, to work in wood and metals, to observe the courses of the stars, and all other such arts and sciences, which if any man attempts to follow according to his private opinion, and not according to the rules of that art, which are independent of him and of his opinions, being discovered from the unchangeable laws of things as they are, he will fail. But yet, as the myth relates, they became only a more cunning sort of animals; not being wholly freed from their original slavery to a certain subjective opinion about themselves, that each man should, by means of those arts and sciences, please and help himself only. Fearing, therefore, lest their increased strength and cunning should only enable them to prey upon each other all the more fiercely, he stole fire from heaven, and gave to each man a share thereof for his hearth, and to each community for their common altar. And by the light of this celestial fire they learnt to see those celestial and eternal bonds between man and man, as of husband to wife, of father to child, of citizen to his country, and of master to servant, without which man is but a biped without feathers, and which are in themselves, being independent of the flux of matter and time, most truly facts as they are. And since that time, whatsoever household or nation has allowed these fires to become extinguished, has sunk down again to the level of the brutes: while those who have passed them down to their children burning bright and strong, become partakers of the bliss of the Heroes, in the Happy Islands. It seems to me then, Phaethon and Alcibiades, that if we find ourselves in anywise destitute of this heavenly fire, we should pray for the coming of that day, when Prometheus shall be unbound from Caucasus, if by any means he may take pity on us and on our children, and again bring us down from heaven that fire which is the spirit of truth, that we may see facts as they are. For which, if he were to ask Zeus humbly and filially, I cannot believe that He would refuse it. And indeed, I think that the poets, as is their custom, corrupt the minds of young men by telling them that Zeus chained Prometheus to Caucasus for his theft; seeing that it befits such a ruler, as I take the Father of gods and men to be, to know that his subjects can only do well by means of his bounty, and therefore to bestow it freely, as the kings of Persia do, on all who are willing to use it in the service of their sovereign."

"So then," said Alcibiades, laughing, "till Prometheus be unbound from Caucasus, we who have lost, as you seem to hint, this heavenly fire, must needs go on upon our own subjective opinions, having nothing better to which to trust. Truly, thou sophist, thy conclusion seems to me after all not to differ much from that of Protagoras."

S. "Ah dear boy! know you not that to those who have been initiated, and, as they say in the mysteries, twice born, Prometheus is always unbound, and stands ready to assist them; while to those who are self-willed and conceited of their own opinions, he is removed to an inaccessible distance, and chained in icy fetters on untrodden mountain-peaks, where the vulture ever devours his fair heart, which sympathises continually with the follies and the sorrows of mankind? Of what punishment, then, must not those be worthy, who by their own wilfulness and self-confidence bind again to Caucasus the fair Titan, the friend of men?"

"By Apollo!" said Alcibiades, "this language is more fit for the tripod in Delphos, than for the bema in the Pnyx. So fare-thee-well, thou Pythoness! I must go and con over my oration, at least if thy prophesying has not altogether addled my thoughts."

But I, as soon as Alcibiades was gone, for I was ashamed to speak before, turning to Socrates said to him, all but weeping:

"Oh Socrates, what cruel words are these which you have spoken? Are you not ashamed to talk thus contemptuously to one like me, even though he be younger and less cunning in argument than yourself; knowing as you do, how, when I might have grown rich in my native city of Rhodes, and marrying there, as my father purposed, a wealthy merchant's heiress, so have passed my life delicately, receiving the profits of many ships and warehouses, I yet preferred Truth beyond riches; and leaving my father's house, came to Athens in search of wisdom, dissipating my patrimony upon one sophist after another, listening greedily to Hippias, and Polus, and Gorgias, and Protagoras, and last of all to you, hard-hearted man that you are? For from my youth I loved and longed after nothing so much as Truth, whatsoever it may be; thinking nothing so noble as to know that which is Right, and knowing it, to do it. And that longing, or love of mine, which is what I suppose Protagoras meant by the spirit of truth, I cherished as the fairest and most divine possession, and that for which alone it was worth while to live. For it seemed to me, that even if in my search I never attained to truth, still it were better to die seeking, than not to seek; and that even if acting by what I considered to be the spirit of truth, and doing honestly in every case that which seemed right, I should often, acting on a false conviction, offend in ignorance against the absolute righteousness of the gods, yet that such an offence was deserving, if not of praise for its sincerity, yet at least of pity and forgiveness; but by no means to be classed, as you class it, with the appetites of brutes; much less to be threatened, as you threaten it, with infinite and eternal misery by I know not what necessary laws of Zeus, and to be put off at last with some myth or other about Prometheus. Surely your mother bare you a scoffer and pitiless, Socrates, and not, as you boast, a man-midwife fit for fair youths."

Then, smiling sweetly, "Dear boy," said he, "were I such as you fancy, how should I be here now, discoursing with you concerning truth, instead of conning my speech for the Pnyx, like Alcibiades, that I may become a demagogue, deceiving the mob with flattery, and win for myself houses, and lands, and gold, and slave-girls, and fame, and power, even to a tyranny itself? For in this way I might have made my tongue a profitable member of my body; but now, being hurried up and down in barren places, like one mad of love, from my longing after fair youths, I waste my speech on them; receiving, as is the wont of true lovers, only curses and ingratitude from their arrogance. But tell me, thou proud Adonis—This spirit of truth in thee, which thou thoughtest, and rightly, thy most noble possession—did it desire truth, or not?"

P. "But, Socrates, I told you that very thing, and said that it was a longing after truth, which I could not restrain or disobey."

S. "Tell me now, does one long for that which one possesses, or for that which one does not possess?"

P. "For that which one does not possess."

S. "And is one in love with that which is oneself, or with that which is not?"

P. "With that which is not oneself, thou mocker. We are not all, surely, like Narcissus?"

S. "No, by the dog! not quite all. But see now: it appears that when any one is in love with a thing, and longs for it, as thou didst for truth, it must be something which is not himself, and which he does not possess?"

P. "True."

S. "You, then, while you were loving facts as they are, and longing to see them as they are, yet did not possess that which you longed for?"

P. "True, indeed; else why should I have been driven forth by the anger of the gods, like Bellerophon, to pace the Aleian plain, eating my own soul, if I had possessed that for which I longed?"

S. "Well said, dear boy. But see again. This truth which you loved, and which was not yourself or part of yourself, was certainly also nothing of your own making?—Though they say that Pygmalion was enamoured of the statue which he himself had carved."

P. "But he was miserable, Socrates, till the statue became alive."

S. "They say so; but what has that to do with the argument?"

P. "I know not. But it seems to me horrible, as it did to Pygmalion, to be enamoured of anything which cannot return your love, but is, as it were, your puppet. Should we not think it a shameful thing, if a mistress were to be enamoured of one of her own slaves?"

S. "We should; and that, I suppose, because the slave would have no free choice whether to refuse or to return his mistress's love; but would be compelled, being a slave, to submit to her, even if she were old, or ugly, or hateful to him?"

P. "Of course."

S. "And should we not say, Phaethon, that there was no true enjoyment in such love, even on the part of the mistress; nay, that it was not worthy of the name of love at all, but was merely something base, such as happens to animals?"

P. "We should say so rightly."

S. "Tell me, then, Phaethon—for a strange doubt has entered my mind on account of your words. This truth of which you were enamoured, seems, from what has been agreed, not to be a part of yourself, nor a creation of your own, like Pygmalion's statue—how then has it not happened to you to be even more miserable than Pygmalion till you were sure that truth loved you in return?—and, moreover, till you were sure that truth had free choice as to whether it should return or refuse your love? For, otherwise, you would be in danger of being found suffering the same base passion as a mistress enamoured of a slave who cannot resist her."

P. "I am puzzled, Socrates."

S. "Shall we rather say, then, that you were enamoured, not of truth itself, but of the spirit of truth? For we have been all along defining truth to be 'facts as they are,' have we not?"

P. "We have."

S. "But there are many facts as they are, whereof to be enamoured would be base, for they cannot return your love. As, for instance, that one and one make two, or that a horse has four legs. With respect to such facts, you would be, would you not, in the same position as a mistress towards her slave?"

P. "Certainly. It seems, then, better to assume the other alternative."

S. "It does. But does it not follow, that when you were enamoured of this spirit, you did not possess it?"

P. "I fear so, by the argument."

S. "And I fear, too, that we agreed that he only who possessed the spirit of truth saw facts as they are; for that was involved in our definition of the spirit of truth."

P. "But, Socrates, I knew, at least, that one and one made two, and that a horse had four legs. I must then have seen some facts as they are."

S. "Doubtless, fair boy; but not all."

P. "I do not pretend to that."

S. "But if you had possessed the spirit of truth, you would have seen all facts whatsoever as they are.

For he who possesses a thing can surely employ it freely for all purposes which are not contrary to the nature of that thing; can he not?"

P. "Of course he can. But if I did not possess the spirit of truth, how could I see any truth whatsoever?"

S. "Suppose, dear boy, that instead of your possessing it, it were possible for it to possess you; and possessing you, to show you as much of itself, or as little, as it might choose, and concerning such things only as it might choose: would not that explain the dilemma?"

P. "It would assuredly."

S. "Let us see, then, whether this spirit of truth may not be something which is capable of possessing you, and employing you, rather than of being possessed and employed by you. To me, indeed, this spirit seems likely to be some demon or deity, and that one of the greatest."

P. "Why then?"

S. "Can lifeless and material things see?"

P. "Certainly not; only live ones."

S. "This spirit, then, seems to be living; for it sees things as they are."

P. "Yes."

S. "And it is also intellectual; for intellectual facts can be only seen by an intellectual being."

P. "True."

S. "And also moral; for moral facts can only be seen by a moral being."

P. "True also."

S. "But this spirit is evidently not a man; it remains therefore, that it must be some demon."

P. "But why one of the greatest?"

S. "Tell me, Phaethon, is not God to be numbered among facts as they are?"

P. "Assuredly; for he is before all others and more eternal and absolute than all."

S. "Then this spirit of truth must also be able to see God as he is."

P. "It is probable."

S. "And certain, if, as we agreed, it be the very spirit which sees all facts whatsoever as they are. Now tell me, can the less see the greater as it is?"

P. "I think not; for an animal cannot see a man as he is, but only that part of him in which he is like an animal, namely, his outward figure and his animal passions; but not his moral sense or reason, for of them it has itself no share."

S. "True; and in like wise, a man of less intellect could not see a man of greater intellect than himself as he is, but only a part of his intellect."

P. "Certainly."

S. "And does not the same thing follow from what we said just now, that God's conceptions of himself must be the only perfect conceptions of him? For if any being could see God as he is, the same would be able to conceive of him as he is: which we agreed was impossible."

P. "True."

S. "Then surely this spirit which sees God as he is, must be equal with God."

P. "It seems probable; but none is equal to God except himself."

S. "Most true, Phaethon. But what shall we say

now, but that this spirit of truth, whereof thou hast been enamoured, is, according to the argument, none other than Zeus, who alone comprehends all things, and sees them as they are, because he alone has given to each its inward and necessary laws?"

P. "But, Socrates, there seems something impious in the thought."

S. "Impious, truly, if we held that this spirit of truth was a part of your own self. But we agreed that it was not a part of you, but something utterly independent of you."

P. "Noble would the news be, Socrates, were it true; yet it seems to me beyond belief."

S. "Did we not prove just now concerning Zeus, that all mistakes concerning him were certain to be mistakes of defect?"

P. "We did, indeed."

S. "How do you know, then, that you have not fallen into some such error, and have suspected Zeus to be less condescending towards you than he really is?"

P. "Would that it were so! But I fear it is too fair a hope."

S. "Do I seem to thee now, dear boy, more insolent and unfeeling than Protagoras, when he tried to turn thee away from the search after absolute truth, by saying sophistically that it was an attempt of the Titans to scale heaven, and bade thee be content with asserting shamelessly and brutishly thine own subjective opinions? For I do not bid thee scale the throne of Zeus, into whose presence none could arrive, as it seems to me, unless he himself willed it; but to believe that he has given thee from thy childhood a glimpse of his own excellence, that so thy heart, conjecturing, as in the case of a veiled statue, from one part the beauty of the rest, might become enamoured thereof, and long for that sight of him which is the highest and only good, that so his splendour may give thee light to see facts as they are."

P. "Oh Socrates! and how is this blessedness to be attained?"

S. "Even as the myths relate, the nymphs obtained the embraces of the gods; by pleasing him and obeying him in all things, lifting up daily pure hands and a thankful heart, if by any means he may condescend to purge thine eyes, that thou mayest see clearly, and without those motes, and specks, and distortions of thine own organs of vision, which flit before the eyeballs of those who have been drunk over-night, and which are called by sophists subjective truth; watching everywhere anxiously and reverently for those glimpses of his beauty, which he will vouchsafe to thee more and more as thou provest thyself worthy of them, and will reward thy love by making thee more and more partaker of his own spirit of truth; whereby, seeing facts as they are, thou wilt see him who has made them according to his own ideas, that they may be a mirror of his unspeakable splendour. Is not this a fairer hope for thee, oh Phaethon, than that which Protagoras held out to thee—that neither seeing Zeus, nor seeing facts as they are, nor affirming any truth whatsoever, nor depending for thy knowledge on any one but thine own ignorant self, thou mightest nevertheless be so fortunate as to escape punishment: not knowing, as it seems to me, that such a state of ignorance and blindfold rashness, even if Tartarus were a dream of the poets or the priests, is in itself the most fearful of punishments?"

P. "It is, indeed, my dear Socrates. Yet what are we to say of those who, sincerely loving and longing after knowledge, yet arrive at false conclusions, which are proved to be false by contradicting each other?"

S. "We are to say, Phaethon, that they have not loved knowledge enough to desire utterly to see facts as they are, but only to see them as they would wish them to be; and loving themselves rather than Zeus, have wished to remodel in some things or other his universe, according to their own subjective opinions. By this, or by some other act of self-will, or self-conceit, or self-dependence, they have compelled Zeus, not, as I think, without pity and kindness to them, to withdraw from them in some degree the sight of his own beauty. We must, therefore, I fear, liken them to Acharis, the painter of Lemnos, who, intending to represent Phœbus, painted from a mirror a copy of his own defects and deformities; or perhaps to that Nymph, who finding herself beloved by Phœbus, instead of reverently and silently returning the affection, boasted of it to all her neighbours, as a token of her own beauty, and despised the god; so that he, being angry, changed her into a chattering magpie; or again to Arachne, who having been taught the art of weaving by Athene, pretended to compete with her own instructress, and being metamorphosed by her into a spider, was condemned, like the sophists, to spin out of her own entrails endless ugly webs, which are destroyed, as soon as finished, by every slave-girl's broom."

P. "But shall we despise and hate such, Oh Socrates?"

S. "No, dearest boy, we will rather pity and instruct them lovingly; remembering always that we shall become such as they the moment we begin to fancy that truth is our own possession, and not the very beauty of Zeus himself, which he shows to those whom he will, and in such measure as he finds them worthy to behold. But to me, considering how great must be the condescension of Zeus in unveiling to any man, even the worthiest, the least portion of his own loveliness, there has come at times a sort of dream, that the divine splendour will at last pierce through and illumine all dark souls, even in the house of Hades, showing them, as by a great sunrise, both what they themselves, and what all other things are, really and in the sight of Zeus; which if it happened, even to Ixion, I believe that his wheel would stop, and his fetters drop off of themselves, and that he would return freely to the upper air, for as long as he himself might choose."

Just then the people began to throng into the Pnyx; and we took our places with the rest to hear the business of the day, after Socrates had privately uttered this prayer:

"Oh Zeus, give to me and to all who shall counsel here this day, that spirit of truth by which we may behold that whereof we deliberate, as it is in thy sight!"

"As I expected," said Templeton, with a smile, as

I folded up my manuscript. "My friend the parson could not demolish the poor Professor's bad logic without a little professional touch by way of finish."

"What do you mean?"

"Oh—never mind. Only I owe you little thanks for sweeping away any one of my lingering sympathies with Mr. Windrush, if all you can offer me instead is the confounded old nostrum of religion over again."

"Heydey, friend! What next?"

"Really, my dear fellow, I beg your pardon. I forgot that I was speaking to a clergyman."

"Pray don't beg my pardon on that ground. If what you say be right, a clergyman above all others ought to hear it; and if it be wrong, and a symptom of spiritual disease, he ought to hear it all the more. But I cannot tell whether you are right or wrong, till I know what you mean by religion; for there is a great deal of very truly confounded and confounding religion abroad in the world just now, as there has been in all ages; and perhaps you may be alluding to that."

Templeton sat silent for a few minutes, playing with the tackle in his fly-book, and then murmured to himself the well-known lines of Lucretius:

"Humana ante oculos fœde cum vita jaceret
In terris oppressa gravi sub Relligione
Quæ caput a cœli regionibus ostendebat,
Horribili super aspectu mortalibus instans.

There!—blasphemous reprobate fellow, am I not?"

"On the contrary," I said, "I think that in the

sense in which Lucretius intended that the lines should be taken, they contain a great deal of truth. He had seen the basest and foullest crimes spring from that which he calls *Relligio,* and he had a full right to state that fact. I am not aware that one blasphemes the Catholic and Apostolic Faith by saying that the devilries of the Spanish Inquisition were the direct offspring of that 'religious sentiment' which Mr. Windrush's school—though they are at all events right in saying that its source is in man himself, and not in the 'regionibus Cœli'—are now glorifying, as something vhich enables man to save his own soul without the interference of 'The Deity'—indeed, whether 'The Deity' chooses or not."

"Do leave these poor Emersonians alone for a few minutes, and tell me how you can reconcile what you have just said with your own dialogue."

"Why not?"

"Is not Lucretius glorying in the notion that the gods do not trouble themselves with mortals, while you have been asserting that 'The Deity' troubles Himself even with the souls of heathens?"

"Certainly. But that is quite a distinct matter from his dislike of what he calls *Relligio.* In that dislike I can sympathise fully: but on his method of escape Mr. Windrush will probably look with more complaisance than I do, who call it by the ugly name of Atheism."

"Then I fear you would call me an Atheist, if you knew all. So we had better say no more about it."

"A most curious speech, certainly, to make to a parson, or soul-curer by profession!"

"Why, what on earth have you to do but to abhor and flee me?" asked he, with a laugh, though by no means a merry one.

"Would your having a headache be a reason for the medical man's running away from you, or coming to visit you?"

"Ah, but this, you know, is my 'fault,' and my 'crime,' and my 'sin.' Eh?" and he laughed again.

"Would the doctor visit you the less, because it was your own fault that your head ached?"

"Ah, but suppose I professed openly no faith in his powers of curing, and had a great hankering after unaccredited Homœopathies, like Mr. Windrush's; would not that be a fair cause for interdiction from fire and water, sacraments and Christian burial?"

"Come, come, Templeton," I said; "you shall not thus jest away serious thoughts with an old friend. I know you are ill at ease. Why not talk over the matter with me fairly and soberly? How do you know till you have tried, whether I can help you or not?"

"Because I know that your arguments will have no force with me; they will demand of me or assume in me, certain faculties, sentiments, notions, experiences —call them what you like; I am beginning to suspect sometimes with Cabanis that they are 'a product of the small intestines'—which I never have had, and never could make myself have, and now don't care whether I have them or not."

"On my honour, I will address you only as what you are, and know yourself to be. But what are these faculties, so strangely beyond my friend Templeton's reach? He used to be distinguished at college for a very clear head, and a very kind heart, and the nicest sense of honour which I ever saw in living man; and I have not heard that they have failed him since he became Templeton of Templeton. And as for his Churchmanship, were not the county papers ringing last month with the accounts of the beautiful new church which he had built, and the stained glass which he brought from Belgium, and the marble font which he brought from Italy; and how he had even given for an altar-piece his own pet Luini, the gem of Templeton House?"

"Effeminate picture!" he said. "It was part and parcel of the idea——"

Before I could ask him what he meant, he looked up suddenly at me, with deep sadness on his usually nonchalant face.

"Well, my dear fellow, I suppose I must tell you all, as I have told you so much without your shaking the dust off your feet against me, and consulting Bradshaw for the earliest train to Shrewsbury. You knew my dear mother?"

"I did. The best of women."

"The best of women, and the best of mothers. But, if you recollect, she was a great Low-Church saint."

"Why 'but'? How does that derogate in any wise from her excellence?"

"Not from her excellence; God forbid! or from the excellence of the people of her own party, whom she used to have round her, and who were, some of them, I do believe, as really earnest, and pious, and charitable, and all that, as human beings could be. But it did take away very much indeed from her influence on me."

"Surely she did not neglect to teach you."

"It is a strange thing to say, but she rather taught me too much. I don't deny that it may have been my own fault. I don't blame her, or any one. But you know what I was at college—no worse than other men, I dare say; but no better. I had no reason for being better."

"No reason? Surely she gave you reasons."

"There—you have touched the ailing nerve now. The reasons were what you would call paralogisms. They had no more to do with me than with those trout."

"You mistake, friend, you mistake, indeed," said I.

"I don't mistake at all about this; that whether or not the reasons in themselves had to do with me, the way in which she put them made them practically so much Hebrew. She demanded of me, as the only grounds on which I was to consider myself safe from hell, certain fears and hopes which I did not feel, and experiences which I did not experience; and it was my fault, and a sign of my being in a wrong state—to use no harder term—that I did not feel them; and yet it was only God's grace which could make me feel them: and so I grew up with a dark secret notion that I was a very bad boy; but that it was God's fault and not mine that I was so."

"You were ripe indeed then," said I sadly, "like hundreds more, for Professor Windrush's teaching."

"I will come to that presently. But in the meantime—was it my fault? I was never what you call a devout person. My 'organ of veneration,' as the phrenologists would say, was never very large. I was a shrewd dashing boy, enjoying life to the finger-tips, and enjoying above all, I will say, pleasing my mother in every way, except in the understanding what she told me—and what I felt I could not understand. But as I grew older, and watched her, and the men round her, I began to suspect that religion and effeminacy had a good deal to do with each other. For the women, whatsoever their temperaments, or even their tastes might be, took to this to me incomprehensible religion naturally and instinctively; while the very few men who were in their clique were—I don't deny some of them were good men enough—if they had been men at all: if they had been well-read, or well-bred, or gallant, or clear-headed, or liberal-minded, or, in short, anything but the silky, smooth-tongued hunt-the-slippers nine out of ten of them were. I recollect well asking my mother once, whether there would not be five times more women than men in heaven—and her answering me sadly and seriously, that she feared there would be. And in the meantime she brought me up to pray and hope that I might some day be converted, and become a child of God—— And one could not help wishing to enjoy oneself as much as possible before that event happened."

"Before that event happened, my dear fellow? Pardon me, but your tone is somewhat irreverent."

"Very likely. I had no reason put before me for regarding such a change as anything but an unpleasant doom, which would cut me off, or ought to do so, from field sports, from poetry, from art, from science, from politics—for Christians, I was told, had nothing to do with the politics of this world—from man and all man's civilisation, in short; and leave to me, as the only two lawful indulgences, those of living in a good house, and begetting a family of children."

"And did you throw off the old Creeds for the sake of the civilisation which you fancied that they forbid?"

"No. I am a Churchman, you know; principally on political grounds, or from custom, or from—the devil knows what, perhaps—I do not."

"Probably it is God, and not the devil, who knows why, Templeton."

"Be it so—— Frightful as it is to have to say it—— I do not so much care—— I suppose it is all right: if it is not, it will all come right at last. And in the meantime, I compromise, like the rest of the world; and hear Jane making the children every week-day pray that they may become God's children, and then teaching them every Sunday evening the Catechism, which says that they are so already. I don't understand it—— I suppose if it was important, one would understand it. One knows right from wrong, you know, and other fundamentals. If that were necessary, one would know that too."

"But can you submit quietly to such a barefaced contradiction?"

"I? I am only a plain country squire. Of course I should call such dealing with an Act of Parliament a lie and a sham—— But about these things, I fancy, the women know best. Jane is ten thousand times as good as I am——you don't know half her worth—— And I haven't the heart to contradict her—nor the right either; for I have no reasons to give her; no faith to substitute for hers."

"Our friend, the High-Church curate, could have given you a few plain reasons, I should think."

"Of course he could. And I believe in my heart the man is in the right in calling Jane wrong. He has honesty and common sense on his side, just as he has when he calls the present state of Convocation, in the face of that prayer for God's Spirit on its deliberations, a blasphemous lie and sham. Of course it is. Any ensign in a marching regiment could tell us that from his mere sense of soldier's honour. But then—if she is wrong, is he right? How do I know? I want reasons: he gives me historic authorities."

"And very good things too; for they are fair phenomena for induction."

"But how will proving to me that certain people once thought a thing right prove to me that it is right? Good people think differently every day. Good people have thought differently about those very matters in every age. I want some proof which will coincide with the little which I do know about science and philosophy. They must fight out their own battle, if they choose to fight it on mere authority. If one could but have the implicit faith of a child, it would be all very well: but one can't. If one has once been fool enough to think about these things, one must have reasons, or something better than mere ipse dixits, or one can't believe them. I should be glad enough to believe; do you suppose that I don't envy poor dear Jane from morning to night?—but I can't. And so——"

"And so what?" asked I.

"And so, I believe, I am growing to have no religion at all, and no substitute for it either; for I feel I have no ground or reason for admiring or working out any subject. I have tired of philosophy. Perhaps it's all wrong—at least I can't see what it has to do with God, and Christianity, and all which, if it is true, must be more important than anything else. I have tired of art for the same reason. How can I be anything but a wretched dilettante, when I have no principles to ground my criticism on, beyond bosh about 'The Beautiful'? I did pluck up heart and read Mr. Ruskin's books greedily when they came out, because I heard he was a good Christian. But I fell upon a little tract of his, 'Notes on Sheepfolds,' and gave him up again, when I found that he had a leaning to that 'Clapham sect.' I have dropped politics: for I have no reason, no ground, no principle in them, but expediency. When they asked me this summer to represent the interests of the county in Parliament, I asked them how they came to make such a mistake as to fancy that I knew what was their interest, or anyone else's? I am becoming more and more of an animal; fragmentary, inconsistent, seeing to the root of nothing, unable to unite things in my own mind. I just do the duty which lies nearest, and looks simplest. I try to make the boys grow up plucky and knowing—though what's the use of it? They will go to college with even less principles than

I had, and will get into proportionably worse scrapes, I expect to be ruined by their debts before I die. And for the rest, I read nothing but "The Edinburgh" and "The Agricultural Gazette." My talk is of bullocks. I just know right from wrong enough to see that the farms are in good order, pay my labourers living wages, keep the old people out of the workhouse, and see that my cottages and schools are all right; for I suppose I was put here for some purpose of that kind —though what it is I can't very clearly define—— And there's an end of my long story."

"Not quite an animal yet, it seems?" said I with a smile, half to hide my own sadness at a set of experiences which are, alas! already far too common, and will soon be more common still.

"Nearer it than you fancy. I am getting fonder and fonder of a good dinner and a second bottle of claret—about their meaning there is no mistake. And my principal reason for taking the hounds two years ago was, I do believe, to have something to do in the winter which required no thought, and to have an excuse for falling asleep after dinner, instead of arguing with Jane about her scurrilous religious newspapers—— There is a great gulf opening, I see, between me and her—— And as I can't bridge it over I may as well forget it. Pah! I am boring you, and over-talking myself. Have a cigar, and let us say no more about it. There is more here, old fellow, than you will cure by doses of Socratic Dialectics."

"I am not so sure of that," I replied. "On the contrary, I should recommend you in your present state of mind to look out your old Plato as quickly as possible, and see if he and his master Socrates cannot give you, if not altogether a solution for your puzzle, at least a method whereby you may solve it yourself. But tell me first—What has all this to do with your evident sympathy for a man so unlike yourself as Professor Windrush?"

"Perhaps I feel for him principally because he has broken loose from it all in desperation, just as I have. But, to tell you the truth, I have been reading more than one book of his school lately; and, as I said, I owe you no thanks for demolishing the little comfort which I seemed to find in them."

"And what was that then?"

"Why—in the first place, you can't deny that however incoherent they may be they do say a great many clever things, and noble things too, about man, and society, and art, and nature."

"No doubt of it."

"And moreover, they seem to connect all they say with—with—I suppose you will laugh at me—with God, and spiritual truths, and eternal Divine laws: in short, to consecrate common matters in that very way, which I could not find in my poor mother's teaching."

"No doubt of that either. And therein is one real value of them, as protests in behalf of something nobler and more unselfish than the mere dollar-getting spirit of their country."

"Well, then, can you not see how pleasant it was to me to find someone who would give me a peep into the unseen world, without requiring as an entrance-fee any religious emotions and experiences? Here I had been for years, shut out; told that I had no business with anything eternal, and pure, and noble, and good; that to all intents and purposes I was nothing better than a very cunning animal who could be damned; because I was still 'carnal,' and had not been through all Jane's mysterious sorrows and joys. And it was really good news to me to hear that they were not required after all, and that all I need do was to be a good man, and leave devotion to those who were inclined to it by temperament."

"Not to be a good man," said I, "but only a good specimen of some sort of man. That, I think, would be the outcome of Emerson's 'Representative Men,' or of those most tragic 'Memoirs of Margaret Fuller Ossoli.'"

"How then, hair-splitter? What is the mighty difference?"

"Would you call Dick Turpin a good man, because he was a good highwayman?"

"What now?"

"That he would be an excellent representative man of his class; and therefore, on Mr. Emerson's grounds, a fit subject for a laudatory lecture."

"I hate reductiones ad absurdum. Let Turpin take care of himself. I suppose I do not belong to such a very bad sort of men, but that it may be worth my while to become a good specimen of it?"

"Certainly not; only I think, contrary to Mr. Emerson's opinion, that you will not become even that, unless you first become something better still, namely, a good man."

"There you are too refined for me. But can you not understand, now, the causes of my sympathy even with Windrush and his 'spirit of truth'?"

"I can, and those of many more. It seems that you thought you found in that school a wider creed than the one to which you had been accustomed?"

"There was a more comprehensive view of humanity about them, and that pleased me."

"Doubtless, one can be easily comprehensive if one comprehends good and bad, true and false, under one category, by denying the absolute existence of either goodness or badness, truth or falsehood. But let the view be as comprehensive as it will, I am afraid that the creed founded thereon will not be very comprehensive."

"Why then?"

"Because it will comprehend so few people; fewer even than the sect of those who will believe, with Mr. Emerson, that Harvey and Newton made their discoveries by the 'Aristotelian method.' The sect of those who believe that there is no absolute right and wrong, no absolute truth external to himself, discoverable by man, will, it seems to me, be a very narrow one to the end of time; owing to a certain primæval superstition of our race, who, even in barbarous countries, have always been Platonists enough to have some sort of instinct and hope that there was a right and a wrong, and truths independent of their own sentiments and faculties. So that, though this school may enable you to fancy that you understand Lady Jane somewhat more, by the simple expedient of putting on her religious experiences an arbitrary interpretation of your own, which she would indignantly and justly deny, it will enable her to understand you all the less, and widen the gulf between you immeasurably."

"You are severe."

"I only wish you to face one result of a theory, which, while it pretends to offer the most comprehensive liberality, will be found to lead in practice to the most narrow and sectarian Epicurism for a cultivated few. But for the many, struggling with the innate consciousness of evil, in them and around them—an instinctive consciousness which no argumentation about 'evil being a lower form of good' will ever explain away to those who 'grind among the iron facts of life, and have no time for self-deception'—what good news for them is there in Mr. Emerson's cosy and tolerant Epicurism? They cry for deliverance from their natures; they know that they are not that which they were intended to be, because they follow their natures; and he answers them with: 'Follow your natures, and be that which you were intended to be.' You began this argument by stipulating that I should argue with you simply as a man. Does Mr. Emerson's argument look like doing that, or only arguing as with an individual of that kind of man, or rather animal, to which some iron Fate has compelled you to belong?"

"But, I say, these books have made me a better man."

"I do not doubt it. An earnest cultivated man, speaking his whole mind to an earnest cultivated man, will hardly fail of telling him something he did not know before. But if you had not been a cultivated man, Templeton, a man with few sorrows, and few trials, and few unsatisfied desires—if you had been the village shopkeeper, with his bad debts, and his temptations to make those who can pay for those who cannot,—if you had been one of your own labourers, environed with the struggle for daily bread, and the alehouse, and hungry children, and a sick wife, and a dull taste, and a duller head—in short, if you had been a man such as nine out of ten are—what would his school have taught you then? You want some truths which are common to men as men, which will help and teach them, let their temperament or their circumstances be what they will—do you not? If you do not, your complaint of Lady Jane's exclusive Creed is a mere selfish competition on your part, between a Creed which will fit her peculiarities, and a Creed which will fit your peculiarities. Do you not see that?"

"I do—go on."

"Then I say you will not find that in Professor Windrush's school. I say you will find it in Lady Jane's Creed."

"What? In the very Creed which excludes me?"

"Whether that Creed excludes you or not is a question of the true meaning of its words. And that again is a question of Dialectics. I say it includes you and all mankind."

"You must mistake her doctrines, then."

"I do not, I assure you. I know what they are; and I know, also, the misreading of them to which your dear mother's school has accustomed her, and which has taught her that these Creeds only belong to the few who have discovered their own share in them. But whether the Creeds really do that or not—whether Lady Jane does not implicitly confess that they do not by her own words and deeds of every day, that, I say, is a question of Dialectics, in the Platonic sense of that word, as the science which discovers the true and false in thought, by discovering the true and false concerning the meanings of words, which represent thought."

"Be it so. I should be glad to hold what Jane holds, for the sake of the marvellous practical effect on her character—sweet creature that she is!—which it has produced in the last seven years."

"And which effect, I presume, was not increased by her denying to you any share in the same?"

"Alas, no! It is only when she falls on that—when she begins denouncing and excluding—that all the old faults, few and light as they are, seem to leap into ugly life again for the moment."

"Few and light, indeed! Ah, my dear Templeton, the gulf between you and happiness looks wide; but only because it is magnified in mist."

"Which you would have me disperse by lightning-flashes of Dialectics, eh? Well, every man has his nostrum."

"I have not. My method is not my own, but Plato's."

"But, my good fellow, the Windrush school admire Plato as much as you do, and yet certainly arrive at somewhat different conclusions."

"They do Plato the honour of patronising him, as a Representative Man; but their real text-book, you will find, is Proclus. That hapless philosophaster's *a priori* method, even his very verbiage, is dear to their souls; for they copy it through wet and dry, through sense and nonsense. But as for Plato—when I find them using Plato's weapons, I shall believe in their understanding and love of him."

"And in the meanwhile claim him as a new verger for the Reformed Church Catholic?"

"Not a new verger, Templeton. Augustine said, fourteen hundred years ago, that Socrates was the philosopher of the Catholic Faith. If he has not seemed so of late years, it is, I suspect, because we do not understand quite the same thing as Augustine did, when we talk of the Catholic Faith and Christianity."

"But you forget, in your hurry of clerical confidence, that the question still remains, whether these Creeds are true."

"That, too, as I take it, is a question of Dialectics, unless you choose to reduce the whole to a balance-of-probabilities argument—rather too narrow a basis for a World-faith to stand upon. Try all 'mythic' theories, Straussite and others, by honest Dialectics. Try your own thoughts and experiences, and the accredited thoughts and experiences of wise men, by the same method. Mesmerism and 'The Development of Species' may wait till they have settled themselves somewhat more into sciences; at present it does not much matter what agrees or disagrees with them. But using this weapon fearlessly and honestly, you will, unless Socrates and Plato were fools, arrive at absolute eternal truths, which are equally true for all men, good or bad, conscious or unconscious; and I tell you—of course you need not believe me till you have made trial—that those truths will coincide with the plain honest meaning of the Catholic Creeds, as determined by the same method—the only one, indeed, by which they or anything else can be determined."

"You forget Baconian induction, of which you are so fond."

"And pray what are Dialectics, but strict Baconian induction applied to words, as the phenomena of mind, instead of to things, the phenomena of——"

"What?"

"I can't tell you; or, rather, I will not. I have my own opinion about what those trees and stones are; but it will require a few years' more verification before I tell."

"Really, you and your Dialectics seem in a hopeful and valiant state of mind."

"Why not? Can truth do anything but conquer?"

"Of course—assuming, as every one does, that the truth is with you."

"My dear fellow, I have seldom met a man who could not be a far better dialectician than I shall ever be, if he would but use his Common Sense."

"Common Sense? That really sounds something like a bathos, after the great big Greek word which you have been propounding to me as the cure for all my doubts."

"What? Are you about to 'gib' after all, just as I was flattering myself that I had broken you in to go quietly in harness?"

"I am very much minded to do so. The truth is, I cannot bring myself to believe that the universal panacea lies in an obscure and ancient scientific method."

"Obscure and ancient? Did I not just say that any man might be a dialectician? Did Socrates ever appeal to any faculty but the Common Sense of man as man, which exists just as much in England now, I presume, as it did in Athens in his day? Does he not, in pursuance of that method of his, draw his arguments and illustrations, to the horror of the big-worded Sophists, from dogs, kettles, fishwives, and what not which is vulgar and commonplace? Or did I, in my clumsy attempt to imitate him, make use of a single argument which does not lie, developed or undeveloped, in the Common Sense of every clown; in that human Reason of his, which is part of God's image in him, and in every man? And has not my complaint against Mr. Windrush's school been, that they will not do this; that they will not accept the ground which is common to men as men, but disregard that part of the 'Vox Populi' which is truly 'Vox Dei,' for that which is 'Vox Diaboli'—for private sentiments, fancies, and aspirations; and so casting away the common sense of mankind, build up each man, on the pin's point of his own private judgment, his own inverted pyramid?"

"But are you not asking me to do just the same, when you propose to me to start as a Scientific Dialectician?"

"Why, what are Dialectics, or any other scientific method, but conscious common sense? And what is common sense, but unconscious scientific method? Every man is a dialectician, be he scholar or boor, in as far as he tries to use no words which he does not understand, and to sift his own thoughts, and his expression of them, by that Reason which is at once common to men, and independent of them."

"As M. Jourdain talked prose all his life without knowing it. Well——I prefer the unconscious method. I have as little faith as Mr. Carlyle would have in saying: 'Go to, let us make'—an induction about words, or anything else. It seems to me no very hopeful method of finding out facts as they are."

"Certainly; provided you mean any particular induction, and not a general inductive and severely-inquiring habit of mind; that very 'Go to' being a fair sign that you have settled beforehand what the induction shall be; in plain English, that you have come to your conclusion already, and are now looking about for facts to prove it. But is it any wiser to say: 'Go to, I will be conscious of being unconscious of being conscious of my own forms of thought'? For that is what you do say, when, having read Plato, and knowing his method, and its coincidence with Common Sense, you determine to ignore it on common-sense questions."

"But why not ignore it, if mother-wit does as well?"

"Because you cannot ignore it. You have learnt it more or less, and cannot forget it, try as you will, and must either follow it, or break it and talk nonsense. And moreover, you ought not to ignore it. For it seems to me, that you were sent to Cambridge by One greater than your parents, in order that you might learn it, and bring it home hither for the use of the M. Jourdains round you here, who have no doubt been talking prose all their life, but may have been also talking it very badly."

"You speak riddles."

"My dear fellow, may not a man employ Reason, or any other common human faculty, all his life, and yet employ them very clumsily and defectively?"

"I should say so, from the gross amount of human unwisdom."

"And that, in the case of uneducated persons, happens because they are not conscious of those faculties, or of their right laws, but use them blindly and capriciously, by fits and starts, talking sense on one point and nonsense on another?"

"Too true, Heaven knows."

"But the educated man, if education mean anything, is the man who has become conscious of those common human faculties and their laws, and has learnt to use them continuously and accurately, on all matters alike."

"True, O Socraticule!"

"Then is it not his especial business to teach the right use of them to the less educated?—unless you agree with the old Sophists, that the purpose of education is to enable us to deceive or coerce the uneducated for our own aggrandisement."

"I am therefore, it seems, to get up Platonic Dialectics simply in order to teach my ploughmen to use their common sense?"

"Exactly so. Teach yourself first, and every one

around you afterwards, not the doctrines, nor the formulæ—though he had none—but the habit of mind which Socrates tried in vain to teach the Athenian youth. Teach them to face all questions patiently and fearlessly: to begin always by asking every word, great or small, from 'Predestination' to 'Protection,' what it really means. Teach them that 'By your words you shall be justified, and by your words you shall be condemned,' is no barren pulpit-text, but a tremendous practical law for every day, and for every matter. Teach them to be sure that man can find out truth, because God his Father and Archetype will show it to those who hunger after it. Try to make them see clearly the Divine truths which are implied, not only in their creeds, but in their simplest household words; and——"

"And fail as Socrates failed, or rather worse; for he did teach himself: but I shall not even do that."

"Do not despair in haste. In the first place, I deny that Socrates taught himself, for I believe that One taught him, who has promised to teach every man who desires wisdom; and in the next place, I have no fear but that the sound practical intellect which that same One has bestowed on the Englishman, will give you a far better auditory in any harvest field, than Socrates could find among the mercurial Athenians of a fallen age."

"Well, that is, at all events, a comfort for poor me. I will really take to my Plato again, till the hunting begins."

"And even then, you know, you don't keep two

packs; so you will have three days out of the six wherein to study him."

"Four, you mean—for I have long given up reading Sunday books on Sunday."

"Then you read your Bible and Prayer-book; or even borrow some of Lady Jane's devotional treatises; and try, after you have translated the latter into plain English, to make out what they one and all really do mean, by the light which old Socrates has given you during the week. You will find them wiser than you fancy, and simpler also."

"So be it, my dear Soul-doctor. Here come Lewis and the luncheon."

And so ended our conversation.

THE END.